Picking Up Airs

Picking Up Airs

Hearing the Music
in Joyce's Text

Edited by

Ruth H. Bauerle

University of Illinois Press   Urbana and Chicago

© 1993 by the Board of Trustees of the University of Illinois
Manufactured in the United States of America
C 5 4 3 2 1

This book is printed on acid-free paper.

Title page illustration from the Paris *Tribune*, 26 February 1932.
Used by permission of the Chicago Tribune Company. All rights
reserved.

Library of Congress Cataloging-in-Publication Data

Picking up airs : hearing the music in Joyce's text / edited by
   Ruth H. Bauerle.
      p. cm.
   Includes bibliographical references.
   ISBN 0-252-01984-9
     1. Joyce, James, 1882–1941—Knowledge—Music. 2. Music and
   literature. I. Bauerle, Ruth H.
   ML80.J75P5 1993
   823'.912—dc20   92-23294
                                       CIP
                                       MN

For Dick and our extending family:

Jim, Ruthanne, Philip, and Matthew
Ellen, David, and Claire

and for

Adaline Glasheen and Mabel Worthington,
the First Ladies of Joyce scholarship

. . . pricking up ears to my phono on the ground and picking up airs from th'other over th'ether . . .

Finnegans Wake 452.12–13

Contents

American Popular Music in *Finnegans Wake*   128
  Ruth Bauerle

Appendixes

Acknowledgments

Because this volume has been a happy collegial enterprise, my first thanks go to the essayists represented here, who responded with alacrity to the invitation to contribute, and to editorial queries along the way. Special thanks are due Dublin journalist John S. Doyle who discovered the original words and music of "Invisibility" from *Turco the Terrible,* in a battered suitcase full of music abandoned at a Dublin flea market. Doyle generously made the music available for this volume. Vincent Deane, editor of *A "Finnegans Wake" Circular,* alerted us to Mr. Doyle's find. Deane also graciously shared his unpublished transcription of Joyce's notes of Sigmund Spaeth's *Read 'Em and Weep* in Joyce's Notebook V-B-41. Michael O'Kelley, of University College, Dublin, provided the E-mail link between Ohio and Dublin to speed the arrangements. Other colleagues in Joyce studies have aided us with useful suggestions or perceptive readings of the drafts; these include Murray Beja, Cheryl Herr, Matthew J. C. Hodgart, James Hurt, and Hugh B. Staples.

David Sanjek of Larchmont, New York, answered queries about his father's research in American music. At Ohio Wesleyan I have also benefitted from the musical knowledge of my neighbor and colleague, Professor Robert C. Lawrence, who by a Joycean coincidence studied with Jacques Jolas, brother of Joyce's friend Eugene Jolas. Other aid was given by Todd Wilson and Theresa Hurt and by typists Tamara Lockhardt and Elah Daniels. Technical assistance in manuscript preparation was provided by Barbara Pearson at Miami University and Rosemary Zahn at the University of Erlangen/Nürnberg. John Kneisly, R. J. Pardee, and Harold Wiebe were the computer gurus at Ohio Wesleyan.

The staffs of Beeghly Library and Sanborn Music Library at Ohio Wesleyan University, especially Bernard Derr, Elizabeth Barker, Denise

Green, and Carol Hallenbeck, aided the work, as did the Ohio State University Libraries, the Delaware County Library, the Columbus Public Library, and the British Library. Barbara Deal and Marty Chan provided FAX services.

Permissions officers at many publishing houses dealt patiently with inquiries, but I owe particular thanks to Mrs. Roma Woodnutt of the Society of Authors, who is modestly omniscient about permissions in the United Kingdom. Martha Finan, managing editor of the *Kenyon Review,* Jessica Lind of the University of Washington Press, and Jan Wilson of Pennsylvania State University Press were particularly helpful. Pennsylvania State University Press also generously lent their copy of the drawing of James Joyce for our cover.

At the University of Illinois Press, Managing Editor Theresa Sears's staff aided repeatedly. Caroline Cole and Margaret Sarkissian dealt with my vexations competently and cheerfully. Harriet Stockanes was an experienced copyright specialist. Louis Simon provided expert copyediting. Most important, Dr. Judith B. McCulloh, executive editor at the Press, believed in this book from the first and offered unwavering encouragement.

My growing family continues to be supportive; but my husband, Dick, has been, as always, unfailingly and especially helpful with his suggestions. If, despite all this help, errors remain, they are to be blamed solely on my own shortsightedness.

I gratefully acknowledge the following publishers and individuals who granted permission to reprint certain materials.

Words and Music

For "At My Time of Life" by T. W. Connor and "Young Men Taken in and Done For" by Harry King, used through the kindness of EMI Music Publishing.

For "Our Lodger's Such a Nice Young Man" by Fred Murray and Lawrence Barclay, copyright © 1897, reproduced by permission of Francis Day and Hunter, Ltd., London WC2H OEA.

For "A Thing He Had Never Done Before" by C. W. Murphy, used through the kindness of International Music Publications.

Quotations

From "Around Theatres" and "The Triumph of the 'Variety Show'" by Max Beerbohm. Copyright by Mrs. Eva Reichmann. Used by permission of Sir Rupert Hart-Davis.

From *The Critical Writings* by James Joyce, ed. Ellsworth Mason and Richard Ellmann. Copyright © 1959 by Harriet Weaver and F. Lionel Monro, administrators of the Estate of James Joyce. Used by permission of the Society of Authors on behalf of the James Joyce Estate.

"Various excerpts" from *Dubliners* by James Joyce. Copyright © 1916 by B. W. Huebsch; definitive text copyright © 1967 by the Estate of James Joyce. Used by permission of Viking Penguin, a division of Penguin Books USA, Inc.

From *Essays and Introductions* by W. B. Yeats. Copyright © 1961 by Mrs. W. B. Yeats. Used by permission of A. P. Watt, Ltd., Literary Agents, and Macmillan Publishing Co.

From *Exiles* by James Joyce. Copyright © 1918 by B. W. Huebsch, renewed 1946 by Nora Joyce; notes copyright © 1951, renewed 1979 by Viking Penguin, Inc. Used by permission of Viking Penguin, a division of Penguin Books USA, Inc.

From *Finnegans Wake* by James Joyce. Copyright © 1939 by James Joyce; copyright renewed © 1967 by George Joyce and Lucia Joyce. Used by permission of Viking Penguin, a division of Penguin Books USA, Inc.

From "The Hours of James Joyce" by Jacques Mercanton, trans. Lloyd C. Parks. Copyright © 1962, 1963 by the *Kenyon Review*. Used by permission of the *Kenyon Review*.

From *James Joyce's The Index Manuscript: "Finnegans Wake" Holograph Workbook VI.B.46,* ed. Danis Rose. Copyright © 1978 by the Trustees of the Estate of James Joyce. Used by permission of the Society of Authors on behalf of the James Joyce Estate.

From the *Letters of James Joyce, Volume One* by James Joyce. Copyright © 1957, 1966 by The Viking Press; copyright renewed 1985 by Viking Penguin, Inc. Used by permission of Viking Penguin, a division of Penguin Books USA, Inc.; by the Society of Authors on behalf of the James Joyce Estate; and by Faber and Faber Limited.

From *Letters of James Joyce, Volume Two* by James Joyce, Copyright © 1966 by F. Lionel Monro as Administrator of the Estate of James

Cover Photo

A Note on References

Standard editions of James Joyce's work and of the Ellmann biography are cited in parentheses within the text of the essays in the form listed below. All other references are incorporated in endnotes following each essay.

CW   James Joyce. *The Critical Writings of James Joyce,* ed. Ellsworth Mason and Richard Ellmann. New York: Viking Press, 1967.

D   James Joyce. *Dubliners,* ed. Robert Scholes. New York: Viking Press, 1967, 1969.

E   James Joyce. *Exiles.* New York: Penguin, 1973.

FW   James Joyce. *Finnegans Wake.* New York: Viking Press, 1939. London: Faber and Faber, 1939.

JJ2   Richard Ellmann. *James Joyce,* rev. ed. New York: Oxford University Press, 1982.

Letters 1   James Joyce, *Letters of James Joyce,* Vol. 1, ed. Stuart Gilbert. New York: Viking Press, 1957; reissued with corrections 1966.

Letters 2   James Joyce, *Letters of James Joyce,* Vol. 2, ed. Richard Ellmann. New York: Viking Press, 1966.

P   James Joyce. *A Portrait of the Artist as a Young Man,* ed. by Chester G. Anderson with Richard Ellmann. New York: Viking Press, 1964, 1968.

SH   James Joyce. *Stephen Hero,* ed. John J. Slocum and Herbert Cahoon. New York: New Directions, 1944, 1963.

U   James Joyce. *Ulysses,* ed. Hans Walter Gabler et al. New York: Random House, 1986.

Introduction: Some Notes

We Haven't Heard in Joyce's Music

Ruth Bauerle

"Sometimes I have the sense that every word in *Finnegans Wake* is a musical allusion" remarked the late Mabel Worthington at the Fourth International James Joyce Symposium in 1973. She spoke with mixed wonder and despair—wonder that even Joyce's mind could crowd so much music into the *Wake;* despair as to whether anyone other than Joyce himself would ever be able to identify it all.

As she suggested, a large quantity of music has lain unrecognized in James Joyce's texts over the years. Partly this resulted because the initial cataloging, primarily in *Song in the Works of James Joyce,*[1] provided such an extensive listing of Joyce's musical allusions, some 3,500 in all. There have been subsequent additions by other scholars[2] and a revision of that portion of Hodgart and Worthington's volume covering Joyce's writing through *Ulysses.*[3] Dr. Kathleen McGrory's revision of the listings for *Finnegans Wake* has also been underway for nearly twenty years. Vincent Deane, editor of *A "Finnegans Wake" Circular,* regularly reproduces music he has discovered in Dublin. *James Joyce: A Student's Guide* included only a portion of the new allusions discovered by Matthew Hodgart's researches into the role of opera in *Finnegans Wake;*[4] but the whole of Hodgart's research is to be presented in a forthcoming book.

As the number of scholars listing musical allusions has increased, the definitions of "allusion" have enlarged and shifted.[5] The most obvious form, of course, is the direct quotation in the same words as the original, as "with the greatest of ease" (*FW* 228.29) is lifted directly from "The Daring Young Man on the Flying Trapeze." Joyce may vary this direct quotation by shifting the spelling of one or more of the words, as when "efter the ball" (*FW* 209.13) or "ladle broom jig" (*FW* 231.32) replaces "After the Ball" or "Little Brown Jug." In the latter instance, a new variant appears in the allusion as words with similar sounds are substituted for the originals ("ladle" for "little," "broom" for "brown," "jig" for "jug").

A step farther into the forest of allusion may leave us dependent more on the rhythm than on the words. In "Tyro a tora" (*FW* 603.34) the only clues are the initial t's (two T's = T for two) and the rhythm, which is distinctly that of the song's second chorus. Similarly it is the rhythm of "it couldn't glow on burning . . . for it couldn't stay alight" (*FW* 427.15–16) that calls to mind "Casey Jones"[6] even though the total passage suggests an allusion to "The Cat Came Back." A similar rhythmic echo at *FW* 379.18–19 ("ho, ho, ho, ah, he, he!") recalls "Little Brown Jug."

If such textual and rhythmic allusions use our aural memories to evoke music, whole scenes in Joyce sometimes depend upon a more generalized allusion, both to the content of a musical composition, and to the effect created by that music. As I have pointed out elsewhere,[7] the Museyroom episode of *Finnegans Wake* gains a whole level of irony when read to the melody of Thomas Moore's "While History's Muse." By Moore's account, the "Genius of Ireland" weeps to see the blots of Irish shame on the leaves of History's volume until the Muse writes Wellington's name "with a pencil of light that illumed all the volume." At this the "Genius of Ireland" apostrophizes the Iron Duke as the "Star of my Isle," insisting that "there is not / One dishonouring blot / On the wreath that encircles my Wellington's name." Moore goes on to urge Wellington

> At the foot of that throne, for whose weal thou has stood,
> Go plead for the land that first cradled thy fame—
> And bright o'er the flood
> Of her tears and her blood
> Let the rainbow of Hope be her Wellington's name!

Kate, Joyce's historical muse, keeps a different memorial to Wellington, one commemorating his rejection of the land of his birth as a stable ("bornstable ghentleman," *FW* 10.17–18), portraying the duke as a bumbling womanizer and giving Waterloo's victory to the "cursigan" (*FW* 10.18).

At this level, allusion becomes the underlying myth of Joyce's stories, the music echoing in our mind as we read, and enriching the tonality of the prose. The music is sometimes operatic, sometimes popular, often both. But it is nearly always there. For Bloom is as much a Mozartian character as he is Homeric. *Finnegans Wake,* though universal myth, is first of all an Irish-American song of drink and resurrection; the *Wake*'s river, though Irish, is also Wagnerian. It is indeed in this largest form that Joyce's musical allusion is most important. The small bits he weaves into his prose at point after point, especially in *Finnegans Wake,* provide wonderful comic moments and enrich the texture of his language, to be sure. But these broad allusions to a song, an opera, or both at once, provide counterpoint and harmony to deepen the effect of the story. At those resonant levels of the mind and heart where human beings respond to music, these allusions have an almost atavistic power, not just for the people Joyce had known as Dubliners, but for all humankind.

In Joyce's mind, the musical allusions not merely deepened the meaning; they also broadened the appeal of his work. The opera-lover familiar with *Don Giovanni* had access to *Ulysses* via Mozart, just as the classicist entered that novel through Homer, or the Renaissance scholar by way of *The Divine Comedy.* Even the fan of Dan Leno or George "Champagne Charlie" Leybourne would find enough of the familiar in the Joycean prose to encourage continued reading.

Joyce's dependence upon music increased as his blindness forced him more and more into an oral/aural world. It is partly for this reason that *Finnegans Wake* includes more music than all the other works combined. Yet it is also probable that Joyce, in his prophetic way, was increasingly appreciative of music's ability to draw responses from deep within human consciousness. Thirty-year-old Joyce scholars, warbling about "the dear dead days beyond recall" on Bloomsday, achieve a more vivid recall of the early years of an author who died two decades before they were born, and of a Dublin which, as it is being progressively destroyed, is being rebuilt in our memories from Joyce's books and songs. "Love's Old Sweet Song" calls up for us a lost world that, while we sing, is not lost.

Joyce, we might say, anticipated by decades the work of neurologist Oliver Sacks, the "Meistersinger" of the Bronx's Beth Abraham Hospital, who has used music to break through the isolation of his patients. A sixty-five-year-old patient who had uttered no syllable through four decades nevertheless sang for Sacks every word of "Love's Old Sweet Song."[8] Though no scientist, Joyce knew that music would reach through silences, through blindness, and beyond infirmities to his readers' deepest selves.

Although musical allusions take many forms in Joyce's work, at times it is difficult to be certain the allusions are there at all. In the wake of Michael O'Shea's brilliant presentation on "Elvis Presley as the Original of HCE and Model for Shaun" at the Miami conference on "Joyce and Comedy" (Joycemas: 2 February 1991), the identifier must realize that quicksand lies on all sides. In instances where a song was composed after Joyce began his own work of composition, on *Finnegans Wake* for example, it is possible by studying the *James Joyce Archive* to ascertain whether the allusive passage entered the text before or after the song's publication. Just such study has generated appendix 4, listing "Musical Delusions in *Finnegans Wake*." Though the *Wake* passages in that list seem, often quite convincingly, to be musical allusions, each was in Joyce's text before the referent song could have been known to Joyce. In other instances it is probably more useful not to attempt to define "allusion," but instead to clarify "coinciding." Strictly speaking, coinciding happens in a situation where Joyce's text overlays a body of knowledge or information we know or presume Joyce to have had. In this sense, every allusion is a coinciding—a place where his text deliberately corresponds with his knowledge of music. When an entry in Joyce's notebook or his own marking on a draft or proof exists, we know the coinciding to be deliberate, intentional, and therefore an allusion. This is true of many, but not all, of his references to the music in Sigmund Spaeth's *Read 'Em and Weep* (see appendix 1). With other examples, such as *La Calumnia è un Vermicelli* (FW 199.28–29), the likeness is so strong to *La Calunnia è un venticello,* Rossini's aria from *The Barber of Seville,* that we have no doubt the coinciding is intended by Joyce.

Joyce's knowledge of music was widespread, however; and even those of us who are less musical than he have experienced the melody that persists in the mind throughout daily activities. For a writer, in such a case, the melody may also force itself into the written text, influencing the rhythm, the vocabulary, the phrasing. It becomes, then, an unintentional or unconscious coinciding, but allusive nevertheless. Oftentime the only "evidence" for such coinciding "texts"—Joycean and musical—is their recognition by a reader who has the same bodies of information at hand—the knowledge of Joyce's text, and a Joycean familiarity with the songs or arias known to the man who wrote those texts. Others may cry, "Unlikelihud!" Such allusions need to be identified and published, nevertheless, as a means of making more scholars aware of Joyce's possible intent, and until we can be certain such instances are among the "Presleys."

As early as *Dubliners* we can find in Joyce's writing both operatic and popular music, though long unrecognized, underlying the texts. In the sense that these are, at least now, "unprovable" allusions, they may be Presleys. Yet familiarity with this music enriches our understanding of Joyce's stories, and the music was so easily available in Joyce's world that it seems quite likely that he wrote with these musical parallels in mind.

For example, the song "Peek-a-Boo," identified by Hodgart and Worthington at *U* 3.298, probably also forms the background of the domestic scene in "A Little Cloud." Composed and performed with great popularity by the American W. J. Scanlan, "Peek-a-Boo" (1898) describes a man's return home from business to a "bright bouncing boy," to hugs and kisses and games of hide and seek:

> Oh! my heart's always light
> When I'm home with my wife,
> There joy and peace ever reign;
> With my boy on my knee
> I'm as happy as can be,
> I never knew [*sic*] care or pain;
> He's pretty he's gentle
> He's kind and he is good,
> And ev'rything nice him I bring;
> Oh, if he attempts to cry
> When I am standing by,
> Just to please him I commence to sing:
>
> CHORUS:
> Peek-a-Boo, Peek-a-Boo,
> Come from behind the chair;
> Peek-a-Boo, Peek-a-Boo,
> I see you hiding there.[9]

Like Scanlan, Joyce depicts a return home, but one where a cloud of quarrels and tensions hides all happiness. Neither singing nor any other paternal effort quiets the child's cries. Joyce had lived too long in

John and May Joyce's troubled household to leave Scanlan's saccharine picture unchallenged. The Joycean version is not merely closer to the reality he knew, but illustrative of the grimness he found in so much of Dublin life. To the reader familiar with Scanlan's song, as Joyce and his 1914 readers were, the picture in "A Little Cloud" grows darker and meaner against the rosy light of "Peek-a-Boo."

Dubliners drew from opera, too, again to bring romanticism down to earth. Puccini, whose music Joyce loved passionately, provided the dramatic kernel at the center of "The Boarding House": a young man of limited finances but high aspiration; a knock on his door, a young woman's request to light her candle at his flame; subsequent passion, quarrels, and disaster. Whereas Rodolfo of *La Bohème* lives in a romantic garret and writes poetry, Bob Doran has a room at Mrs. Mooney's and aspires only to retain his "sit" at "a great Catholic wine-merchant's office" (*D* 65). Mimi's timorous knock on Rodolfo's door is truly shy; Polly Mooney's seems a shrewd plan to take advantage of Doran's weakness. Rodolfo brings his own warmth to Mimi's chilled hands; Polly waits up for Doran with "a little tumbler of punch" calculated not merely to warm but to inflame. Rodolfo and Mimi love, but do not marry. Doran and Polly marry, but do not love. At the end of *La Bohème,* as his mistress dies of consumption, Rodolfo's impassioned cry of "Mimi!" is flung against the powerful C-sharp minor chords of the orchestra. By contrast, *Ulysses* shows the sniveling breakdown of Doran, "lowest blackguard in Dublin when he's under the influence" (*U* 12.384–85). Though Doran is able to express maudlin sympathy for Mrs. Dignam, he can barely walk straight, "boosed at five o'clock" (*U* 12.800–801). Against Puccini's bang, Joyce sets Dublin's whimper. (The whimper, too, is drawn from music, as Ulrich Schneider demonstrates below.) Either Doran or Polly, now described by Thersites as a "little sleep-walking bitch" and a "concubine of a wife" (*U* 12.398, 12.812) might well envy Mimi's early death.

Could Joyce rely upon his readers to make the association between *La Bohème* and "The Boarding House"? Probably more so when he wrote the story in 1905 than with readers three-quarters of a century later. *La Bohème* was an enormously popular opera from its first production in 1896 in Turin. Italian productions followed within the year in Buenos Aires, Alexandria, Moscow, and Lisbon. In less than fifteen months it had been translated into English, and was presented by the

Carl Rosa Opera Company in Manchester on 22 April 1897, with Puccini himself supervising the production. Two months later Berliners
heard it in German; that same summer it was done, in Italian, in Rio
de Janeiro and Mexico City. In October 1897, the opera opened in
London's Covent Garden and also in Los Angeles. (In 1899 the London
production was in the original Italian, and by 1923 the opera passed
its 150th performance at Covent Garden.) Vienna also saw *La Bohème*
in October 1897, though Prague had to wait till February 1898 for a
Czech production. In Barcelona it was presented in both Italian (April
1898) and Spanish (1905); in Athens, in Italian (1898); in New York
in both Italian and English in the same year, 1898. Also in 1898,
Parisians heard it in French; but the performance was in Italian in
Malta, Warsaw, Smyrna, and Valparaiso, Chile, although Zagreb heard
it in Croatian. Three years after its premiere, *La Bohème* made its way
in 1899 to Helsinki, St. Petersburg, Algiers, Tunis, and Bucharest
(all in Italian), and the next year to Antwerp and Brussels (French). In
its fifth year, 1901, Puccini's success was performed in Riga (German),
Geneva (French), Port Said (Italian), Stockholm (Swedish), and Lem-
berg (Polish). The next half decade saw performances in Ljubjana (Slo-
venian), Budapest (Hungarian), and Zurich (German), as well as a
translation (without performance) into Bulgarian. By 1926, when Puccini died, *La Bohème* had been translated, additionally, into Serbian,
Danish, Russian, Lettish, Finnish, and Lithuanian, and had been performed in one language or another in Oslo, Sofia, Kaunas, Belgrade,
Johannesburg, Tallinn [Reval], and Copenhagen. [10]

Given the Dublin interest in music, including opera, evidenced in
the conversation in "The Dead," it seems inescapable that Dubliners
were familiar with *La Bohème* in Joyce's youth; even if he did not encounter the opera there, however, he must certainly have come to know
it during his stay in Paris in 1903, or during his European residence
from 1904 onwards.

In *Ulysses*, as in *Dubliners*, popular music has a larger role than we
have generally realized. "There Is a Flower That Bloometh," as was
pointed out in *The James Joyce Songbook*, provides one of the most important themes for the whole novel, that of memory in conflict with
guilt. [11] Bloom, Molly, and Stephen live as much in memory as in the
present during the hours of 16 June 1904. Each sets happy memories
against those burdened by guilt, echoing the song's warning against

allowing guilty thoughts to make of memory "a poisoned flower." Moreover, by reversal, W. V. Wallace's song offers Bloom his pseudonym, a Bloom that flowers.

Not only "parlor songs" but also music hall ballads lend musicality to *Ulysses*.[12] "At My Time of Life," sung in the halls as a "dame" number by a male dressed as a substantial middle-aged woman, becomes a song associated with the "womanly" Leopold Bloom. I first noted the song in a short paper at the centennial James Joyce Symposium (Dublin, 1982); it has since been sung with great comic effect by Donna Janusko at several Joyce conferences.[13] Ulrich Schneider, who discovered the song independently at the same time, analyzes it thoroughly in his essay in this volume.

Another music hall melody sings quietly while Bloom rests "wrapped in the arms of Murphy" (*U* 16.1727), and Molly, also enveloped by a Murphy, opens her soliloquy with, "Yes because he never did a thing like that before as ask to get his breakfast in bed" (*U* 18.1–2). "A Thing He Had Never Done Before," by C. W. Murphy, describes a rare occurrence when "darling papa" comes home shockingly sober. The chaos engendered by Papa's sobriety incorporates a number of themes from *Ulysses:* aquaphobia, recognition of a spouse who returns home in a changed state, death of a child, even paternal suicide. Each theme has in its own way cast a gray shadow over the first Bloomsday; the thematic echo, in Molly's opening notes, is comic in tone, reminding us that *Ulysses* is a laugh-filled epic.

Joyce's love of music hall was surpassed only by his passion for opera. It is therefore no surprise that, when writing, he inserted operatic references so casually that some have remained unnoted for seven decades. Thus in *Exiles* (which he called his "comedy") he parodies *Carmen* by having Richard Rowan fling one of Robert Hand's roses at Bertha's feet (*E* 67.31). Carmen throws the flower in a manner both seductive and contemptuous toward Don José. As Joyce uses the gesture in *Exiles,* it retains the note of contempt while vitiating Hand's seductive purpose in bringing the flowers.

The same element of *Carmen* suggests heartache rather than comedy in the "Sirens" episode of *Ulysses,* where Bloom reflects, as Simon Dedalus sings *M'appari:* "Tenors get women by the score. Increase their flow. Throw flower at his feet. When will we meet?" (*U* 11.686–87). This may refer, as we have heretofore assumed, to the scores of sweethearts available to the man with a sweet tenor voice. It is also a clear allusion to a particular musical score—*Carmen*—and even to the aria, Don José's *La fleur que tu m'avais jetée,* in which he recalls the flower thrown him by Carmen. Those who have heard an artist like Jussi Björling sing the aria will understand Bloom's reasoning.[14] Bizet's opera provides a passionate background against which Martha Clifford's small flower "thrown" to Bloom (*U* 5.239–40) may be seen in all its pathos. The aria also heightens our perception of Bloom's relationship to Molly; for though Carmen once threw a flower to Don José, the aria marks a moment in the opera when she is turning away from him to follow her toreador. Bloom can identify with Don José's rejection at the same time he envies the ability of a tenor like Boylan to sing duets with Molly.

By recalling Martha's flower, the aria also summons the coy phrases from Martha's letter: "When will we meet? . . . What perfume does your wife? I want to know" (*U* 11.687–89). The first question recalls a meeting in the offing—Molly's four o'clock appointment. In the background Simon Dedalus's tenor becomes a description of the jingling Boylan as "all delighted." Boylan may have a tenor's charm for Molly, but Bloom, under the sway of Bizet's aria, still has the power of musical judgment tinged with bravado: "He can't sing for tall hats" (*U* 11.687–88). Nevertheless, for Molly, this afternoon, Boylan's voice, like Si Dedalus's tenor at the Ormond, will rise "sighing, changed: loud, full, shining, proud" (*U* 11.693).

Considerable attention has been given to *Don Giovanni's* presence in *Ulysses,* but even here scholars have ignored important musical background. Thus, through many discussions of the "actual" number of lovers Molly has taken during her marriage,[15] we have overlooked the fact that the list offered by Bloom ("Ithaca" 17.2133–43) is a Joycean parody of *Madamina! il catalogo,* wherein Leporello, seeking to console Donna Elvira about her abandonment by Don Giovanni, details the Don's conquests. That Joyce's purpose is as jocular as that of Leporello is suggested by the similarity of language. As recitative prior to the aria, Leporello sings: "*Eh consolotevi! non siete voi, non foste, e non sarete nè la prima, nè l'ultima* (Be consoled! You are, were, and will be neither the first nor the last)" (*Don Giovanni,* I.2).[16] Joyce introduces Bloom's catalog thus: "each imagining himself to be first, last, only and alone whereas he is neither first nor last nor only nor alone in a series originating in and repeated to infinity" (*U* 17.2129–31). In Mozart's *opera buffa* the servant Leporello takes a certain pride in Don Giovanni's amatory prowess. Bloom, who has identified with Leporello elsewhere in

Ulysses,[17] experiences an analogous pride in Molly's sexual attractive-
ness to other men, despite his genuine pain at her affair with Boylan.
Use of the aria not only affords Joyce another opportunity to reverse the
customary sexual roles, but makes possible the (s)laughtering of this
Penelope's suitors.

There is still another important but unnoted allusion to *Don Giovanni* in *Ulysses*. It is clear throughout the book that Molly's duet with
J. C. Doyle in *Là ci darem* symbolizes her duet with Boylan in "Love's
Old Sweet Song." Yet at the end of "Penelope" the woman who began
her monologue with a music hall ballad ends in an operatic duet with
the sleeping Bloom: "yes I said yes I will Yes" (*U* 18.1608–9).

"I will." *Voglio*. True it may be that Bloom has been mis-
remembering *Là ci darem* all day when he wonders whether Molly mis-
pronounces *"voglio"*;[18] he perhaps even mistranslates it at *U* 5.224
when, considering the cabbies' subservience to their customers, he
thinks "no will of their own. *Voglio e non."* Yet Bloom and Molly trans-
late alike, making *voglio* a matter of will. Whatever her stage pronunciation, in bed Molly's last "yes" is given to Bloom with a "voglio"—
yes, she will. This is also a reversal of the attitude of Don Giovanni's
servant Leporello, who has sung *Non voglio più servir.*[19] Molly will serve
Bloom breakfast.

If we have been slow to make complete listings of musical allusions
in Joyce's works, we have also lagged in comprehensive interpretations
of how he employed these allusions. Three and a half decades have produced a relatively small group of interpretive essays, starting with Zack
Bowen's "The Bronzegold Sirensong."[20] Both Bowen and I have provided extensive analyses of individual songs in their Joycean contexts.[21]
Carole Brown and Leo Knuth have studied Joyce's use in *Finnegans Wake*
of the songs sung by John McCormack.[22] Anthony Burgess's address to
the 1982 James Joyce Centennial Symposium in Dublin offered bril-
liant insights into *Finnegans Wake* as musical composition.[23] Recently
James Van Dyck Card has scrutinized all the music associated with
Molly Bloom to evaluate her professional standing and musical taste.[24]
There have also been fine impressionistic and background studies of
Joyce and music.[25] Timothy Martin's detailed volume on Joyce's use of
Richard Wagner's music appeared in 1991.[26] Nevertheless, much of the
music, even where allusions have been identified, remains unstudied.
In part scholars have been deterred by the mass of music to be investi-
gated. The catholicity of Joyce's musical taste also delayed study: how

could one encompass American variety songs like "Becky Do the Bombashay," rowdy music hall numbers like "At My Time of Life," and themes from Puccini's last opera (contemporary with *Finnegans Wake*), *Turandot?*

Picking Up Airs approaches the problem of multiplicity by bringing together comprehensive analyses of particular aspects of musical allusion in Joyce. Zack Bowen's opening essay is an imaginative interpretation of music as a comic element in *Ulysses,* particularly in "Sirens" and "Circe." After Bowen analyzes "Circe" as being like a Christmas pantomime written by Joyce, Henriette Lazaridis Power provides a closely focused study of a popular pantomime of Joyce's day, showing how both theme and structure of *Turco the Terrible* are repeatedly significant in *Ulysses.*

Ulrich Schneider moves to a closely related form of popular music. He brings his substantial knowledge of continental and British music hall to an examination of the role of music hall songs in *Dubliners* and *Ulysses,* demonstrating how frequently Joyce's themes and plots echo the story lines of popular ballads.

Timothy Martin turns to Joyce's ambivalent attitudes toward Wagner, scrutinizing particularly Wagner's influential role in the intellectual world of Joyce's youth, and the presence of *Die Meistersinger* and the *Ring* cycle in Joyce's writing. Finally, in a study of *Finnegans Wake,* my own essay focuses on American popular music, especially the melodies Joyce found in Sigmund Spaeth's *Read 'Em and Weep,* heard in concerts by American singers, or found in the air around him during his Paris years.

Because Joyceans love to sing, we also include words and music of four of the songs discussed in these essays, including Edwin Hamilton's and T. J. Jackson's lively "Invisibility," from the original Michael Gunn production of *King Turco the Terrible.* This "eccentric song and dance," as the cover describes it, had not been available in its entirety until discovered recently in Dublin by John S. Doyle, who generously made it available to us.

In one sense, moving from the music hall to Wagner to Gershwin may seem a very scattered analysis of musical influences upon James Joyce. It would be more accurate to say, however, that all of these essays are in some sense an extension of Cheryl Herr's influential work in *Joyce's Anatomy of Culture.*[27] For in Joyce's world—whether in Dublin, Trieste, Zurich, or Paris—opera was a part of popular culture, as the conversation about singers in "The Dead" makes clear. In the United States, whether in the frontier days of the nineteenth century, or in the cities of an industrialized nation, "grand opera" came to have distinctly snobbish connotations. In nineteenth- and early twentieth-century Europe, however, it was not merely the social elite who frequented opera houses, nor was it only in opera houses that opera might be heard. When London's Oxford Music Hall opened in 1861, for example, a star of the program was the Scottish soprano Euphrosyne Parepa, who had made operatic appearances in Malta and London.[28] She later married Carl Rosa, with whom she founded and managed the Carl Rosa Opera Company, for whose popular Dublin appearances one had to book ahead, as Corley points out in "Eumaeus" (*U* 16.202). On the same opening program at the Oxford was operatic baritone George Santley, who later sang the title role in the first London production of Wagner's *Der Fliegende Holländer.* Gounod's *Faust* made its first English appearance at Charles Morton's Canterbury Music Hall, Lambeth, when selections from the opera were presented in a concert, and Morton included other opera and ballet selections in his bills at the Canterbury.[29] Nor was Morton the only impressario interested in opera. The London Hippodrome commissioned a one-act opera by Leoncavallo, *I Zingari,* which opened in 1912 with the composer conducting. On the same bill was the American Ragtime Octette, a group of white musicians who introduced the ragtime fad to England.[30]

Readers of these essays will note a familiar Joycean paradox: where one scholar sees operatic references in a line, another will perceive music hall, and yet another may find American popular song. Thus for Ulrich Schneider the meanness of tone in "The Boarding House" is a reflection of similar tales in numerous music hall ballads; by contrast, to me the story makes significant use of *La Bohème,* as noted above. It is not necessary to reject one interpretation so as to accept the other. Joyce was no Kierkegaard, and with music, as with so much else in his work, Joyce's answer was less often "either/or" than "yes." Just as he found his wife's and his daughter's slight visual squints pleasing, he took great comic delight in the squinting allusion that could look in two or more directions simultaneously.

To aid readers in finding discussions of the allusions in a given passage of Joyce's work, we provide indexes of the passages in Joyce's works discussed in these essays, as well as of the titles and composers mentioned. Appendixes also give page/line lists of the American music, because many of these are newly identified allusions.

All of this, we hope, will make James Joyce's "auradramas" sound more melodiously in the readers' ears. We trust that these essays, each a substantial study of one group of Joyce's musical allusions, will prompt others to comparable inquiry until Joyce's readers finally hear something of what Joyce heard as he composed his works.

Notes

A brief draft of this essay was read at Joyce conferences in 1987 in Milwaukee and Zurich.

1. Matthew J. C. Hodgart and Mabel Worthington, *Song in the Works of James Joyce* (New York: Columbia University Press for Temple University Publications, 1959).

2. For a survey of scholarship on Joyce and music prior and subsequent to *Song in the Works of James Joyce,* see Ruth Bauerle, "From Silence to Song," *Re-Viewing Classics of Joyce Criticism,* ed. Janet Dunleavy (Urbana: University of Illinois Press, 1991), 200–215.

3. Zack Bowen, *Musical Allusions in the Works of James Joyce: Early Poetry through "Ulysses"* (Albany: State University of New York Press, 1974).

4. Matthew J. C. Hodgart, *James Joyce: A Student's Guide* (London: Routledge and Kegan Paul, 1978).

5. My husband, who has taught for more than four decades, defines a professor as "one who thinks otherwise."

6. Hodgart and Worthington, 146.

7. Ruth Bauerle, *The James Joyce Songbook* (New York: Garland, 1982, 1984), 608–12.

8. Susan L. Crawley, "The Amazing 'Power of Music,'" *AARP Bulletin* 33:2 (February 1992): 20, 13. See also Oliver Sacks, *Awakenings* (Rpt. New York: HarperCollins, 1990).

9. According to Sigmund Spaeth (*A History of Popular Music in America* [New York: Random House, 1948], 216–18), Scanlan was born in Springfield, Massachusetts, in 1856. He was already performing by age thirteen as the "Temperance Boy Songster." Eventually he became not only performer but producer, and wrote "Peek-a-Boo" in 1881 for a show called *Friend and Foe.* Edward Marks (*They All Sang* [New York: Viking, 1934], 12) describes Scanlan as "a new Irish singing comedian" in 1881. Though he probably was of Irish parentage and wrote and sang many "Irish" songs, Scanlan's career seems

to have been almost entirely in variety theaters in the United States. Music and complete lyrics for "Peek-a-Boo" may be found in the Ultra-Modern Library's collection, *Songs of the Gay 90's*. Hodgart and Worthington list "Peek-a-Boo" as a music hall song, suggesting it also achieved popularity in the British halls.

10. Alfred Loewenberg, *Annals of Opera, 1597–1940*, 2 vols., 2d ed. (Geneva: Societas Bibliographica, 1943), 1:cols. 1188–90. That was only Puccini's record. Leoncavallo wrote an opera with the same title from the same source (Henri Murger's 1847–49 novel, *Scènes de la vie de Bohème*), though this 1897 opera was far less popular than Puccini's of the previous year. See Harold Rosenthal and John Warrack, *Concise Oxford Dictionary of Opera*, 2d ed. (New York: Oxford University Press, 1979), 54.

11. Bauerle, *James Joyce Songbook*, 253–56. In the 1984 edition of *Ulysses* the song appears at 5.62, 13.438–39, 14.1344–55, 15.898, 15.902, 15.2489–90, 15.3027–40, 18.775. On the importance of memory as a theme in *Ulysses*, see Jean Kimball, "Autobiography as Epic: Freud's Three-Time Scheme in *Ulysses*," *Texas Studies in Literature and Language* 31 (Winter 1989): 475–96.

12. Composer and author Anthony Burgess acknowledged the music hall ambience of *Ulysses* in the music he composed for *The Blooms of Dublin*, a musical setting of Joyce's story, broadcast on Radio Telefis Eireann and BBC for the Joyce centennial on 16 June 1982. In "staying close to the tonalities of the music hall," writes Burgess, he hoped to achieve "the kind of thing Joyce might have envisaged, or eneared, for his characters." See Anthony Burgess, *You've Had Your Time* (New York: Grove Weidenfield, 1991), 371.

13. Ruth Bauerle, "Some Unnoted Songs in *Ulysses*" (unpublished paper). Robert Janusko, Ulrich Schneider, and I have identified the song at *U:* 13.435–37, 15.329–30, 15.2795, 16.540–44, and *FW:* 87.12, 130.35–132.1, 531.23, 607.12. It is problematical whether the song is also alluded to when Bloom picks up a "Bit of stick" (*U* 13.1252) and "with his stick gently vexed the thick sand at his foot" until "the stick fell in silted sand, stuck" (*U* 13.1256, 13.1270). Though it is possible that he intended to write "I. AM. A. stick-in-the-mud" as his message for Gerty (*U* 13.1258, 13.1264), we shall never know. Sticks are, of course, significant images throughout "Nausicaa."

14. Jussi Björling on Victor LM 105, "Great Tenor Arias"; Victor LM 2003, "Björling Sings at Carnegie Hall."

15. Robert M. Adams, "The Twenty-five Lovers of Molly Bloom," *Surface and Symbol: The Consistency of James Joyce's "Ulysses"* (New York: Oxford University Press, 1962), 35–43; Richard Ellmann, *James Joyce*, rev. ed. (New York, Oxford University Press, 1982), 377.

16. Mozart, *Don Giovanni, Opera Libretto Library* (New York: Avenel Books, 1980), 3:398.

17. Adams, 98.

18. *U* 4.27–28. See also Adams, 71; and Vernon Hall, "Joyce's Use of Da Ponte and Mozart's *Don Giovanni,*" *Publications of the Modern Language Association* 66 (March 1951): 78–84.

19. Adams, 71.

20. Zack Bowen, "The Bronzegold Sirensong: A Musical Analysis of the 'Sirens' Episode in Joyce's *Ulysses,*" *Literary Monographs* 1, ed. Eric Rothstein and Thomas K. Dunseath (Madison: University of Wisconsin Press, 1967), 245–98, 319–20.

21. Bowen, *Musical Allusions in the Works of James Joyce,* and Bauerle, *James Joyce Songbook*.

22. Carole Brown [Knuth], "Will the Real Signor Foli Please Stand up and Sing 'Mother Machree'?" *A Wake Newslitter* 17 (December 1980): 99–100. Carole Brown Knuth and Leo Knuth, *The Tenor and the Vehicle. A Wake Newslitter* Monograph no. 5 (Colchester, Essex: A Wake Newslitter Press, 1982). Knuth and Knuth, "More Wakean Memories of McCormack: A Centenary Tribute," *A Wake Newslitter* Occasional Paper no. 4, September 1984.

23. The address may be found, titled "Re Joyce," in Anthony Burgess, *This Man and Music* (New York: Avon Books, 1985; orig. publisher McGraw-Hill, 1983), 134–49.

24. James Van Dyck Card, "Molly Bloom, Soprano," *James Joyce Quarterly* 27 (Spring 1990): 595–602.

25. See, for instance, Arthur Nestrovski, "Blindness and Inwit: James Joyce and the Sirens," *Iowa Review* 18 (Winter 1988): 18–26; and Reed Way Dasenbrock, "Mozart contra Wagner: The Operatic Roots of the Mythic Method," *James Joyce Quarterly* 27 (Spring 1990): 517–31.

26. Timothy Martin, *Joyce and Wagner* (Cambridge: Cambridge University Press, 1991).

27. Cheryl Herr, *Joyce's Anatomy of Culture* (Urbana: University of Illinois Press, 1986).

28. Raymond Mander and Joe Mitchenson, *British Music Hall* ([New York]: London House and Maxwell, 1966; London: Studio Vista Ltd., 1965), 16. Rosenthal and Warrack, *Concise Oxford Dictionary of Opera,* s.v. "Parepa."

29. Mander and Mitchenson, [46], caption 11.

30. Ibid., [152], caption 226.

Words and Music

"At My Time of Life"
Words and music: T. W. Connor

1. Now ev - er since I 'tied the knot,' and which it ain't a

day,   I've sat - is - fied   my   hus - band   in   my

good old - fash - ioned   way,   But   since   he's   seen   a

gal   in 'bags,'   it's   knocked him,   sure   as   fate,   He

says   I ain't worth that,   be - cause   I   am *not* up to   date.

There was none o' yer 'High - ty Fligh - ty' girls, yer

p - f

'Hi - Tidd - ley Hi - ty' girls, When my old

'Stick - in - the - mud' took me for a wife, Now

fan - cy me a smok - ing 'fags,' rid - ing bikes and

wear - in' bags, A - leav - ing off my bits o' rags, At

my time o' life! There was life!

Now ever since I "tied the knot," and which it ain't a day,
I've satisfied my husband in my good old-fashioned way,
But since he's seen a gal in "bags," it's knocked him, sure as fate,
He says I ain't worth that, because I am *not* up to date.

FIRST CHORUS:
There was none o' yer "Highty Flighty" girls,
yer "Hi-Tiddley Hity" girls,
When my old "Stick-in-the-mud" took me for a wife,
Now fancy me a-smoking "fags,"
riding bikes and wearin' bags,
A-leaving off my bits o' rags,
At *my* time o' life!

I likes my drop o' "stimulant," as *all* good ladies do,
A 'arf a quartern, "two out," used to do between the two;
But now he says it's only "roughs," as patronizes "pubs,"
For all "New Women" wot *is* "class" belongs to swagger clubs!

SECOND CHORUS:
There was none o' yer "Highty Flighty" girls,
yer "Hi-Tiddley Hity" girls,
When my old "Thing-a-my-bob" took me for a wife,
Now fancy me old "Mother Scrubs"
a-jineing these 'ere Totties' clubs,
Fancy me deserting the "pubs,"
At *my* time o' life!

He'd like to see me got up with a cigarette to puff,
A "dicky dirt" and tie, (as if I wasn't guy enough!)
Says I'd look well in "bloomers" and a "call me Charlie" hat!
If *I'd* proposed it he'd 'a said, "Get out, yer gay old cat!"

THIRD CHORUS:
There was none o' yer "Highty Flighty" girls,
yer "Hi-Tiddley Hity" girls,
When my old "Four-penny-bit" took me for a wife,
Now fancy me a-sportin' shirts!
playing billiards, backing "certs,"
A-going about without my skirts,
At *my* time o' life!

"A Thing He Had Never Done Before"
Words and music: C. W. Murphy

Allegro moderato

The wind it blowed, the snow it snowed, the light-ning it did light, The rain came down as us - u - al, and, breth-ren, well it might; For had not dar - ling pa - pa come home so - ber that same night, A thing he had nev-er done be - fore! It took us all our time to hold the bull - dog Pat - sy Burke; And ma - ma tore her hair and start - ed rav - ing like a Turk, When pa - pa calm - ly told us that he'd been and done some work, A thing he had nev - er done be - fore! 'Twas a thing he had nev-er done be - fore, Though he'd of - ten been to pris-on, to be sure; It killed our sis - ter Ruth, when he

went and spoke the truth, A   thing he had nev-er done be - fore.

The wind it blowed, the snow it snowed, the lightning it did light,
The rain came down as usual, and, brethren, well it might;
For had not darling papa come home sober that same night,
A thing he had never done before!
It took us all our time to hold the bulldog Patsy Burke;
And mama tore her hair and started raving like a Turk,
When papa calmly told us that he'd been and done some work,
A thing he had never done before!

> FIRST CHORUS:
> 'Twas a thing he had never done before,
> Though he'd often been to prison, to be sure;
> It killed our sister Ruth,
> When he went and spoke the truth,
> A thing he had never done before.

That very same papa was overjoyed last Sunday morn,
He'd never been so jolly since the day that I was born,
For he got his only pair of trousers out of pawn,
A thing he had never done before!
When mama saw that papa was a-treading virtue's path,
She said, Salvation Army–like, "Oh! what a soul he harth!"
She sold the clock for fourpence and then went and had a bath,
A thing she had never done before!

> SECOND CHORUS:
> 'Twas a thing she had never done before,
> Not even in the good old days of yore,
> She thought she'd like a treat,
> So she took on water neat,
> A thing she had never done before!

When mama came home from the baths the old home went amiss;
Pa didn't recognise her so he shouted, "Who is this?"

He chucked her underneath the chin, and gave her a kiss,
A thing he had never done before!
"Ah! Harold, don't you know me? 'Tis your loving wife," she cried,
But dear papa had fainted, then to cheer him up we tried,
And as soon as he recovered, he committed suicide—
A thing he had never done before!

THIRD CHORUS:
'Twas a thing he had never done before,
To hop the twig unto another shore,
He'd a haircut and a shave,
When we laid him in his grave,
A thing we had never done before.

"Young Men Taken in and Done For"
Words and music: Harry King

As smart a man as ever lived was I when in my prime,
Until I met Miss Lucy Jaggs, she knocked me out of time.
I called there for apartments for I'd noticed once or twice,
A card stuck in the window, and on it this device:

CHORUS:
"Young men taken in and done for,"
Oh! I never thought that she,

The girl I left my happy home for,
Would have taken in and done for me.

Being a lonely single man, I wanted lodgings bad,
So Lucy Jaggs's mother then soon showed me what she had.
I'd not stayed there above a week when Lucy came to me
And fondly kissed me on my cheek, then sat me on her knee.

CHORUS

Of course, just like a stupid, I must go and tie the knot
That brings us bliss and happiness—but that's all tommy rot.
I don't believe my wife loves me, it's the truth I'm telling you.
A wife can't love her husband much if she beats him black and blue.

CHORUS

"Invisibility"
Words: Edwin Hamilton
Music: T. J. Jackson

I'm sure it would be nice To__ be a-ble to van-ish from

sight,   To   be   a - ble to stop in the   whis - key shop   'Till

af - ter e - lev - en   at   night.   To   con - sult an at - tor - ney

and   Dis - ap - pear when he speaks   of   fees, _____   To

trav - el by rail, in the   lim - it - ed mail, And   van - ish at "tick - ets,

please."___   In - vi - si - bil - i - ty   you'll say   is

just   the thing   for   me,   For   I   am   the boy   that

can   en - joy   In - vi - si - bil - i - ty.___

I'm sure it would be nice
   To be able to vanish from sight,
To be able to stop in the whiskey shop
   'Till after eleven at night.
To consult an attorney and
   Disappear when he speaks of fees,
To travel by rail, in the limited mail,
   And vanish at "tickets, please."

   CHORUS:
   Invisibility you'll say
   Is just the thing for me,
   For I am the boy
   That can enjoy
   Invisibility.

Should I happen to break the laws,
   (As the best of us often do,)
I'd wait till the bobby was out in the lobby,
   And then disappear from view.
Should the weather become too hot
   For clothing however small,
It would be a treat to do Grafton Street
   Without any clothes at all.

CHORUS

I am sure it would be fine
   Should your landlord call for rent,
To disappear and never to hear
   What the deuce it was he meant.
Or to vanish to Sandymount
   Should the Gas collector call
With his three months bill, and your cash was nil
   And you'd nothing "at all at all."

CHORUS

Music as Comedy in *Ulysses*

Zack Bowen

Joyce's interest in music is evident in all of his published works, from the appropriately titled *Chamber Music* to *Finnegans Wake,* which derives its title and some of its central themes from an Irish-American comic song. Joyce composed an original song for the *Wake,* "The Ballad of Persse O'Reilly," which, along with "Finnegan's Wake," encapsulates the whole story of fall and resurrection. In relying on musical motifs to advance his comic theme, Joyce was following a pattern he had already set in *Ulysses,* in which approximately 700 allusions to musical compositions, mostly to songs popular in Ireland during Joyce's time, make it appear a predominantly musical work.[1] While critics have pointed to numerous musical allusions in *Ulysses,* the extent to which these allusions advance the novel's comic impulse has not received much attention.

This essay will develop the connection between the musical allusions in *Ulysses* and the comedic spirit that informs the book. I have belabored the point elsewhere that *Ulysses* is predominantly a comic novel.[2] When one considers that among the myriad allusions to music most have comic overtones, the idea of characterizing the novel as a musical comedy is not so farfetched as it seems. Even the funeral dirge, "The Pauper's Drive," repeated a number of times on the way to Glasnevin, is alluded to in counterpoint to the jostling of the fast-paced carriage as it proceeds at a near gallop toward the cemetery, and to the street organ sending after the carriage "a rollicking rattling song of the halls. Has anybody here seen Kelly? Kay ee double ell wy," to which Bloom adds, "Dead March from *Saul,*" while the street organ continues with the music hall song, "He's as bad as old Antonio. He left me on my ownio"

(*U* 6.373–75). The effect of mixing the two dirges with a comic song, in the context of Bloom's satirical mind, is ultimately laughable. An absent, perhaps dead Kelly, the dead pauper, the funeral march from *Saul,* even Bloom's father's suicide generate a grim atmosphere that is mitigated by the comic effect of the music surrounding the scene.

In this essay I discuss four variations on Joyce's combination of music and comedy: the entire novel as an example of musical comedy; the "Sirens" episode as another variation on the musical comedy form; "Circe" as a particular model of musical comedy—the post-Christmas music hall pantomime; and a prime example of how music is used for comic-satiric purposes in debunking religious ritual and glorifying drinking ritual as a substitute. These four comedic structures of *Ulysses* are exemplified by individual instances of the comedy of farce, hyperbole and confusion.

Romance and Reunification

Ulysses anticipates the experiments of the *Wake* in a number of ways, not the least of which is to foreshadow Joyce's later reliance on music to summarize and refine themes and encapsulate plot. The most accurate analogy that can be drawn to characterize the structure of *Ulysses* musically is not opera, in which every word is generally sung, but musical comedy, in which spoken dialogue is integrated with music, which comically lightens the tone even as it develops themes and plot. The evolution from opera, itself a bastard form of drama set to music, is through a gradual popularization and violation of the traditional tenets of operatic form, which demands that credulity be suspended to allow the unrealistic conceit of singing every word in the drama itself. The operetta moved from operatic form by permitting some spoken dialogue to intervene between musical selections, and it was only a short step, once the blend of spoken dialogue and music became established, merely to suspend the action while appropriate music was sung and played. The resultant form is loosely called "the musical." This further popularized version made use of the verisimilitude of traditional drama, at the same time it required that the audience suspend belief in realistic action while songs were sung. The idea of the bowdlerized action interspersed with incongruous music caused the music itself to act in most instances as a sort of comic relief, even when spurned lovers lamented their woes. Thus, most musicals shed their tragic trappings for the more familiar comic mode. Those that did not admit of comedy did not survive as serious drama. It is difficult today to take seriously the sober-faced Jeannette MacDonald in billowing gossamer and Nelson Eddy in his Mountie's uniform singing "The Indian Love Call." Although comedy per se was not the only form the musicals took, it certainly was the predominant one.

While Joyce does not have every character literally sing a song or two, many in fact do, and the protagonist, Bloom, not only alludes to lyrics, but often to the music from which the lyrics came. The stream of conscious thought technique allows readers to experience the music as well as the lyrics, as Bloom and Molly mentally sing the songs to themselves. That Joyce often intended music as well as words is apparent from his quotations of lyrics that hyphenate one syllable words to indicate that the words are sung to more than one note: *"Comes lo-ove's old . . ."* (*U* 5.161), *"Co-ome thou lost one"* (*U* 7.59), *"Glowworm's la-amp is gleaming, love"* (*U* 8.590), and so on. We read the passages as if we hear the music as well as words. With all these tunes going on in the minds of the characters and in the spoken and sung dialogue, it would be hard to think of *Ulysses* as other than a musical.

Structurally, musical comedy usually occurs in two acts. At the end of the first, the lovers traditionally part, having experienced some seemingly insurmountable difficulty or mistake or parental or societal intransigence that seems, for all intents and purposes, to doom their love. The second act brings about their reconciliation. "Sirens" is the episode corresponding to the end of the first act, when "All Is Lost Now," to borrow a song from the chapter. At the four o'clock hour of assignation, the song marks the low point of Bloom's day, a point at which music becomes paramount. I discuss this in the "Sirens" section, below; but for now, however, it is enough to call to mind Bloom's recovery, his proof of his worthiness of the romantic fulfillment that inevitably awaits him at the conclusion of a traditional musical comedy. Bloom's trials in Bella Cohen's, in Barney Kiernan's, on Sandymount Strand, in Holles Street, the cabman's shelter, and elsewhere prove his valor, his compassion, and his magnanimity, thus enabling his triumphal homecoming and reconciliation with his beloved in their bower of bliss, marred by only a few flakes of potted meat. Bloom's generally hapless escapades are even funnier if seen as a parody of the musical comedy form, with Molly's flatulence ringing down the curtain to the concluding bars of the traditional restatement of the original musical motif, "Love's Old Sweet Song," just the tune for twilight, when the lights are low.

If the main musical comedy story line lies, as tradition dictates, in the romance between Leopold and Molly, the subplot consists of the almost-as-popular reconciliation between father and son. Of course neither Joyce's plot nor subplot is anything like what a musical comedy audience was used to hearing, since the romance is hardly apparent; the search for father-son reconciliation is, on the conscious level, confined to Bloom; and any satisfactory traditionally happy resolution to either dilemma is so understated as to seem almost nonexistent. Even so, "Love's Old Sweet Song" and the selections from *Don Giovanni* are the romantic leitmotifs of the Blooms' love relationship—with all its comic complexities—beginning with the introduction of the song and the opera in connection with Boylan's concert tour and the adulterous four o'clock rehearsal of the program. Echoes of the music reverberate throughout the day, concluding with Molly's lengthy rendition of "looooves old . . ." (*U* 18.897) "sweet soooooooooooong" (*U* 18.877), with a prolonged fart under the cover of a passing train in the distance: "I wish hed sleep in some bed by himself with his cold feet on me give us room even to let a fart God or do the least thing better yes hold them like that a bit on my side piano quietly sweeeee theres that train far away pianissimo eeeee one more tsong" (*U* 18.905–8). The musical affinities between song and flatulence have been the subject of several gaseous attacks, most noticeably at the end of the "Sirens" episode, always to exquisite comic effect.

The second predominant musical motif, *Don Giovanni,* is an entire opera, in which Bloom mentally participates, singing the songs of the cuckolded Masetto when Bloom feels the pangs of his wife's infidelity with Boylan, and then taking the Don's and Masetto's parts as he reconstructs Zerlina-Molly's line in the duet from "I would" to "I will" after Bloom is certain of the four o'clock assignation. Later Bloom sings the Don's part in the duet when he is feeling like an amorous lover in his affair with Martha Clifford; and finally, thinking of the inevitable seduction of his own daughter, Milly, Bloom sings the Commendatore's recitative lines as he pictures himself avenging her loss of innocence.[3] At the risk of minimizing Bloom's pain over the Boylan affair, the music, by creating an appropriate yet ludicrous picture of Bloom as a noble sufferer, far from inspiring additional pathos, goes a long way toward comically mitigating the damages and creating the idea that the marriage will survive satisfactorily, if not ideally.

The major songs relevant to the romantic motif are supplemented by a series of minor variations on the theme: "The Young May Moon," sung by Molly and Boylan as they touch each other's hands in the darkness while walking along the Tolka with Bloom (*U* 8.588–91); "The Last Rose of Summer," a comic leitmotif for the tortured husband; the "Seaside Girls" as temptress figures in Bloom's continuing ineffectual attempts to go astray himself; "Goodbye Sweetheart Goodbye," as the peripatetic Boylan's traveling music; and "Home, Sweet Home" to represent in the most maudlin comic terms the situation at Number Seven Eccles Street; as well as a host of other melodies ancillary to aspects of the lovers' activities.

Augmenting the idea that the music of *Ulysses* is used for musical comedic purpose is its contribution to funny hyperbolic comparison. Examples that come immediately to mind are the association of the cursing blind piano tuner with the near-sainted Croppy Boy who has cursed only "three times since last Easter Day"; the figure of Jesus/Mario, and subsequently Bloom's parody figure singing *M'appari;* Bloom as *Don Giovanni* and Lionel; Dublin as the Holy City; and the comparisons among Mercadante's "Seven Last Words of Christ," Robert Emmet's last words, and Bloom's last, flatulent statement at the end of "Sirens."

As a final addendum to the musical comedy form, all the essentially comic characters of the novel are associated with comic music or more serious music transformed by the circumstances into comedy: Buck Mulligan establishes his harlequin role by singing his "Ballad of Joking Jesus"; Simon Dedalus sings Lionel's role in *Martha;* D. B. Murphy is associated with "Has Anybody Here Seen Kelly?" or "Kelly From the Isle of Man," by the old tarpaulin's reference to Antonio; John Alexander Dowie's theme song is "Washed in the Blood of the Lamb," which Bloom comically confuses with his own name; and the citizen owns a dog named "Garryowen," the title of a song of riot and drunken debauchery in the Owen's Garden (Garryowen) suburb of Limerick.

The conscious exaggeration provided by musical allusion, coupled with Bloom's off-key memory regarding lyrics and composers, as well as the music associated with comic characters, provides more than mere comic relief to serious matters; in aggregate, through parody and association, the repeated comic references become the stuff of full-blown musical comedy.

"Sirens": The Encapsulated Form

The medley overture to "Sirens" is precisely the prose fiction parallel to the type of overture that precedes the action of musical comedies. Composed of leitmotifs from sixty-seven thematic and descriptive passages from the entire chapter, and set to twenty-one musical leitmotifs or excerpts from eleven songs, the overture anticipates the concentrated use of music throughout the episode, which contains one hundred fifty-eight references to forty-seven songs. Although I earlier rejected the notion that "Sirens" was a light or comic opera,[4] I am now ready to embrace the idea that it is in fact a musical comedy, exactly as the presence of the overture indicates. In my youth, I saw Bloom's plight as being so pathetic that it admitted no happy conclusion; but in my dotage, his dilemma does not seem so serious to me that it would deny a comic interpretation. Certainly the conclusion of "Sirens" is one of the high comic points of the novel, ending on an up—or rather down—beat of flatulent exuberance not unlike the novel as a whole. In fact, though varied in tone and quality, Molly's final gaseous response to "Love's Old Sweet Song," the romantic leitmotif of the novel, comes from precisely the same bodily instrumental section as Bloom's answer to the "Love and War" pathos generated by the "Sirens'" singers.

"Sirens" follows the traditional musical comedy pattern of preliminary exposition by two minor characters, Misses Douce and Kennedy; followed by the introduction of the protagonist of the romantic dilemma, Bloom; again followed by a minor character associated with the subplot (the father-son relationship), Simon Dedalus. These elements form a story line connected with and commenting on the main plot: Bloom as surrogate father for Stephen, and Simon as the grieving Lionel who has lost his love.

Boylan, Bloom's rival and antagonist, appears briefly on the scene and then leaves to the traveling music of "Goodbye Sweetheart Goodbye," on his way to cuckold Bloom. Boylan's exit from the Ormond coincides with the arrival of Ben Dollard, who introduces the topic of Molly to the company, and who sings the prophetic song, "Love and War," which sets the action for the rest of the "Sirens" comedy. Dollard starts to sing the tenor's part in the duet, the part of the lover (identified with Bloom): "While love absorbs my ardent soul, I think not of the morrow." But Dollard is a bass, and after being admonished by Cowley, begins the bass response to the tenor: "While war absorbs. . . ." When the two singers unite in the last stanza, they vow to blend both Love and War, like the immortal lovers, Venus and Mars, summoning "Bacchus, all divine, / To cure both pains with rosy wine, . . . [and] / . . . sing and laugh the hours away." Thus the mood of "Sirens" shifts from love to war to their combined counterpart in patriotism, the transition oiled with booze and song. As the music at the conclusion of the chapter commemoratively links the final sacrifice of an Irish patriot with Jesus' end, Bacchus's carbonated burgundy has at least the penultimate word.

Simon's detested brother-in-law, Richie Goulding, arrives to commiserate musically with Bloom as they listen to "All Is Lost Now" at the four o'clock hour of assignation, the low point of Bloom's day and the traditional conclusion of the first act. At the beginning of the second act, Simon sings the great love lament, *M'appari*, from the opera *Martha*, as Richie and Poldy listen in an adjoining room: "When first they saw, lost Richie Poldy, mercy of beauty, heard from a person wouldn't expect it in the least, her first merciful lovesoft oftloved word" (*U* 11.678–80). Though "sorrow from them each seemed to from both depart when first they heard" (*U* 11.677–78), the song offers more than mere consolation; it also presents an issue out of Bloom's affliction in the form of Martha Clifford, with whom, Bloom remembers, he is just about to communicate: "*Martha* it is. Coincidence. Just going to write" (*U* 11.713). However, thoughts of Molly soon overcome Martha's attraction, and the song, especially in the context of the action of the opera as a whole, promises a happy resolution of Siopold's affliction.

Boylan's rap on the door at Number Seven coincides with yet another modulation of tone and theme, as Dollard begins his long rendition of "The Croppy Boy," linking the war motif to the search for the father, Stephen Dedalus, and the intertwined subplot of *Ulysses*, a novel based on the ancient epical archetype of universal homecoming, faithfulness, and familial reconciliation. After the false priest-father's betrayal of the innocent croppy boy, Bloom will have no part of the final sentimental stanza: "Get out before the end. Thanks, that was heavenly" (*U* 11.1122). He leaves pathos to the drinker-patriots, whose sentiments turn comic as they chink glasses to the tune of "The Memory of the

Dead," while Bloom tootles away in commemoration of Emmet's last words, happy that a passing tram covers the sound and affords him the "oppor."

"Sirens" could rightly be termed a modernist musical comedy, untraditional only in its anti-sentimental conclusion. The rest of the comic trappings are there. It is also a musical within a musical, a score and a libretto for the action and the musical setting of the rest of the novel, and an encapsulation of the character traits that define the long-suffering but ultimately defiant modern comic hero.

"Circe": The Panto Brand of Musical Comedy

"Circe" has often been associated with the art of pantomime, but less often recognized by critics in terms of its affinity with that particularly British and Irish phenomenon by the same name: the entertainments staged right after Christmas and running until the beginning of Lent. The best work on the pantomimes are an early essay by David Hayman and the fuller development of their various influences on Joyce by Elliott Gose and Cheryl Herr.[5] Exhibited immediately after the winter solstice and its Christian counterpart, Christmas, the pantos reflect the ancient comic spirit of rebirth, recognized at the turn of the century by Cornford[6] and brought brilliantly to our attention by Bakhtin.[7] Pantomime as a form of drama (distinguished from the much later development of British "Pantos") was a precursor of both Attic and medieval continental drama. As aspects of the saturnalia, pantomime has long featured harlequins, comedy, and music, precisely as the productions do today. The earliest version of the English pantomime form as we know it today was the 1702 Drury Lane production of "Tavern Bilkers," written by John Weaver.[8] The form has not changed a great deal since in tenor or tone. It was always an extremely popular form with the general populace and condemned as crass, dull, and vulgarly plebeian by people like Cibber and Fielding. Of exactly the sort of carnival spirit Bakhtin relates in his descriptions of the early processions, pantomimes represent a sort of leveling Bacchanalia in which officialdom was satirized.[9] The tremendous popularity of the productions in the nineteenth century and later was in part due to their proximity to the Christmas holidays, which made them treats for children, to whose mentalities they catered. The tender age of a large segment of the audience meant that stories that were popular with youngsters, such as variations on

Sinbad and Aladdin, Cinderella, and a variety of fairy tales, were standard fare year after year, often with two or more theaters in the same town simultaneously playing pantos with the same title.[10] While the same general plot with minor variations was often repeated annually, the songs and the topical jokes varied from year to year.

The pantomimes were so popular that their revenues could carry the entire season for the theater, and since they made a lot of money, a great deal of expense was lavished on their production, especially on spectacular scenes and mechanical devices. These promoted a tradition of including Utopian scenes or visions, frequently transformed on the stage from the drab or dismal circumstances under which the characters labored to a realization of the millennium when their fondest hopes are realized: constant celibates were united or reunited with lovers, the poor acquired fabulous wealth and the downtrodden secured power, and so forth. Pantos represented a return to innocence and childhood for adults, and a fairy-tale vision of reality for children. With all this sweetness and light there still remained less savory overtones from ancient times, harlequin figures of subversion, and a satiric questioning of the order of events and traditions under the guise of comedy.

David Hayman and Cheryl Herr see the appearance of Rudy as a transformation scene typical of pantomime activities, while Elliott Gose cites two direct references to pantomime in "Circe" to support his contention that Joyce made extensive use of the form.[11] The conventions of later nineteenth- and twentieth-century pantomime, particularly as practiced in Ireland, also regularly included an assertive if ludicrous harlequin character known as the Widow Twankey, portrayed by a male comedian.[12] Hayman and Herr also point out that the principal boy is normally played by a girl. The similarities to the role reversals between Bloom and Bello in "Circe" are obvious. Elliott Gose has linked Bloom's successive cycles of rise and fall in "Circe" with the traditional scapegoat activities of early comedy and saturnalia, from which pantomime is descended.[13] In assuming the role of pig-donkey and being ridden around by Bello, Bloom is also closely allied with another ancient tradition, the Wicker-basket donkeys, revived in the later pantomimes. Bloom's role as the combination of clown-harlequin and scapegoat under constant attack and vilification comes close to meriting the praise of The Veiled Sibyl: "I'm a Bloomite and I glory in it. I believe in him in spite of all. I'd give my life for him, the funniest man on earth" (*U* 15.1736–37). Bloom is a funny man. Such remarks have traditionally been reserved for the great harlequins of British and Irish pantomime, comedians such as the Grimaldis, James Byrne, and Dan Leno, whose popularity rivaled that of Will Rogers and Bob Hope as esteemed vaunted public figures and Presidential Medal winners. My concern here, however, is with the music of these comedies, the mainstay of the celebrations of antiquity, and no less important in Christmas pantomimes and in Joyce's version of that genre in "Circe."

The "Circe" episode opens with opposing versions of morality parodied in Cissy Caffrey's bawdy "The Leg of the Duck," and Stephen's mockery of the church in his rendition of the "Asperges" for paschal tide.[14] Joyce's panto is hardly the party-line saccharine that whole parishes travel in school buses to Dublin to see each year, but is much closer to the gross saturnalia of the form's ancient ancestor. Molly, the embodiment of Bloom's dream, appears early in traditional Eastern Costume to intone "The Shade of The Palm" and reestablish the *Don Giovanni* motif as the love song of the panto, repeated again in part by Mrs. Breen, while Bloom, in a subplot variation of the theme, assumes the Don's role, having established himself as a dashing quasi-military type with his borrowed and perverted toast to "Ireland, home, and beauty": a Celtic version of the phrase "For England, home and beauty" immortalized in the popular song "The Death of Nelson."

When the military, Privates Carr and Compton, come on the scene they are heralded by the Navvy's rendition of the Irish patriotic song, "The Boys of Wexford," as prelude and leitmotif for the coming strife between Ireland and England: Stephen's comic altercation with the privates. A number of songs related to Bloom establish his sexual and political prowess, and at the apex of his rise to power, the references to "The Holy City" occur as the climax of perhaps the most important politically related transformation in "Circe," the establishment of the New Bloomusalem. The construction of the *"colossal edifice with crystal roof, built in the shape of a huge pork kidney, containing forty thousand rooms"* (*U* 15.1548–49) is as miraculous as any fabulous pantomime transformation ever seen on the Irish stage. The song itself is about transformation of the Holy City and the ups and downs of its Redeemer and the capital of the "Nova Hibernia." The lyrics relate a dream of happy children singing antiphonally with choirs of angels, the beatific vision interrupted in the second stanza by a dark vision of a cross on a "lonely hill" that silenced the happy little chanters until a new city took its place with the light of God shining on its streets, free and open to all, the New Jerusalem (Bloomusalem, *U* 15.1544–48) "that would not pass away."[15] It is the culmination of Stephen's (and perhaps Joyce's) youthful vision of creating the new city of Dublin and the uncreated conscience of the Irish race, now comically transformed into satiric parody involving a middle-aged harlequin scapegoat in a pantomime. A monumental example of the ancient carnivalistic leveler, the comic audacity of the vision is one of the gems of modern literature. As the gramophone later picks up the song, and all the participants at Bella's are exhorted by Elijah to join in singing of the new millennium, the machine malfunctions, and the anguished "Ahhkkk!" (*U* 15.2214) of the whores is the last we hear in "Circe" of Bloom's magnificent if degraded comic vision.

Another harlequin in the form of Virag makes his appearance accompanied by a spate of comic music hall songs, "Lily of the Valley," "Sally in Our Alley," "What Ho! She Bumps!" and "Slap! Bang! Here We Are Again Boys!" One of the repeated complaints regarding the wholesomeness of pantomimes was the use of music hall comedians and songs of occasionally unsavory nature to brighten the lives of the adults and inadvertently tarnish those of the children who came to the pantos, an art form conceived by the turn of the twentieth century to be an embodiment of childish purity, but ironically one whose saturnalian, low comic origins were always lurking just underneath the surface.

When Bello revives the donkey-ride tradition of earlier pantomimes, she blends the early licentious tradition with feigned childish innocence by invoking the nursery rhymes, "Ride a Cock Horse" and "This is the Way the Ladies Ride," again underscoring the puerile nature of Bloom's fantasy and the pantomime it imitates: "Gee up! A cockhorse to Banbury cross. I'll ride him for the Eclipse stakes. . . . The lady goes a pace a pace and the coachman goes a trot a trot and the gentleman goes a gallop a gallop a gallop a gallop" (*U* 15.2944–49). When Bloom is reduced to the infantile state of wetting his pants, Bello's retort again is in terms of a low music hall song: "The sawdust is there in the corner for you. I gave you strict instructions, didn't I? Do it standing, sir! I'll teach you to behave like a jinkleman! If I catch a trace on your swaddles. Aha! By the ass of the Dorans you'll find I'm a martinet" (*U* 15.3022–25). "Doran's Ass" relates the story of Paddy Doran's brief affair with a jackass. Doran, drunk, mistakes a jackass for his girl, spends the night making love with the animal, and finally weds the girl two days later.[16] Joyce returns the songs of saturnalia to their original place in the pantomime.

Amid a cacophony of other melodies, the soldiers return to the tune of "My Girl's a Yorkshire Girl," and Stephen enters the fray under the musical auspices of the image of the hanged croppy boy, while old Gummy Granny, a degraded parody of the Shan Van Vocht, intones lines from "The Wearing of the Green." In the middle of the altercation Father Malachi O'Flynn, a combination of Stephen's blasphemous tow-ermate and the perfect priest celebrated in the song that bears his name, performs the black mass of ritual sacrifice as Stephen is martyred in the fray. The accompanying music is a combination of anti-papist blasphemy, "Kick the Pope," and a well-known Roman Catholic hymn, "Daily, Daily Sing to Mary."[17] His wounded lips still intoning the line from Fergus's song, Stephen is metamorphosed by the misunderstand-ing Bloom into a combination of Cinderella (a pantomime favorite), Hamlet (Stephen's self-generated surrogate), and a brother mason, all in the final grand transformation—as Hayman claims—of the pantomime.

"Circe" has more references to music than any other chapter except "Sirens." Like "Sirens," the episode is not only rife with song, but bears resemblance to a musically dominated dramatic form. Pantomimes are made up of the stuff of transformation, of adherence both to the mod-ern form of sweet morality and a comic subversive ritual form far older than the nineteenth- and early twentieth-century Dublin stage. As musical celebrations of comic saturnalia and rebirth, they delve deep into the psyche of human nature, an establishment-defying impulse, happy to do battle with seriousness and shame.

From Ritual to Rotgut: Music as Comic Corrective

Long before the beginning of recorded religious worship, music played a major role in nearly all ceremonial rites. Omnipotent powers were traditionally invoked through sound as well as action, and incantation and musical drama figured heavily into nearly every ceremony.

As time went on, music and its metric counterpart in spoken chant became so identified with tradition that they assumed the property of ritual itself, so that certain works of music incorporated the whole cere-mony. For example, chants or choruses evolved from mere response to spoken words, increasingly chanted themselves, to become the entirety of the rite. High masses were conducted entirely in music. What began as religious invocation was metrically and musically enhanced to give it additional dignity. This dignity accorded music assumed a life of its own, and music became a principal vehicle of worship.

At best, however, music used in this manner was always in a sense a profanation, a contrivance of humans to enhance their already imperfect path to bravery or omnipotent truth. As such, in the wrong hands (the mind of the satirist) music was open to the balancing corrective of comedy. When priests turned to an art form that they conceived as more closely emulating the perfection they were trying to express than spoken words could hope to offer, they relied on the bonus factor that music has always had the power to arouse emotion, and the emotion produced by religious music and incantation proved more potent than any vehicle of reason arising from common discourse. In the comic imagination, however, music was likely to produce precisely the opposite effect.

Thus it was often claimed that music had the property of having been itself divinely inspired, the words and the tune, in a sense, having been composed by the deity. Comic writers from Chaucer to Huxley have had a satiric field day with the excesses that arose from such claims. For instance, Spandrell in *Point Counter Point* kills himself after having been convinced that the perfection of Beethoven's A Minor Quartet represents some ultimate good, which proves the existence of evil and allows him to die triumphant. The dubious validity of attaching spiritual importance to a ritual by musical means, or, more blatantly, creating a musical ritual, was recognized by Joyce in *Ulysses*, where characters attempt to accord their bibulous activities a certain ritual dignity by invoking religion, patriotism, and love, and enhancing the whole lot musically.

Here the characters are themselves following the patterns of tradition. Like religion, war and its counterpart, patriotism, draw upon music for dignity and enhanced emotion, from the drums, bugles, and pipes of the army going into battle, to the songs that swell the nationalistic hearts of those at home. When patriotic feelings are artificially aroused through musical tactics, the wedding of slaughter and music have an ultimately manipulative origin, not unlike the religion-music combination. We are trained to march rather than shuffle off to battle.

The comic battles of *Ulysses* are barroom and bedroom oriented, with the occasional skirmish in the street. In terms of selecting an ideal national hero, cuckoldry and drunken pontificating or brawling are hardly the stuff of inspiration. But Joyce chose Odysseus as his proto-typical hero, an adulterer fearful of cuckoldry, a reluctant draftee, and a man interested almost entirely in his own well-being and possessions, who used the worship of a ritual idol to dupe the credulous Trojans, and who defied the gods whenever he thought he could get away with it. Odysseus is about as close to a comic character as an epic hero is ever likely to be.

The background to the modern day Odysseus's wanderings is a city with a cast of characters who have gone far beyond musically desacral-izing ritual. Traditional institutions and rites are almost always under-cut in the novel, and their modern replacements bear the brunt of even harsher satire. While the Greeks used the ritual hecatomb as an excuse for a good meal and party, their consumption was the result of piety, not its cause. In *Ulysses* drinking is the end of the ritual, patriotism and war the excuse, and music the comic ritualizing device that rationalizes and adds the requisite piety and dignity to the whole occasion, just as it did with religious worship over the course of history. The sacrificial wine and wafer have merely been replaced by g.p.'s and sardines.

There is insufficient space here to dwell at length on the role of mu-sic in the novel's depiction of traditional religious ritual per se, except to describe briefly how Joyce comically uses Protestant music, nursery rhymes, bawdy ballads, and nonsense songs as an undercutting back-drop to the two ecclesiastical rites Bloom attends and desacralizes in All Hallows and in the cemetery chapel. In contrast to its usual ritual-enhancing value, Bloom consciously uses music satirically to degrade formal worship on these occasions. Holy Communion prompts his ref-erence to a couple of mealtime nursery rhymes: "The priest bent down to put it into her mouth, murmuring all the time. Latin. The next one. Shut your eyes and open your mouth" (*U* 5.348–50). Bloom is thinking of course of the nursery song, "Open your mouth / And close your eyes / And I'll give you something / To make you wise." However, his next reflections are a bit more convoluted: "Look at them. Now I bet it makes them feel happy. Lollipop. It does. Yes, bread of angels it's called. There's a big idea behind it, kind of kingdom of God is within you feel. First communicants. Hokypoky penny a lump" (*U* 5.359–62). Bloom's last line refers to another nursery rhyme called the "King of the Cannibal Islands":

> Hokey, pokey, whisky thum,
> How d'you like potatoes done?
> Boiled in whiskey, boiled in rum
> Says the King of the Cannibal Islands.

The cannibalistic aspects of the Eucharist are referred to again by Bloom on the next page. While his interpretation of the rite is not far off the mark anthropologically, coupling the idea with the nursery rhymes comically trivializes the concept and transforms the worshipers into children.

When Bloom spies a parishioner asleep near the confessional, his thoughts travel to a Protestant hymn, "Safe in the Arms of Jesus": "Blind faith. Safe in the arms of kingdom come. Lulls all pain. Wake this time next year" (*U* 5.367–68). The Protestant hymn paints a typically sentimental picture in its own profanation of Catholic ritual:

> Safe in the arms of Jesus,
> Safe on his gentle breast,
> There by his gentle love o'er shaded
> Sweetly my soul shall rest.

Sacred somnolence to the unbeliever's eye can take on highly satiric connotations.

Finally, in a gratuitous indignity, Bloom, watching the priest's lace garment, speculates on a bawdy ballad: "Suppose he lost the pin of his. He wouldn't know what to do" (*U* 5.371–72). Admittedly the song lyrics, "O Mary Lost the Pin of Her Drawers. / She didn't know what to do to keep it up," have been in Bloom's mind since he got Martha's letter with the pin in it, but its use here is to deflower both priest and ritual.

Again, in the cemetery chapel Bloom debunks priest and ritual via nursery rhymes: "A server bearing a brass bucket with something in it came out through a door. The whitesmocked priest came after him, tidying his stole with one hand, balancing with the other a little book against his toad's belly. Who'll read the book? I, said the rook" (*U* 6.589–92). In verse five of the rhyme the Rook volunteers to perform the priestly duties:

> Who'll be the parson?
> I, said the Rook,
> With my bell and book
> I'll be the parson.

Thus Bloom, whom we are eventually invited to compare with Christ, becomes the great desacralizer, ironically undercutting religious symbolism with music, the device traditionally employed to enhance ritual.

The other comic aspect of music addressed earlier is its utility in augmenting or creating ritual from the profane, notably to draw upon love, war, and their combination in patriotism to give dignity to the boozy libations of their alcoholic celebrants. Bloom himself foreshadows this musical motif: "Drinkers, drinking, laughed spluttering, their drink against their breath. More power, Pat. Coarse red: fun for drunkards: guffaw and smoke. Take off that white hat. His parboiled eyes. Where is he now? Beggar somewhere. The harp that once did starve us all" (*U* 8.603–7). Bob Doran, the memory of whose drunken figure prompts the passage, is following the ritual Irish trek from innocence to alcoholism. Pat Kinsella's Harp Theatre, a favorite watering hole, becomes in Bloom's mind the alcoholic grave of the celebrants. In the last line of the above passage, Bloom's pun on the name of the theater and the Thomas Moore song of the lost grandeur of Ireland turns drunkenness into a national tragedy. At the Harp Theatre, where music became drinking ritual, the music of Irish patriotism died:

> The harp that once through Tara's halls
> The soul of music shed,
> Now hangs as mute on Tara's walls
> As if that soul were fled,
> So sleeps the pride of former days,
> So glory's thrill is o'er,
> And hearts that once beat high for praise,
> Now feel that pulse no more.

The modern-day ritual perversion of patriotic music to the ends of debauch in places like Kinsella's Harp prompts Bloom's modification of the lyrics to "The harp that once did starve us all."

The two major barroom scenes, "Cyclops" and "Sirens," counterpoint the two ecclesiastical scenes in All Hallows and cemetery chapel. The citizen serves as high priest of tippling in the latter scene, a role recognized immediately by the barfly narrator:

—There he is, says I, in his gloryhole, with his cruiskeen lawn and his load of papers, working for the cause. (*U* 12.122–23)

The musical allusion to "The Cruiskeen Lawn" deals with a traditional Scotch-Irish song, translated literally, "my full little jug." [18] The metaphor works because the citizen's cause is getting someone to buy him a drink. What follows is certainly one of the most ritualized invocations ever depicted in literature:

> —Stand and deliver, says he.
> —That's all right, citizen, says Joe. Friends here.
> —Pass, friends, says he.
> Then he rubs his hand in his eye and says he:
> —What's your opinion of the times?
> Doing the rapparee and Rory of the hill. But, begob, Joe was equal to the occasion.
> —I think the markets are on a rise, says he, sliding his hand down his fork.
> So begob the citizen claps his paw on his knee and he says:
> —Foreign wars is the cause of it.
> And says Joe, sticking his thumb in his pocket:
> —It's the Russians wish to tyrannise.
> —Arrah, give over your bloody codding, Joe, says I. I've a thirst on me I wouldn't sell for half a crown.
> —Give it a name, citizen, says Joe.
> —Wine of the country, says he.
> —What's yours? says Joe.
> —Ditto MacAnaspey, says I.
> —Three pints, Terry, says Joe.
>
> (*U* 12.129–47)

The barfly, miffed that Joe, evidently the only one with money, is holding off buying a round by prolonging the introductory conversation, admonishes his potential benefactor for not sticking to the ritual rules: drinks first, conversation later. That it will be patriotic conversation is signaled by the use of passwords and signs that parody those of the Ribbonmen. The code is augmented musically with the reference to "The Irish Rapparees" and "Rory of the Hill," [19] since both the first song and the citizen have a carping nationalistic quality about them, and the second song celebrates a national hero, famous for harassing landlords, evictors, and the tenants who paid them.

Having begun the ritual, it is not long before the citizen leads his followers around to a Talmudic diatribe on Irish history and patriotism, beginning with a brief musical overture: "So of course the citizen was only waiting for the wink of the word and he starts gassing out of him about the invincibles and the old guard and the men of sixtyseven and who fears to speak of ninetyeight . . ." (*U* 12.479–81). The last clause refers to the first line of "The Memory of the Dead," a song of which all great Irish drinker-heroes are fond because it embodies the ritual of fierce alcoholic patriotism:

> Who fears to speak of Ninety-eight?
> Who blushes at the name?
> When cowards mock the patriot's fate,
> Who hangs his head for shame?
> He's all a knave, or half a slave,
> Who slights his country thus;
> But a true man, like you, man,
> Will fill your glass with us.

According to the song, it is unpatriotic not to drink, so when the citizen begins his long harangue, it will be in the company of like-minded drinkers. Bloom unknowingly violates ritual in two ways: first by accepting a cigar instead of a drink, thus proving himself no "true man," and second by not buying at least the obligatory round or two after a false report of his winning big on Throwaway. Bloom's problems begin and end with his Semitism, but are aggravated by the fact that he knows as little about the secular booze-patriotism ceremonies as he did about the Roman Catholic rituals in "Lotus Eaters."

When the citizen, fed up with Bloom's out-of-place sweet reasonableness, finally invokes ritual incantation, it is to the words of "Where Is the Slave So Lowly?," Thomas Moore's song of fallen Ireland:

> —*Sinn Fein!* says the citizen. *Sinn fein amhain!* The friends we love are by our side and the foes we hate before us.
> The last farewell was affecting in the extreme. From the belfries far and near the funereal deathbell tolled unceasingly while all around the gloomy precincts rolled the ominous warning of a hundred muffled drums punctuated by the hollow booming of pieces of ordnance. . . .
> Considerable amusement was caused by the favourite Dublin streetsingers L-n-h-n and M-ll-g-n who sang *The Night before Larry was Stretched* in their usual mirthprovoking fashion. (*U* 12.523–29, 12.541–43)

The description of the execution turns decidedly toward mirth with the reference to "The Night Before Larry Was Stretched." [20] The song is a curious mixture of pathos, ribaldry, and grisly realism. It was intended to be funny, but at the same time in its description of the last violent jerks of the hanged man, its gallows humor fits both the comic and sinister aspects of the scene at Kiernan's. The episode ends happily enough with Bloom's miraculous escape, but the invocation of all the biblical imagery at the end does not completely dispel our distaste for the barroom secular rituals of contemporary Ireland.

We have already discussed how the "Sirens" episode is a mini-musical comedy in its own right. It further serves the comic genre as the high mass of musically inspired drinking ritual. Presided over by two priests, Simon Dedalus and Ben Dollard, who sing of love, war, and patriotism, the sentimentality generated by the music includes all three subjects in one final comic musical climax, punctuated by Bloom's wind instrument.

When Simon and his friends take the Ormond stage at four o'clock, the most emotion-laden hour of Bloom's day, their love songs produce enhanced pathos, only to be cheapened by the sentimentality of amorous sacrifice transferred to patriotic and finally to religious sacrifice. There is only so much sentiment to be tolerated by readers bombarded for thirty-five pages by the romantic musical losses of sweethearts and martyrs, and so the episode inevitably turns comic. If, as we have seen, Simon touches Bloom with his version of Lionel's cry for his lost love in *M'appari,* Bloom has only become much more cynical toward the croppy boy's suffering during Dollard's ballad of youthful martyrdom, and resolves to "Get out before the end," in exactly the same way he exited All Hallows to beat the collection plate.

The alcoholic connotations of the musical ritual of "Sirens" are considerably more muted than they are in the company of lower class brawlers at Barney Kiernan's. One difference is that while a body of musical reference is invoked in "Cyclops," in the musical comedy of "Sirens" the music is performed as well as alluded to. The citizen merely pronounces a catechism enhanced by musical allusion, while the musical litany of emotion is performed in "Sirens." This is not meant to imply that Simon and company do not like their booze, or that the afternoon will not become increasingly patriotic as the drinking continues. We have already noted that beginning with such love songs as

"When the Bloom Is on the Rye," "The Shade of the Palm," "Goodbye Sweetheart Goodbye," and *M'appari,* the chapter undergoes a gradual metamorphosis into the melodies of war.

War-like themes begin early with the triumphal arrival of Boylan to the martial strains of "See the Conquering Hero Comes," carrying the double meaning of amorous as well as belligerent triumphs, and proceed through the transitional duet, "Love and War," to the pathos of the sacrificial croppy boy, whose only serious crime was loving his country above his king. The music degenerates into the patriotic nostalgia we are to hear later in "Cyclops," and finally into the last words of Christ, intoned to the text of Robert Emmet's gallows statement, and accompanied by Bloom's fortissimo flatulence.

The conclusion of the "Sirens" ritual is much the same as it is in "Cyclops":

> —True men like you men.
> —Ay, ay, Ben.
> —Will lift your glass with us.
> They lifted.
> Tschink. Tschunk.
>   (*U* 11.1276–80)

But again Bloom puts his own variation and final commentary on the chapter and its ceremonies, when he discovers Emmet's last words in Lionel Marks's window, sets them to the tune of Mercadante's profanation of Christ's death, and waits for the tram noise to crescendo before adding his own final blast of self-generated hot air to the performance.

Throughout the novel Joyce uses Bloom as the agent of comic desacralization, not only to debunk the Quixotic motifs of his would-be son, but to explode the mythologies and rituals of Joyce's countrymen. Where they have used music to heighten as well as create ritual, Bloom's satiric views comically explode literally as well as figuratively the profanation of tradition for ignoble purpose. And the demythologizing process is accomplished largely through the same means used to create it, notably music. As readers we can examine the debris in full knowledge of its sentimental pretenses, and yet be mightily moved despite ourselves. Is it genius or schlock? In a work in which musical comedy plays so great a role, I'm not sure there's a great deal of difference.

Notes

1. For the texts and applications to *Ulysses* of the songs alluded to in this essay, see Zack Bowen, *Musical Allusions in the Works of James Joyce: Early Poetry through "Ulysses"* (Albany: State University of New York Press, 1974). For reproductions of the actual music and the history of many of these songs, see Ruth Bauerle, *The James Joyce Songbook* (New York: Garland, 1982, 1984).

2. For detailed definitions and analyses of the various aspects of comedy, see "*Ulysses* and Comic Theory," in Zack Bowen, *"Ulysses" as a Comic Novel* (Syracuse, N.Y.: Syracuse University Press, 1989), 17–44.

3. See Bowen, *Musical Allusions,* 2, 86–87, 89, 91, 95, 117, 140–41, 142, 150, 167, 192–93, 256, 273–74, 319, 345; and Vernon Hall, "Joyce's Use of Da Ponte and Mozart's *Don Giovanni,*" *Publications of the Modern Language Association* 66 (March 1951): 78–84.

4. Bowen, *Musical Allusions,* 53.

5. David Hayman, "Forms of Folly in Joyce: A Study of Clowning in *Ulysses,*" *ELH* 34 (1967): 260–83; Elliott B. Gose, Jr., *The Transformation Process in Joyce's "Ulysses"* (Toronto: University of Toronto Press, 1980), 137–66; Cheryl Herr, *Joyce's Anatomy of Culture* (Urbana: University of Illinois Press, 1986), 96–135.

6. Francis Macdonald Cornford, *The Origin of Attic Comedy,* ed. Theodore H. Gaster (Garden City, N.Y.: Doubleday Anchor Books, 1961).

7. Mikhail Bakhtin, *Problems of Dostoevski's Poetics,* ed. and trans. Caryl Emerson (Minneapolis: University of Minnesota Press, 1984); and *Rabelais and His World,* trans. Helene Iswolsky (Cambridge, Mass.: The MIT Press, 1968).

8. See R. J. Broadbent, *A History of Pantomime* (London: Simpkin, 1901; rpt. New York: The Citadel Press, 1965) for an interesting idiosyncratic history of the genre, from which much of my brief account is taken.

9. Bakhtin, *Rabelais and His World,* 34.

10. Broadbent, 195–96.

11. Gose, 149.

12. See Herr, 136–88, on transvestism and transformation.

13. Gose, 146.

14. Joyce errs in calling this the "introit" for the Easter season, which would be *Resurrexi, et adhuc tecum sum, alleluia: posuisti super me manum tuam, alleluia.*

15. The lyrics of the song "Bloomusalem," which I performed at the Joyce conference in Vancouver (June 1991), were of course of my own composition.

16. "Doran's Ass," in Colm O Lochlainn, *Irish Street Ballads* (Dublin: Three Candles Limited, 1939), 166–67, 217.

17. "Kick the Pope" and "Daily, Daily Sing to Mary" are in the Bowen Collection, Richter Library, University of Miami.

18. "The Cruiskeen Lawn," in Bauerle, 423–25.

19. Charles Gavan Duffy, "The Irish Rapparees," in Padraic Colum, ed., *A Treasury of Irish Verse* (New York: Liveright, 1922), 279–80, 353; Anon., "Rory of the Hill," in Georges-Denis Zimmermann, *Songs of Irish Rebellion* (Hatboro, Pa.: Folklore Associates, 1967), 268–69. From an 1868 Broadside in the National Library of Ireland.

20. Bauerle, 454–56.

Pantomime Songs and the Limits of Narrative in *Ulysses*

Henriette Lazaridis Power

I am the boy
That can enjoy
Invisibility.

These words were once sung on the stage of a Christmas pantomime by an actor who was visible to the spectators. Immediately after the song, when the actor had "become" invisible, he was still visible to the spectators.[1] In Joyce's *Ulysses,* when Stephen remembers his mother's stories of Edward Royce singing this song as Turko the Terrible,[2] Royce and his Turko finally achieve the invisibility the song proclaims. The words of the song stand to remind the readers of Joyce's text that Royce's Turko—and any other figure evoked in a narrative—must be invisible to his or her audience. At the same time, the reference to Royce's song makes us aware that any song evoked in a narrative, strictly speaking, goes unheard. Of course, the real invisibility of a creature of narrative, and the inaudibility of a written and unperformed song are necessities of written discourse. But in the case of Turco's complicated invisibility and inaudibility, and in the case of his ghostly presence in *Ulysses,* Joyce not only heightens our awareness of the limits of narrative, but also suggests ways in which song in general and pantomime song in particular can serve as a form of discourse that eludes or challenges the limits of the written text.

While Joyce alludes extensively to the pantomime itself—particularly in *Finnegans Wake,* where the titles of pantomimes appear frequently throughout the text and where "The Mime of Mick, Nick, and the Maggies" takes the form of a panto as one of its patterns—his references to the music of the pantomime in *Ulysses* are few. They are, nevertheless, significant in the sense that they center on the performances of Edward Royce as the visible invisible Turco. Joyce seems to have had a particular interest in Royce, asking Constantine Curran for a libretto of *Turko the Terrible* [*sic*] as late as 1937 (*Letters 1* 393).[3] In *Ulysses*, Royce becomes an object of shared appreciation for Bloom, May Dedalus, and, probably, Stephen: May most likely saw Royce in the 1873 *Turco the Terrible*; in "Calypso" Bloom may derive his image of the cross-legged Turko from the same production (he was seven years old at the time); in addition to his mother's stories about Royce, Stephen (then ten years old) may have seen him in 1892 as Captain M'Turco in *Sinbad*. As we learn in "Ithaca," it is this production for which Bloom was commissioned to write a topical song. Royce's Turco, then, becomes a shared reference point for these three figures in *Ulysses*, and becomes, as well, a point of departure for Joyce's consideration of the disjunctions between genres and between words and music, writing and the voice.

Before we look closely at Royce's Turco and at the aliases to which his song becomes related in the text, it will be helpful to consider the specific nature of the pantomime itself, as well as to examine the function of songs in the pantomime. The British pantomime of the nineteenth century was a more or less formulaic production, consisting of two parts: first the "opening," an often modernized staging of a fairy tale or folk tale; then the harlequinade, an unrelated piece that borrowed its characters and its emphatically gestural acting style from the conventions of the commedia dell'arte. Between the two parts was the transformation scene—a gradual unfolding of layers of elaborate scenery and the best that Victorian special effects had to offer, transporting the characters of the opening into a magnificent fairy land. Like the transformation scene, the other two portions of the panto offered ample opportunity for spectacular performance: the opening and harlequinade were full of scenes of "comic business," magical effects, songs, "concerted pieces," and, later in the century, even acrobatic acts.[4]

While the pantomime did, like mime, involve a good deal of silent gesturing and posturing, it relied heavily on music for the creation of its spectacular effects. All the same, very little music was actually written especially for pantomime. Most of the songs in a given production would more accurately be defined as "settings"—of new lyrics to melodies with an established popularity. The London audience of the 1901 production of *The Babes in the Wood,* for example, heard the music of "Now What Will Become of Poor Old Ireland" sung with lyrics that drastically changed the meaning of the song. The lyrics ran:

> Baron Bluster, Baron Bluster
> Naughty, naughty chap,
> She has plainly let you know,
> She does not care a rap.
> Pardon us if we giggle and grin—
> You see we love you so.
> If you could buy another face,
> You might win her you know.

The song's concern with Ireland and the Home Rule question is completely removed from the lyrics to describe instead a romantic usurpation—Baron Bluster's failed attempt to woo Phyllis away from her eventual husband, Prince Charming.[5] This particular rewording raises questions about the imperial use to which the pantomime was put, and it leads us to think that the response to the reshaped song would have been markedly different in London and in Dublin. Yet in more innocuous cases of rewording, the audience could—and presumably did—enjoy the familiar and popular tune and admire the often comic revision its lyrics had undergone for the production at hand.

On other, less frequent, occasions, the original words of a song remained intact, yet its new context within the pantomime plot gave those words a new resonance and meaning. When Balfe's very popular "Killarney," for instance, was used in a nineteenth-century Theatre Royal performance of *Robinson Crusoe* in Dublin, the song served not only as a reminder of the county's beauty, but more forcefully as part of the panto's general warning that "No stranger shall upon my realms encroach." Following the singing of the song, the "Spirit of the Lake" joined the rest of the panto's Irish characters in defending the county: "While we live let it be our duty / To the alien ne'er to sell."[6]

In many cases, the conjunction of old melody and new lyrics played on the *dis*junction between the original and the revised subject matter of the song. And where a melody was a particular favorite of the time, it would be introduced into the pantomime plot with little attention to narrative coherence or relevance. The songs of a pantomime production, then, presented the audience with a dual disjunction—between a melody and its new lyrics, and between narrative and song. Certainly, pantomime songs did have a practical purpose in the pantomime, as they seem to have been used to initiate transitions from one scene to the next, or to mark entrances and exits within one scene. But they were most often introduced as rather gratuitous star turns, and the pantomime paused for the virtuoso performance of a favorite song sung with new and clever lyrics. The star-turn quality of the pantomime song became more prominent toward the end of the nineteenth century as the panto began to draw its music not only from popular songs, but from the music hall as well. In the music hall context, the song was an "act" with no underpinning in any narrative at all.[7] Translated into the panto, the song retains its independence from the requirements of a narrative plot.

Even more removed from the exigencies of the pantomime plot were the topical songs of the pantomime. Like the other songs, the topical songs were introduced somewhat gratuitously into the narrative flow of the panto, but rather than alluding in some sense to that plot, the topical songs turned instead to current events. In the midst of a pantomime of *Ali-Baba and the Forty Thieves*, for instance, the genies I, O, and U materialize to sing a song about national and personal debt.[8] The topical song that Bloom would have written (but has not) for *Sinbad* would have combined the history of Brian Boru with the contemporary issues of the visit to Ireland of the Duke and Duchess of York, or of the opening of a new Dublin fish market—in either case, issues far removed from the concerns of the *Sinbad* plot (*U* 17.417–45).

By introducing references to actual and contemporary events, the topical song offered the panto audience a not so implicit reminder that the rest of the panto was fictive. Like any postmodernist metatextual device, the topical song broke the spell of the illusion, making its hearers aware of the real world from which the panto had provided a diversion. More specifically, the song reasserted certain distinctions that the illusion of the pantomime necessarily blurred: distinctions between the fictive and the real, and between the genres of narrative and non-narrative song.

The operation of the topical song in the pantomime is similar to that of any song when it appears in a written narrative. When Royce sings Turko's song in Stephen's recollection of his mother's memory, or when in "Sirens" Miss Douce sings *"O, Idolores, queen of the eastern seas!"* from the musical *Floradora* (*U* 11.226),[9] the apparent shift from writing into music initially goes unquestioned by Joyce's readers. But as we consider more closely the problems of recording Miss Douce's "all but humm[ing]" and "trill[ing]" (*U* 11.378), we become aware of the constraints of the narrative framework and of the fundamental distinction between written words and the voice. The trill and the hum of Miss Douce's voice, like the timbre of Royce's, cannot be translated into the written text. Moreover, as with all translations, something is lost in the shift from one discourse to another. For the move into music is only an apparent one, of course; though the text shifts into song, it remains a written text unable to record the living voice of the singer.

Here the pantomime becomes relevant again in helping us clarify the relationship between singing, speaking, and writing. Along with the comic business of the panto, the musical portion of the performance was the most susceptible to change and revision, and was often left unspecified by the script. The dialogue, on the other hand, remained more or less permanent according to the words set down on the printed page. This distinction between speaking and the more improvisational elements of singing and business emphasizes the association between gesture and the singing voice as the essentially physical rather than verbal elements of the pantomime performance. While the speaking voice can supposedly be recorded, according to narrative conventions, the voice that sings has a dimension more obviously inaccessible to written words.

The "Ithaca" chapter of *Ulysses* addresses the question of the compatibility of voice and writing in its inclusion of the anti-Semitic song about little Harry Hughes (*U* 17.801–28). The narrator demands a recitation of "the first (major) part of this chanted legend," and the words are printed in the text, followed by the musical score for those words. But the recitation of "the second part (minor) of the legend" is accomplished in the text through the citation of four of the song's stanzas, with only the first accompanied by a musical score. Certainly, this format is the standard for song notation, which requires that the score be repeated as successive stanzas of the song are sung. Nevertheless, as part of a literary text, the song about little Harry Hughes creates a disjunction in "Ithaca" between words and music: the music does not match the words recorded in the literary text, and the text, of course, leaves out the voice that must sing the song.

Because of this implicit elusiveness of the singing voice, all of Joyce's borrowings from music are, in a sense, like borrowings from topical songs: the songs within the narrative make explicit not only the fictive nature of the text that frames them, but also the disjunction between voice and words. Like Joyce's early reference in *Ulysses* to the visible singer of a song about invisibility, his reference in "Ithaca" to Bloom's topical song plays with our sense of presence and absence. Turko is there but not there after he sings, and Bloom's song is there in the text of *Ulysses*—but as an *un*written song. The catechistic narrator of "Ithaca" tells us that Bloom has refrained from writing "a topical song (music by R. G. Johnston) on the events of the past, or fixtures for the actual, years, entitled *If Brian Boru could but come back and see old Dublin now*" (*U* 17.417–19). Bloom's reasons for musical reticence are telling—among them an implicit worry that the topical pairing of Brian Boru's fictional visit with the actual Dublin visit of the Duke and the Duchess of York will unpleasantly remind the pantomime audience of Ireland's conquest by the British (*U* 17.431–33). Bloom seems preoccupied with the problem of how to position his song in terms of the Empire and its power alignments. In addition to his concern with the Duke and Duchess of York, he expresses an uncertainty regarding his choice of topical subject matter—"the anticipated diamond jubilee of Queen Victoria . . . [or] the posticipated opening of the new municipal fish market" (*U* 17.428–30). Add to this his sense, perhaps, that the pantomime was, after all, a British import, often replete with imperialist propaganda.[10] Bloom's silence suggests that he is unable to decide whether to celebrate the Empire or to critique it by alluding to Ireland as a degraded nation.

By not writing the topical song, Bloom forgoes the necessity of confronting these problems, and, indirectly, he refrains from suggesting that Ireland's status as independent nation—embodied in part by Brian Boru, the defeater of Norse invaders—is fictive. He resists the creation of a topical song that would heighten the audience's awareness of the disjunction between fictive and real, power and submission. Moreover, the reference to the topical song appears in "Ithaca" almost immediately after the question and answer of the narration identifies "Name, age, race, creed" as the "four separating forces" between Bloom and Stephen (*U* 17.402–3). Bloom's refusal to write a song that will remind its hearers of unpleasant distinctions—of race and creed as well as power between Ireland and England—operates in "Ithaca" to suggest that the apparent distinctions between Bloom and "his temporary guest" (*U* 17.402) need not be noticed.

Bloom is foiled, however, by the narrator of "Ithaca," who details all of his hesitations and preoccupations, and who thus reminds Joyce's readers of the fact that Bloom has no choice but to position himself within the Empire. No matter how he resolves his preoccupations with and hesitations toward his place within imperial power alignments, and no matter how much the comedy of the pantomime can appear to mollify the tensions of Empire, in "Ithaca," Bloom and his unwritten song remain contextualized by the problems of colonialization. By the same token, on the level of narrative, the unwritten song survives in the text to remind us of the problems of translation between discourses. Even the speculative introduction of Bloom's song into *Ulysses* asserts significant distinctions between the singing voice and the written text.

Unlike the reference to the topical song of the pantomime, Joyce's reference to Turco's "Invisibility" song provides a site in the text where distinctions *are* blurred and where certain sympathies or connections are established. *Turco the Terrible; or, Harlequin Prince Amabel* presents the typical pantomime plot of prohibited and then magically achieved love through the story of the tyrannical King Turco and his attempts to disrupt the pleasant world of King Buonocore and his son Amabel. The magic device that assists in the reunion of Amabel and his chosen Violet is a pair of roses—red and white: a sniff of the white rose grants invisibility, while a sniff of the red returns the bearer to visibility.[11] Turco sings the "Invisibility" song once he gains possession of the white rose, expressing his delight in being able to use his invisibility to elude authorities like publicans, attorneys seeking fees, ticket-takers, and bobbies; he goes on to use his invisibility to eavesdrop on a conspiracy against him (*Turco* 19–20). However, the plot of the panto reveals that neither visibility nor invisibility is a consistent and reliable source of power. For earlier, as soon as two allies of Amabel become visible, Turco apprehends them; but as soon as Turco becomes *in*visible, he loses his kingdom to Buonocore (ibid.). Within the panto of *Turco,* then, the distinction between visibility and invisibility is confused by the logistics of a staged performance that must make its "invisible" characters visible to the audience; and it is also blurred by the plot of the panto, which plays with the identification of either visibility or invisibility as a source of power.

The issue of invisibility and visibility is introduced in *Ulysses* through Joyce's explicit reference to Turco's song in "Telemachus." The song is part of Stephen's reverie on his mother and on *"love's bitter mys-*

tery," which he feels to have eluded him in his relationship with her. The reverie is prompted by Buck Mulligan's singing or recitation[12] of Yeats's "Who Goes With Fergus?" and by Stephen's subsequent recollection of his playing of the song for his mother (*U* 1.237–53). Stephen goes on to remember his mother's "secrets"—among them, dancecards, a birdcage, Royce singing Turco's song, a drinking glass, a cored apple full of sugar (*U* 1.255–63). Significantly, these secrets seem to mark absences of some kind, in addition to being reminders of May Dedalus's absence in death: the dancecard prescribes only the partner not the dance, the cage is empty of the bird, the glass is empty, the apple filled though cored, and Royce's Turco is on the verge of becoming invisible. Into this vacated space, May Dedalus's ghost emerges—a vision of a mute, wasted, and foul-smelling corpse whose power resides in her "glazing eyes" and her "hoarse loud breath" (*U* 1.270–76). Even her speech is absent.

But Turco and May's ghost remind us that the space of Stephen's vision is not so vacant after all. It becomes, in fact, a space in which emptiness and fullness, absence and presence become intertwined. For instance, Turco's disappearance into the invisibility proclaimed by the song is never a complete absence since the audience continues to see him after he smells the magic rose. In other words, Royce's Turco is there but invisible. Conversely, May Dedalus is *not* there but visible; her appearance in the vision makes her present to Stephen, but she is present as a sign of absence and silence. Royce's song here seems to have had the power to do two things: to conjure up the ghost of Stephen's mother, and to put into question the distinction between presence and absence, vacancy and completeness. The allusion to Turco's song leads Joyce's reader to reconsider the emptiness and silence of May's birdcage, the hollowness of the filled apple, and, more generally, the ghostliness, the silence, or invisibility of a figure of narrative. It is as if the song provides for the narrative discourse the same kind of disguise that it provides for Turco: having assumed a musical form, the text is more flexible, more able to blur the distinctions that the denotative language of narration relies on.

What is significant about *Turco* and the appearance of the "Invisibility" song in *Ulysses* is the pair of flowers that bring about the conversion from presence to apparent absence (and back) in the pantomime. As in *Turco,* the various forms of flowers that appear in Joyce's text assist in blurring the distinctions that the topical song clarifies and confirms.

Joyce associates the flower fairly consistently with music, and with a kind of language that challenges or frustrates conventional notions of communication. Moreover, the flower introduces to Joyce's text a more physical language in which speech or singing is not so much immaterial breath or voice, but what Bloom calls the "Vibrations" of the material body (*U* 11.794).[13] This associative joining of song with the physical language of flowers reminds us again of the essential distinction between singing and writing; as physical communication, song escapes the permanent denotations of the written text.

The flower that precipitates Turco's song in the panto appears in "Sirens" as Bloom writes to Martha Clifford under the pseudonym of Henry Flower. The explicit musical allusion here is, clearly, to Flotow's *Martha,* whose song *M'appari tutt' amor* runs through the narrative of "Sirens." But Joyce's use of references works also in a less explicit, more associative, manner. The presence in Joyce's writing of something borrowed should alert his readers to the possible influence on the text of something that is not clearly there—something apparently invisible yet related to the visible, legible material. This apparent absence is relevant in the case of the flowers of *Turco the Terrible.*

Like Turco, Bloom uses the flower as an alias—in this case, to produce a different sort of invisibility. By carrying on his correspondence under the assumed name of Henry Flower, Bloom keeps his real self doubly invisible: he avoids physical contact with Martha, and he conceals his own identity. As in the case of Royce playing Turco, Bloom as Flower is simultaneously absent and present; he is the one who writes, but he writes letters that deliberately replace him with someone else. Moreover, Bloom shares Turco's voyeurism, commenting internally in "Sirens," "See, not be seen" (*U* 11.357–58).

Yet Bloom's voyeurism is a source of power here, not disempowerment. For under this disguise or alias, Bloom is able to express himself (as is Martha, presumably) through a different sort of language—what he calls alternately a "language of flow" and a "Language of flowers" (*U* 11.298, 5.261).[14] The language in which Henry Flower and Martha Clifford correspond is intertwined with music—specifically, with the *M'appari* of *Martha,* and more generally, with Bloom's internal humming and murmuring in "Sirens."[15] In the text of "Sirens," Bloom's/ Flower's postscript, for instance, appears as "P.S. The rum tum tum" and "P.P.S. La la la ree. I feel so sad today" (*U* 11.890, 11.894). As the postscript suggests, Bloom's writing under the alias of Flower eludes complete transcription into words. There are several levels of disguise here: Bloom covers his message to Martha of "it will excite me" with a murmur of "best references"; and he covers both the actual message and its disguise with his murmured singing of "La la la ree" (*U* 11.888, 11.894). The written, the spoken, and the sung come together in Bloom's/Flower's letter, indicating to us that written discourse can be overlayed by or interlarded with other discourses that challenge its denotative power. Bloom's use of the alias in "Sirens" stages a sort of surreptitious creeping into written narrative of a physical and musical discourse. As in *Turco,* the F(f)lower provides a disguise that enables the crossing of barriers—between presence and absence, visibility and invisibility, and between what can and what cannot be transcribed into words.

Within *Ulysses,* Turco's song does more than blur distinctions, however. It also establishes connections between apparently disparate characters. While Bloom is associated with May Dedalus by virtue of his spring-like name, it is likely that he also shares May's memory of "old Royce sing[ing] in the pantomime of *Turko the Terrible*" (*U* 1.257–58) since they were both children in 1873. The connection has the effect of giving May's memory a physical presence within the text. The flower of Turco's song is also, of course, part of the link between Bloom and Flower—a link that pairs the cuckold with the adulterer. The pairing of Bloom and his alias creates a confusion of the victim with the vanquished, as Bloom figuratively inhabits both the role of the disempowered cuckold and of the Boylan-like seducer. The same connection is suggested in "Nausicaa," where voyeuristic seduction is mutual between Bloom and Gerty, and where this seduction coincides with Boylan's tryst with Molly.

Finally, both Stephen and Bloom, as children, have seen Royce perform as either Turco the Terrible or Captain M'Turco. This shared experience of Royce and his "Invisibility" song seems to be able to counteract the power of the "four separating forces" between Stephen and Bloom mentioned in "Ithaca." These separating forces of "Name, age, race, creed" (*U* 17.403) are not insignificant. We know from "Cyclops" that Bloom is persecuted for his Jewishness, and we know from various moments in *Ulysses* that he senses himself an outsider in both racial and religious terms. Moreover, the text of "Ithaca" emphasizes these separating forces through its subsequent reference to the topical song and its implicit setting of English race and Protestant creed against Irish race and Catholic creed. Nevertheless, along with all these indications of separation between Stephen and Bloom, *Ulysses* offers scattered images of connection—among them shared visions of the Orient filtered through a memory of *Turco the Terrible* and the *Arabian Nights.* In "Proteus," Stephen thinks of a man like the "Haroun al Raschid" of the *Nights,* along with images of "Street of harlots," "Red carpet spread," "creamfruit," and "melon" (*U* 3.366–69). Bloom, meanwhile, envisions, "Turbaned faces going by. Dark caves of carpet shops, big man, Turko the terrible, seated crosslegged, smoking a coiled pipe. Cries of sellers in the streets. Drink water scented with fennel, sherbet" (*U* 4.88–91).

Significantly, the association between Stephen and Bloom appears to be possible largely in terms of a shared opposition to the Orient. The problematic nature of the connection perhaps explains the apparent contradiction between the two functions of pantomime songs in *Ulysses.* For, in considering the operations of Bloom's topical song and Turko's song in the text, the question remains how it can be that one type of pantomime song should foster connection in Joyce's text while another type should act as an agent of demarcation and disruption. In both songs, the nature of the distinctions—blurred or asserted—is imperial. While the topical song asserts distinctions between English and Irish (or, more generally, between empowered majority and disempowered minority), the image of Turko places "Irish" on the same side as "Jewish" in opposition to the exotic East. Under the politics implied by the topical song, Stephen and Bloom might fall on opposite sides of a cultural distinction; yet according to the politics of Turko and the stereotyped image of the East that he suggests, the two characters share their empowerment against the Other. It is perhaps this political context of the two songs that determines their function in *Ulysses.*

But that is not all. In Joyce's use of both Turco's song and the topical song, we are led to consider the specifics of the overlapping of Empire and pantomime song. Such a consideration would seem, in fact, to be unavoidable since the pantomime can be seen as a part of imperialism, imported from the Home of the Empire and espousing its propaganda.[16] We have seen that, despite his decision to forego the writing of a song that will in some way confront the issue of Empire, Bloom remains contextualized *by* those issues; he remains a relatively powerless figure whose actions are controlled by the dominant political and narrative authority.

At the same time, there is another contextualization and another power relation going on in Joyce's text: a relation between the powers of narrative discourse and of the discourse of the singing voice. As Joyce's use of pantomime songs points out, the discourse of written narrative remains contextualized, determined in some way, by the problem of translating the singing voice into writing. Though Bloom's song shows us the assertion of the dominant power, that dominant representational power is challenged by the potentially marginal discourse that enters the text in the form of song. Joyce's use of pantomime songs serves as an illustration of the ways in which music in general works in his texts to challenge the way the written narrative operates. Despite their suggestion of invisibility and of silence, or perhaps because of it, the references to pantomime song in *Ulysses* become sites in which the limitations of written discourse are tested and made visible.

Notes

1. Edwin Hamilton, *Turco the Terrible; or Harlequin Prince Amabel, the Magic Roses and Oberon, King of the Fairies, Words of the Songs,* 3d ed. Gaiety Theatre (Dublin: 1874), 20. All further references to this work will appear in the text as *Turco.* From the collection of the library of the University of Illinois. I am indebted to Cheryl Herr for providing me with a copy of this text.

2. Since Joyce misspells the name of the pantomime's invisible man, I will adopt his spelling of "Turko" whenever I am referring to the character cited in *Ulysses.* In reference to the pantomime itself, I will spell the name "Turco."

3. The interest in Royce may have, in fact, derived from the similarity of the two men's names—a phonic similarity that Joyce might have delighted in for his writing of the *Wake,* especially with its allusion, through Turko, to disguise and voyeurism.

4. For detailed accounts of the form of the pantomime, see: David Mayer, III, *Harlequin in his Element* (Cambridge: Harvard University Press, 1969); R. J. Broadbent, *A History of Pantomime* (London: Simpkin, 1901); Michael R. Booth, ed. *English Plays of the Nineteenth Century,* vol. 5 (Oxford: Clarendon Press, 1976).

5. The song's other title, according to the *Babes in the Wood* book of words, was "Charlie Parlie"—a nickname, perhaps, for Parnell (Stanley Rogers, *The Babes in the Wood,* Dalston Theatre [London: 1901], 9. Harvard Theatre Collection). All pantomime citations, unless otherwise noted, are from the Harvard Theatre Collection.

6. *Robinson Crusoe.* Theatre Royal (Dublin: [n.y.]), 13, 17.

7. Cheryl Herr, *Joyce's Anatomy of Culture* (Urbana: University of Illinois Press, 1986), 191–92. As Herr points out, these music hall songs tended to introduce to the pantomime a degree of what contemporary viewers considered indecency or vulgarity inappropriate for the essentially childlike world of the pantomime (105–6). Joyce's use of pantomime music should perhaps be considered in the context of this music hall influence. A reference to a panto song in Joyce can be said to carry with it a controversy regarding the issue of what is obscene and what can be seen.

8. Gilbert á Beckett, *Ali-Baba and the Forty Thieves; or, Harlequin and the Genii of the Arabian Nights,* Covent Garden (London: 1866), Boston Public Library, Special Collections.

9. Ruth Bauerle, *The James Joyce Songbook* (New York: Garland, 1982, 1984), 357.

10. Herr notes a song from the Dublin Theatre Royal's 1902 production of *Sleeping Beauty* that asserts the cooperation, pride, and patriotism of all colonies of the British Empire (112–13). The Harvard Theatre Collection offers numerous examples of such Imperialist sentiment.

11. Interestingly, the device of the flowers presents the audience with a complex of confused senses: the white rose is something lacking color that one smells in order to be invisible to sight. Moreover, when the audience sees the white rose worn by an actor, they know they "cannot" see the actor wearing it. Molly's thoughts in "Penelope" of the song "Shall I wear a white rose, shall I wear a red" seem to confirm the color patterning of *Turco*'s roses: she associates white with the invisibility of imaginative and illicit meetings (*U* 18.768, 18.1553–54) and red with the visibility of her real and accepted meeting with Bloom on Howth (*U* 18.1603). I am indebted to Ruth Bauerle for drawing this to my attention.

12. Mulligan seems to be reciting, for Stephen hears simply "the drone of his descending voice"; yet, since Joyce had set the poem to music, it is possible that Mulligan's droning is a deliberately pompous delivery of the song.

13. Like Bloom, Stephen in "Telemachus" thinks of music in terms of its materiality: the "long dark chords" of the song vibrating in the piano (*U* 1.250).

14. As in the case of Turco, smell is part of this disguised activity: Martha's letter asks Bloom "what kind of perfume does your wife use" (*U* 5.258, 11.689).

15. Another element here is that of Bloom's farting ("Pprrpffrrppfff" [*U* 11.1293]) which again reminds us of the physical, material aspect of Bloom's language of F(f)lowers.

16. One need only look at the advertisements included throughout the

pantomime scripts to see this. Dispensing with the subtlety of modern adver-
tising, these ads bluntly proclaim Imperialist sentiment. For instance: "The
Boer of the Transvaal is uncouth and ignorant, but the bore of a Peterson
Patent Pipe is absolutely perfect" (Rogers, *The Babes in the Wood,* and passim
Harvard Theatre Collection).

"A Rollicking Rattling Song of the Halls": Joyce and the Music Hall

Ulrich Schneider

> *"By-the-by, Nancy, will you go with me to a music-*
>   *hall tomorrow night?"*
> *"A music-hall?"*
> *"Yes. It would do us both good, I think."*
> —George Gissing, *In the Year of the Jubilee*

The Music Hall as Criticism of Life

In the year in which *Ulysses* takes place, Stanislaus Joyce entered in his diary the following comment about his elder brother: "Jim considers the music hall, not poetry, as criticism of life."[1] According to Ellmann, Joyce and his father went to London in May 1900, spending "most of their evenings [. . .] at theaters and music halls"; they came back to Dublin, the one with "funny garbled versions of popular songs," the other with the discovery that Matthew Arnold's famous formula no longer applied to modern life and that the music hall had superseded poetry as criticism of life. Ellmann tells us that they saw Eleanora Duse in *La Gioconda* and *La Città Morta* (*JJ2* 77), but we have no information about which music halls father and son visited or what they saw and heard in them.

Music halls had proliferated in London and the industrial centers of Great Britain since the early Victorian period and by 1900 they were still in their heyday.[2] Different explanations of their success have been offered; according to a contemporary observer no other reason was needed, however, than the following very simple one: "The music-hall offers variety—it matters not whether it be good or bad—the theatre, monotony, variety the people prefer, and always have preferred."[3]

If the Joyces did have a tourist guide, say the latest Baedeker for *London and its Environs,* they would have been given a wide enough selection, even if it comprehended only a small section out of the total number of halls. If they restricted themselves only to the halls listed for the West End, they might have visited the London Pavilion at Piccadilly Circus; from there after a short stroll up Shaftesbury Avenue they would have reached the Palace Theatre of Varieties. Turning toward Leicester Square they would have come to the Empire Theatre of Varieties and the Alhambra, both famous for their splendid ballets and, especially the latter, notorious for their "gilded vice"; carrying on toward the river they would soon have passed the newly opened Hippodrome, more circus than music hall, and at Charing Cross and in the Strand they could have chosen between the more traditional music halls, Gatti's ("under the arches") and the Tivoli. In most of these places they would have been admitted to the gallery for sixpence, if they had waited patiently in the long line outside and would not have felt uncomfortable in the rows densely packed with spectators from the lower classes; or they could have paid up to seven and six for better seats. At any rate they would have got their money's worth watching some of the most celebrated music hall stars of the day, perhaps Marie Lloyd, "Our Marie," as Londoners called her affectionately, or Vesta Tilley, "the London Idol," or Dan Leno, "the King's Jester," or Albert Chevalier, "the Coster Laureate," to name just a few.

But the pleasure would not have been unmitigated for a "pro-Boer" such as John Joyce. In May 1900 the "jingoism" building up during the Boer War had reached a feverish climax and, as Stanislaus remembers in *My Brother's Keeper,* already "in the train from Holyhead to London, [John Joyce] had words regarding the war with another traveller, an English jingo, and only my brother's calm dialectic prevented their actually coming to blows."[4] Jingoism was rampant in the music halls; in fact, some hostile critics blamed them for the dissemination of this evil spirit. Thus the liberal and pro-Boer J. A. Hobson wrote:

> Among the large sections of the middle and the labouring classes, the music-hall and the recreative public-house into which it shades off by imperceptible degrees, are a more potent educator than the church, the school, the political meeting, or even the press. . . . Its words and melodies pass by quick magic from the Empire or the Alhambra over the

length and breadth of the land, until the remotest village is familiar with air and sentiment. By such process of artistic suggestion the fervour of Jingoism has been widely fed.[5]

The music halls provided the British Army with the tunes to march to and cheered up the people when things did not go as well as they had expected. When the news reached London that the British troops at Mafeking had finally been relieved on 17 May, "the whole city—the whole country—went mad with enthusiasm. Strangers were clapped on the back and stood drinks; the 'pubs' were filled to overflowing and people danced in the street," as W. Macqueen-Pope remembers in *Twenty Shillings in the Pound*.[6] The music halls did not lag behind in their vociferous excitement as the *Music Hall and Theatre Review* reported on 25 May:

> We do not suppose the oldest inhabitant of musichall land remembers such a scene as that which we witnessed on Saturday night. True to its tradition, the variety stage was instantly and completely sympathetic to the mood of the moment. Instinctively the public crowded the vast pleasure palaces of the metropolis, there to shout itself hoarse with glee. The singers and musicians played fuglemen to the popular demonstration. If the wild shout of joy at the success of British arms that rent the air of London on Saturday night be Jingoism, why then we ardent apologists for the variety stage are Jingoes; and proud of it.[7]

The sexual innuendoes and the stereotyping of the "stage Irishman" were other features of the music hall that offended the Irish Nationalists. *The Leader,* the mouthpiece of Irish Nationalism, complained in 1900 about "Imported Amusements," which not only cost the Irish "half a million sterling a year" but also served—and the music halls in particular—as "regular night-schools for Anglicisation [and] a powerful propaganda for the lowest and grossest moral standards."[8] W. B. Yeats had nothing but contempt for the products of English mass civilization that were such a threat to the indigenous Irish traditions, as we can see from a letter to his father: "When you go from an Irish country district, where there are good manners, old songs, old stories and good talk, the folk mind, to an Irish country town, generalization meets one in music-hall songs with their mechanical rhythm, or in thoughts taken from the newspapers."[9] In *Ulysses* this view is represented by A.E. in his dispute with Stephen: "The rarefied air of the academy and the arena produce the sixshilling novel, the musichall song. France produces the finest flower of corruption in Mallarmé but the desirable life is revealed to the poor of heart, the life of Homer's Phaeacians" (*U* 9.107–10).

Joyce did not ignore the unholy alliance of the music halls with jingoism, but it did not lead him to dismiss them completely as places where British vulgarity and propaganda were disseminated. There were many qualities to be found in the music hall songs: a down-to-earth realism often bordering on "scrupulous meanness," topicality, parody, role-playing and, most of all, a language charged with puns and innuendoes, constantly at the risk of being censored by local authorities and by the music hall managers. When words were forbidden or deficient the music hall singer could rely on an eloquent language of gesture, a "universal language" (*U* 15.105–6) that Joyce explored in all his works as well.[10]

Whether the Irish liked it or not, "imported amusements" were spreading throughout their cities and towns. One should add that this was by no means a one-way street, since the Irish had always contributed substantially to the amusements of the English and had some vested interest in the new show business. Dublin had a long tradition of musical entertainment in its pubs and concert-rooms which did not cease to exist when the new music halls were opened, but survived to enrich their program.

We still know too little about the interconnection between popular culture in England and Ireland, but the example of Dan Lowrey's career is perhaps a case in point, even if not every Irish entertainer was as successful as he was. According to Eugene Watters's and Matthew Murtagh's *Infinite Variety: Dan Lowrey's Music Hall, 1879–97,* Lowrey was born in 1823 in Roscrea, County Tipperary. When the only textile mill there went out of business, Dan's family emigrated to Leeds, which like other industrial towns in England had a large Irish population. After finding work as a dyer in one of the mills, Dan tried another career as a comic singer in one of the many musically licensed pubs that sprang up in the 1840s. Stage Irishmen, whether played by real Irishmen or not, were popular at the time, and Dan in the role of "Pat of Mullingar" could make enough money to open his own singing tavern in 1857 and enlarge it in the following year. Fourteen years later he moved back to Ireland, first opening a music hall in Belfast and finally settling in Dublin in 1878. Just in time for the Christmas season, Dan Lowrey's Star of Erin Music Hall in Dame Street opened its doors. There were other, if somewhat smaller music halls in Dublin as well, among them The Grafton, which went out of business in 1884, and The Harp, which was run by the popular comedian and singer Pat Kinsella before it closed down in 1893. Competition in show business was fierce, and music halls often changed owners and names. Even Dan Lowrey's successful hall was swallowed up in 1897 by one of the huge music hall syndicates that established themselves around the turn of the century. True to the spirit of the time, they changed The Star of Erin into The Empire Palace, which on a full night could hold a clientele of 3,000 instead of the 600 that thronged to Dan Lowrey's place when it was first opened.[11]

Thus the young Joyce did not have to go to London to find out about the music halls. In Joyce's early autobiographical fragment, Stephen Daedalus is familiar with the Dublin music halls and chooses one of them to discuss esthetic questions with his friend, "while the band bawled to the comedian and the comedian bawled to the band" (*SH* 129). No doubt, like his fictional alter ego, Joyce was one of the many artists who discovered the music halls in the 1890s.

As Max Beerbohm, one of the prototypical dandies of the time and Shaw's successor as theater critic for the *Saturday Review*, recollects on the occasion of a later visit to the Tivoli in the Strand:

> Here, in these very stalls, I would often sit with some coaeval *in statu pupillari*. Lordly aloof, both of us, from the joyous vulgarity of our environment, we would talk in under-tones about Hesiod and Fra Angelico, about the lyric element in Marcus Aurelius and the ethics of apostasy as illustrated by the Oxford Movement. Now and again, in the pauses of our conversation, we would rest our eyes upon the stage and listen to a verse or two . . . about a mother-in-law or an upstairs-lodger, and then one of us would turn to the other, saying, "Yes! I see your point about poor Newman, but . . ." or "I cannot admit that there is any real distinction between primitive art and. . . ." Though our intellects may not have been so monstrous fine as we pretended, we were quite honest in so far as neither of us could have snatched any surreptitious pleasure in the entertainment as such. We came simply that we might bask in the glow of our superiority—superiority not only to the guffawing clowns and jades around us, but also to the cloistral pedascules who, no more exquisite than we in erudition, were not in touch with modern life and would have been scared, like so many owls, in that garish temple of modernity, a Music Hall, wherein we, on the other hand, were able to sit without blinking.[12]

Even for an Oxford student the time had come to move out of the sacred halls of poetry into the "garish temple of modernity" in order to update Arnold's criticism of life. In the rapid succession of music hall turns Beerbohm found an artistic expression that was in tune with the accelerating speed of modern city life, with the simultaneity of contradictory impressions, and with the fragmentation of "an age of snippets": "As the penny weekly magazines are to literature, so are the music halls to drama: snippets there, 'turns' here, to perform precisely the same function of catching your attention for one thing and switching it on to another before you know where you are." [13]

Arthur Symons, the editor of *The Yellow Book* and mediator of French Symbolism, who had helped Joyce with the publication of his poems, was proud to admit that he was an "aficionado of the music halls." In the halls he found what he could not find anywhere else in straitlaced Victorian society, "that exquisite sense of the frivolous, the air of Bohemian freedom, that relief from respectability, which one gets here, and nowhere more surely than here." [14] John Davidson, like Symons a member of The Rhymers' Club, explored the music hall as a subject and as an artistic medium by basing his poems upon the rhythm of popular music hall tunes. Kipling discovered "the scheme for a certain sort of song" amid "the smoke, the roar, and the good fellowship of relaxed humanity" that he found at Gatti's music hall. [15] George Moore found in "its communal enjoyment and its spontaneity" traces of the Elizabethan stage that were completely lost in the well-made plays with their conventional language. There was the "imaginativeness of the slang," and instead of "worn-out rhetoric" there were "bright quips and cracks fresh from the back-yard of the slum where the linen is drying, or the 'pub' where the unfortunate wife has just received a black eye that will last her a week." As he summed up: "The music hall is a protest against the villa, the circulating library, the club, and for all this the ' 'all' is inexpressibly dear to me." [16]

All these writers shared the conviction that contemporary poetry and drama had become rather anemic and anachronistic by losing touch with the colloquial speech of the day. They were all, as Linda Dowling argues, reacting against the burden of dead literary language and in search of an authentic speaking voice, looking for a source of invigoration in the music hall. [17] From the nineties one could trace the connection to the more radical avant-garde movements of later decades. Thus the creator of Futurism, Tomaso Marinetti, saw in the music hall or, as it was called by his time, the Theatre of Variety, "a crucible in which are stirring today the elements of a new sensibility which is coming into being." As he declared, "The Theatre of Variety destroys the Solemn, the Sacred, the Serious, the Sublime of Art with a capital A."[18] Needless to say, elements of this sensibility were also stirring in Joyce's works from the very beginning.

In *Joyce's Anatomy of Culture,* Cheryl Herr deals with the popular stage (music hall and pantomime) as one of the major institutions of popular culture in Joyce's Dublin. She develops a semiotic model of culture as an ensemble of "texts of culture" that interact with each other, striving for superiority and exerting their power over the individual. In order to expose these ideological pressures in his anatomy of culture, Joyce developed narrative strategies of subversion such as allusion or parody. In *Joyce, Bakhtin, and Popular Literature,* R. B. Kershner uses Bakhtin's theory to explore the function of popular literature in Joyce's early works (*Dubliners* and *A Portrait*).[19] Indeed, Joyce's works are ideally suited for illustrating Bakhtin's concepts of "heteroglossia" and the "polyphonic novel."

From the very beginning, Joyce was aware of the fact that words "have a certain value in the literary tradition and a certain value in the market-place" (*SH* 33). Stephen adds, "a debased value," but Joyce himself started very early to question Stephen's value judgment. Increasingly the voices and the noises of the literary tradition and of the market-place contributed to the rich polyphony of his works. The linguistic and cultural situation that Joyce found in Ireland, and later in Trieste and Zurich, was propitious for developing such a concept uncompromisingly. In *Culture and Anarchy in Ireland, 1890–1939,* F. S. L. Lyons argues how inadequate Matthew Arnold's concept of culture is for a diagnosis of the situation in Ireland:

> where Arnold saw culture as a unifying force in a fragmented society and as a barrier against anarchy, my thesis is that in Ireland culture—or rather, the diversity of cultures—has been a force which has worked against the evolution of a homogeneous society and in doing so has been an agent of anarchy rather than of unity. . . . The coexistence of several cultures, related yet distinct, has made it difficult, if not impossible, for Irishmen to have a coherent view of themselves in relation to each other and to the outside world.[20]

Precisely for this reason, Joyce in his "anatomy of culture" went further than his Irish contemporaries who still held on to the Romantic idea of organic unity.

Naughty Girls and Lodgers: Some Prototypes from the Music Hall in *Dubliners*

In *Dubliners* we can observe the intrusion of music hall elements in the life of the city.[21] At the period in which the stories are set one could still hear the "nasal chanting of street-singers, who sang a *come-all-you* about O'Donovan Rossa, or a ballad about the troubles in our native land" ("Araby" 31), while the bazaar could boast of a *"Café Chantant"* (34), which was nothing but a music hall whose French name, like the name of the bazaar itself, was intended to lend some exotic flavor to the scene. The two spheres of entertainment were not entirely separate, as many street musicians were thronging to the new music halls, which promised a better income and shelter from the cold. With them they brought their rich repertoire of Irish songs and ballads, while, on the other hand, the latest music hall hits were taken up in the streets and pubs. Music hall elements also found their way into the programs of the "legitimate" theaters in spite of the usual hostility between the managers of the theaters and the managers of the music halls. Eugene Watters and Matthew Murtagh tell us that no sooner had Dan Lowrey opened his music hall than he was sued for selling liquor without a proper license. There was a strong suspicion that the police raid was instigated by John and Michael Gunn, the holders of the old Royal Theatre Patent for Dublin and the managers of the successful Gaiety Theatre. Their hostility to the new rival did not prevent them, however, from including music hall songs and dances in their popular Christmas pantomimes.[22]

It must have been at the Gaiety that Stephen's mother in her youth heard "old Royce sing in the pantomime of Turko the terrible and laughed with the others when he sang:"

> *I am the boy*
> *That can enjoy*
> *Invisibility.*
> (*U* 1.257–62)

Obviously there was no compelling reason why a respectable, devout young Catholic woman should not be seen at such a performance. On the other hand, Mrs. Kearney with her education "in a high-class convent where she had learned French and music" ("A Mother" 136) would never dream of setting foot in the Gaiety on a Pantomime night, let alone in one of the even more vulgar music halls. But when it comes to business even she is shrewd enough to know that she cannot fill four nights in the Antient Concert Rooms with the kind of music her daughter and her Nationalist friends perform. She allows a "comic turn" to be included, and in order "to keep the audience continually diverted [she slips] the doubtful items in between the old favourites" ("A Mother" 138). We can guess that these "doubtful items" were much in the line of the music hall songs despised by people like Mrs. Kearney. Joyce, however, not only queries her "tact" (138), but also her snobbish musical taste. We register a strong touch of irony when we read that "a stirring patriotic recitation delivered by a young lady who arranged amateur theatricals . . . was deservedly applauded." We may feel sorry for the "poor lady [who] sang *Killarney* in a bodiless gasping voice, with all the old-fashioned mannerisms of intonation and pronunciation which she believed lent elegance to her singing," but we can also understand why "the cheaper parts of the hall made fun of her high wailing notes" (147). In a music hall such a singer would have been given the bird immediately, deservedly or not.

When the conversation in "The Dead" turns to the subject of music, Freddy Malins embarrasses everyone by attributing "one of the finest tenor voices he had ever heard" not to an opera singer but to a "Negro chieftain singing in the second part of the Gaiety pantomime." After a curt answer from Mr. Bartell D'Arcy and a sneering remark from Mr. Browne, Mary Jane briskly leads "the table back to the legitimate opera" ("The Dead" 198–99). Singers and entertainers who blackened their faces with burnt cork had become very popular since the 1830s whether they called themselves "Ethiopian Serenaders," "Negro Melodists," "niggers," or "coons"; they could be seen in the streets of the cities, or the piers at the seaside, a staple of every music hall program and Christmas pantomime. Minstrel troupes such as the Christy Minstrels performed year after year at the St. James Hall before an audience that was clearly distinct from the typical music hall audience. Harry Reynolds, himself a former minstrel, sums up this audience: "Straitlaced people who even barred the ordinary theatre patronized St James Hall. It was quite an ordinary experience to observe a dozen clergymen at one time enjoying the minstrels' entertainment; so naturally their flocks followed."[23] In his widely read *Music And Morals,* the very Victorian Rev. H. R. Haweis surmises "that the lasting popularity and deep appreciation of negro fun and pathos in England is mainly due to the genius of *Uncle Tom's Cabin.*"[24] In "The Dead," Gretta Conroy has at least heard of the Christy Minstrels of whom the word "goloshes" reminds her ("The Dead" 181), perhaps because it makes her think of strange words like "golliwogs." According to Tighe Hopkins, in a music hall one could qualify as "the London edition of a negro" simply by wearing ragged clothes, "banging upon a table with a bulgy umbrella, and saying, 'By golly.'"[25]

But most of the characters in *Dubliners* prefer light opera and parlor songs to music hall entertainment and minstrel shows. Frank takes Eveline to a theater in which Michael Balfe's *Bohemian Girl* is being performed ("Eveline" 39). Maria chooses to sing "I Dreamt I Dwelt in Marble Halls" from the same opera, moving Joe to tears and making him declare that "there was no time like the long ago and no music for him like poor old Balfe, whatever other people might say" ("Clay" 106). On the other hand, Corley would certainly have no qualms about picking up "a fine decent tart" ("Two Gallants" 54) in a music hall; and Jack Mooney who is not above "using soldiers' obscenities" and "always sure to be on to a good thing—that is to say, a likely horse or a likely *artiste*" ("Boarding House" 62), seems to be equally at home in the music halls and on the turf. But no particular music hall songs are mentioned, and if music hall artistes are included they remain shadowy outsiders hovering in the margins of the stories. In the crowd at the pub in "Counterparts" we find an English "acrobat and knock-about *artiste*" from the Tivoli and a young woman from the same ensemble dressed in bright colors and ready to earn some extra money through occasional prostitution ("Counterparts" 94–95). They still have a long way to go before they gain even a modicum of the fame and glamor associated with the great music hall stars. Meanwhile they work the halls, being constantly on the move from one town to the other and lodging in cheap places like Mrs. Mooney's boarding house. Their presence no doubt contributes to the bad reputation of this place. On Sunday evenings, when the music halls are closed, they gather for a singsong in Mrs. Mooney's front drawing room, where Polly Mooney can pick up some of their trade. She presents herself in one of the typical poses from the music hall stage and sings:

> *I'm a . . . naughty girl*
> *You needn't sham*
> *You know I am.*
> ("Boarding House" 62)

The role of the "naughty girl" allows Polly, under the watchful eyes of her mother, to flirt with the young men in the audience much more freely than off stage. The blending of girlish innocence and sexual provocation that is essential to this role has become almost habitual and makes her "look like a perverse madonna" (ibid. 62–63). In a music hall duet described by Tighe Hopkins we get not only a glimpse of what Polly's role-playing might have looked like, but also a good example of the perfect teamwork between mother and daughter in search of a husband and provider for the whole family:

> A plump lady and her slim daughter are the next performers. They treat us to a pretty little love song, in which the daughter with much sly ogling of the audience, and many little giggles and rouge-capped blushes, relates to her mother, the capture of . . . [the daughter's] heart by a certain tall young gentleman, with fair hair and a beautiful moustache. To her the mother, in maternal reproof, replies that it is all very wrong, and that she . . . is a very naughty girl, she is. But in another stanza the naughty girl discloses . . . that, though love alone incited her to pledge her plighted troth, the tall young man has whole drawers full of bank notes, and a house in Eaton-square [*sic*], of which the mother shall have the second floor all to herself. On this, mamma not only relents, but proceeds also, with some matronly ogling of the audience, to school her artless offspring in the wiles of love, enforcing her precepts by apt illustrations of the admirable manner in which she enticed and trapped . . . [the daughter's] dear departed father.[26]

Hopkins concludes his description of the duet with the general observation that "what is technically known as the female interest is remarkably strong at the music hall."

Nowhere perhaps is the affinity between Joyce's comic spirit and the music hall greater than in "The Boarding House." In many songs we find young lodgers entangled in affairs with the mother or daughter as in Vesta Victoria's "Our Lodger's Such a Nice Young Man." The picture on the music sheet cover of this song, which can be found in Peter Davison's *Songs of The British Music Hall*,[27] gives us an idea of the blend of girlish innocence and adult knowingness connected with the role of the naughty girl: we see a little girl with golden ringlets wearing a white frock and black stockings and shoes, holding in her left hand what looks like a big hat. With a sweet smile she sings:

> At our house not long ago a lodger came to stay,
> At first I felt as if I'd like to drive him straight away;
> But soon he proved himself to be so very good and kind,
> That, like my dear mamma, I quite made up my little mind.
>
> CHORUS
> Our lodger's such a nice young man, such a good young man
>   is he;
> So good and so kind to all our family!
> He's never going to leave us, Oh dear, oh dear no!
> He's such a good, goody, goody man, mamma told me so.
>
> He made himself at home before he'd been with us a day-
> He kissed mamma and all of us, 'cos papa was away;
> Before he goes to work he lights the fires and scrubs the floor,
> And puts a nice strong cup of tea outside ma's bedroom door.
>
> At night he makes the beds and does the other little jobs,
> And if the baby hurts itself he really cries and sobs;
> On Sunday when ma's cooking and papa is at the club,
> He takes the kids and baths us all inside the washing tub.
>
> We usually go to Margate, in the sea to have a splash,
> This year pa said, "I'm busy!" but I think he had no cash;
> The lodger took us down instead—mamma and baby too,
> And never charged Pa anything—now there's a pal for you.[28]

Like a good music hall singer, Polly Mooney has an excellent sense of timing. As Bob Doran remembers vividly, she had come to his room after her bath, just when he was undressing for bed, "to relight her candle at his, for hers had been blown out by a gust" ("Boarding House" 67). In music hall songs, lighting fires or candles is one of the "little jobs" lodgers are supposed to do, and Polly's stratagem might have been inspired by one of them. *Beside the Seaside* gives a sample of such songs, this time sung by a "naughty" young man,

> staying in a boarding-house where there were six nice little girls for whom he used to light the candles. And as they went up to bed, he sang the [following] chorus:

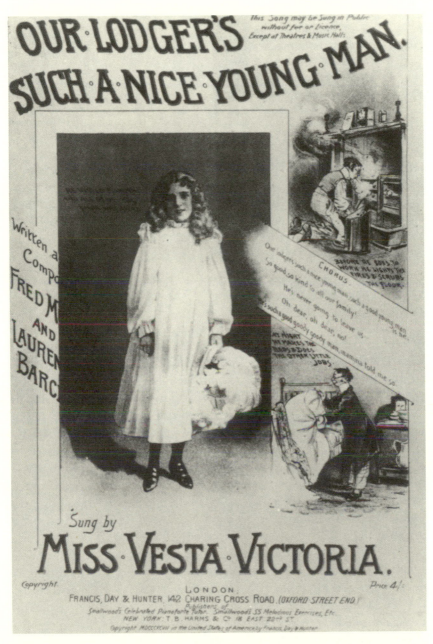

Vesta Victoria in girlish apparel to explain the virtues of the "good goody goody" lodger who is so helpful to Mamma. From Peter Davison, *Songs of the British Music Hall*.

Good-night number one,
Good-night number two,
Good-night number three,
And number four the same to you.
Good-night number five,
Good-night number six,
And ere you retire,
In case of fire,
Don't forget to snuff your little wick. [29]

In Dan Leno's song "Young Men Taken in and Done For," Bob Doran's sad story is already anticipated (see "Words and Music" chapter). Bob Doran has still a flicker of hope that "perhaps they could be happy together" ("Boarding House" 67), but the "scrupulous meanness" of the story makes it plain that such vague hopes will prove to be nothing but "tommy rot," as the music hall song so bluntly puts it. [30]

Voices of the City: Music Hall Songs in *Ulysses*

The year in which *Ulysses* was published was also the year in which Marie Lloyd died, an event of much greater news value at the time. As Walter Macqueen-Pope writes in *The Melodies Linger On,* "All Britain, all the English-speaking world, mourned her. More than 100,000 people filed past her grave when she was buried on an October day in 1922." [31] Such figures are always guesswork, but the fact of Marie Lloyd's immense popularity remains. She was a past mistress in the art of innuendo and body language that added so much to the performance of music hall songs. As the music critic of the *Saturday Review* observed in 1894: "No one else is so clever in suggesting a *sous-entendre;* every trick of her face and voice has its meaning and its undermeaning; no phrase was ever so innocent that she would not pass it on to you as an insinuation." [32] The story goes that for one of the songs out of her "blue bag" she had to appear before the Vigilance Committee of the London County Council, where she sang the objectionable song with a straight face. When nothing offensive could be found, she sang "Come into the Garden Maud" with her usual wealth of gesture, thus demonstrating to the nonplussed committee that obscenity, like beauty, lies in the eye of the beholder. Like many other music hall artistes, Marie Lloyd exploited rather than actually propagated the jingoism of the time. During the years of the Boer War when, as Macqueen-Pope remembers in

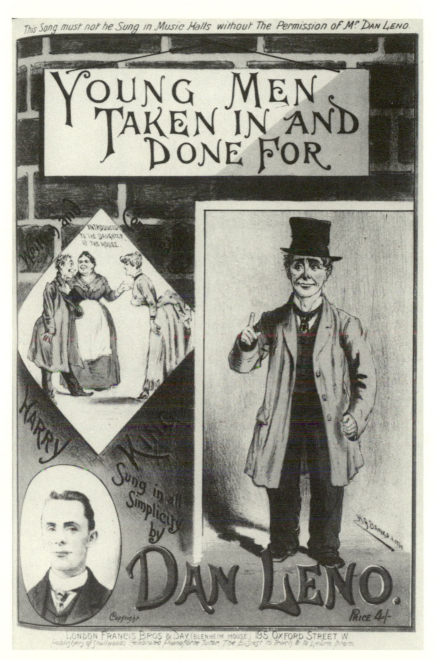

Dan Leno explaining the plight of Bob Doran in "The Boarding House"—and of others tricked the same way. Used with permission of The British Library.

Twenty Shillings in the Pound, "everyone grew learned about khaki,"[33] she came on stage as "The Girl in the Khaki Dress" and sang:

> I am a girl who's rather larky,
> Always dressing myself in khaki,
> Just the same as men who claim
> To fight for their home and Queen.
> Now they're winning a nation's praises,
> You all know what the latest craze is
> Khaki this, and khaki that! Well, I'm on in that scene!
> Khaki boots and stockings on either leg,
> And ev'ry morn, at breakfast time, I have a khaki egg!
> Khaki cuffs and collars, yes, and khaki "dicky dirts,"
> And I've got khaki bloomers on, underneath my skirts.[34]

Needless to say, there is much more comic deflation and parody in the song than affirmation of jingoism.

One of her many admirers was T. S. Eliot, who wrote an obituary that spelled the death of a whole cultural period. The dignity and meaning of lower-class life was expressed well by music hall comedians, but not at all by revue, Eliot argued. As revue and vulgar films displaced the music halls, the lower and middle classes would grow more alike—at a cost to the lower classes, in Eliot's view.[35] Joyce did not share Eliot's contempt for the cinema, but he also felt much closer to the music hall of his youth than to the new variety stage with its revues. While working on *Ulysses* in Zurich he sang music hall songs with Frank Budgen "from those vintage years of popular song associated with the names of Dan Leno, Harry Randall, Tom Costello, Gus Elen, Arthur Roberts, and the other music hall giants of that time."[36] In Zurich Joyce also came across H. Baumann's *Londonismen,* a pioneer work on London dialect, slang and cant. As one of the most recent examples of English as spoken in the streets of London, Baumann quotes Albert Chevalier's *coster song* "Wot Cher, or Knock'd 'em in the Old Kent Road,"[37] a song that Joyce echoed in *Finnegans Wake,* as Hodgart and Worthington registered, as "sock him up, the oldcant rogue" and "bricking up all my old kent road" (*FW* 359.19–20 and 584.6). The exploitation of Cockney was not restricted to Chevalier's songs. In fact most music hall songs thrived on the use of dialect, colloquial speech, and slang. And they not only copied the speech they found in the streets but they enriched it in a reciprocal process. In his *Cockney Past and Present,* Walter Matthews dedicates a whole chapter to "Cockney in the Music Hall" listing many catch phrases that had been added to Cockney by the songwriters and comedians of the music hall and that have often outlasted the popularity of the songs themselves.[38] In spite of William Archer's harsh verdict that "the music hall has produced not one single lyric which has any chance of living in the national memory, except perhaps, as a monument of vulgarity and inanity,"[39] many music hall songs have remained well known until today and even become in Matthew's words, "the true folk-songs of London."[40]

In *Ulysses* music hall songs are associated with Cockney from the very beginning. The versatile Mulligan includes in his repertoire of roles the impersonation of a music hall performer

> singing out of tune with a Cockney accent:
> —*won't we have a merry time,*
> *Drinking whiskey, beer and wine!*
> *On coronation,*
> *Coronation Day!*
> *0, won't we have a merry time*
> *On coronation day!*
>
> (*U* 1.298–305)

Long before his coronation, Edward VII had acquired the reputation of being "a bit of a rake," as even Mr. Henchy has to admit, who comes to his defense in "Ivy Day in the Committee Room" (*D* 132). In his youth the Prince of Wales had shocked some of the more straitlaced Victorians by his penchant for the the music hall. The American writer D. J. Kirwan, who did not wish to be outdone in prudery by his English cousins, remarked after his visit to London in 1870: "The taste of the Prince for music may be imagined from the fact that 'Champagne Charlie,' and 'Not for Joseph,' are his two most cherished melodies." Even worse, the royal rake was also "an admirer of Finette, the famous can-can danseuse of the Alhambra."[41] The royal family was not amused, but even Queen Victoria herself could not help catching the music hall virus, singing "old bits of songs about *Ehren on the Rhine* and come where the booze is cheaper" (*U* 12.1397–98).[42]

The coronation of her successor on 9 August 1902 marked the beginning of a new era, as Macqueen-Pope remembers: "Nobody had sung of being merry on wine and spirits on the occasion of Queen Victoria's Diamond Jubilee. The Victorian bonds were off, and the

Edwardian days were in full flood . . . the nation cheered from its heart, for it loved its new King . . . who went to the races, frequented the Theatre as a regular patron and was well known in the haunts of even the Middle Classes."[43]

Two years before Bloomsday, and only two months before Edward's coronation, the Boer War had finally drawn to an end. The repercussions of the war with its frenzied jingoism are still felt in *Ulysses*. In the debate in the library over Shakespeare, Mr. Best remembers Mallarmé's description of a Hamlet performance in the provinces advertised as *Hamlet ou Le Distrait*. Stephen interrupts impatiently Best's long-winded explanation of the title by substituting "The absent-minded beggar" (9.118–25). No music hall program would have been complete without this song, which was written by Kipling and set to music by Arthur Sullivan in support of the *Daily Mail* War Fund for the British soldiers in South Africa. The song was played *ad nauseam* and even Kipling got sick of it. When asked by an admirer, "Is it possible that I have the honour to meet the author of 'The Absent Minded Beggar?'" he answered, "Yes, I have heard that piece played on a barrel organ and I would shoot the man who wrote it, if it would not be suicide."[44] Kipling presents the British soldier not as a belligerent jingo, but as a poor "absent-minded beggar" who does his duty "out on active service, wiping something off a slate." ("Beggar," incidentally, is the written form of "bugger," which in Cockney usage is a slightly condescending word for chap or bloke; "absent-minded" indicates one of the many foibles of the British soldier, but also that he is easily forgotten by the British at home; moreover it alludes to J. R. Seeley's explanation of British imperialism: "We seem, as it were, to have conquered and peopled half the world in a fit of absence of mind.")[45] Kipling's title provides Stephen with an important cue for his theory in which Shakespeare becomes "a ghost by absence" (*U* 9.174) and Hamlet a blood-thirsty forerunner of English imperialism: "Khaki Hamlets don't hesitate to shoot. The bloodboltered shambles in act five is a forecast of the concentration camp sung by Mr Swinburne" (*U* 9.133–35). Thus the spirit of imperialism can be found not only in the music hall songs of the time but also in the works of Shakespeare and Swinburne. For Joyce, as this example illustrates, the two spheres of art and mass culture are never completely separated but ideologically connected in intricate ways.

In "Circe" these songs are interwoven with others equally popular at

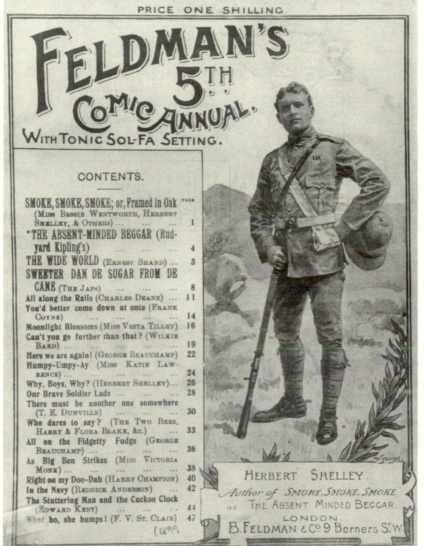

Kipling's "Absent Minded Beggar." Collection of Ulrich Schneider.

the time of the Boer War in the brawl between the British soldiers and the drunken Stephen, which is transmogrified into a fight between Ireland and England. One of the music hall songs that accompanied the soldiers on their way to South Africa was "Good-bye, Dolly I Must Leave You" (also known as "Good-bye, Dolly Gray"), and in this scene Dolly Gray *"from her balcony waves her handkerchief, giving the sign of the heroine of Jericho."* Like the Rahabs, Cissy Caffreys, or Mother Courages of all ages she is not above fraternizing with the enemy. She shouts: "Rahab. Cook's son, good-bye. Safe home to Dolly. Dream of the girl you left behind and she will dream of you" (*U* 15.4418–20), picking up fragments from "The Absent-Minded Beggar" ("Duke's son—cook's son—son of a hundred kings," "We must help the girl that Tommy's left behind him") and other proverbial tags. In this scene in which Stephen is taken for a Pro-Boer by Private Compton, Edward VII interferes as a peacemaker and freemason.[46] In spite of his proclaimed pacifism and neutrality as an umpire, he sides with the British when it comes to the hanging of the croppy boy. He *"dances slowly . . . and sings with soft contentment"* (*U* 15.4560–61) the coronation song introduced by Mulligan in "Telemachus."

As in *Dubliners,* many of the older characters in *Ulysses* hold on to the musical repertoire of their youth. At the Ormond one of the barmaids may be heard trilling the song "The Shade of the Palm" from *Florodora* (*U* 11.226), a musical comedy composed by Thomas Barrett (writing as Leslie Stuart), whose melodies, mostly sung by Eugene Stratton, were also popular in the music hall; Simon Dedalus and his cronies, however, prefer music from earlier operas, traditional songs, and ballads like "The Croppy Boy." When the funeral carriage passes the hoardings in front of the Queen's Theatre, Bloom is much less interested in Eugene Stratton than in Mrs. Bandman Palmer playing in *Leah* (*U* 6.184–85), as he was before on his way to the chemist's when his eyes were "wandering over the multicoloured hoardings" (*U* 5.192–205). Later in the day when Eugene Stratton grimaces "with thick niggerlips at Father Conmee," the very reverend father thinks immediately "of the souls of black and brown and yellow men" (*U* 10.141–44), unaware that underneath his burnt cork Eugene Stratton's soul was probably not blacker than the souls of other white men.

But if the characters do not give much attention to music hall advertisements, Joyce does, and he inserts them as the landmarks of present-day Dublin. In "Wandering Rocks," where the individual characters are enmeshed in the labyrinthine network of the modern city, the presence of these landmarks makes itself strongly felt by repetition. From hoardings in a different area of Dublin, "Mr Eugene Stratton, his blub lips agrin, bade all comers welcome to Pembroke township" (*U* 10.1273–74). He is not the only famous music hall star performing in Dublin on 16 June 1904. From her office Miss Dunne looks "at the large poster of Marie Kendall, charming soubrette" (*U* 10.380–81). Her smiling image also follows the viceregal equipage on its way through Dublin: "A charming soubrette, great Marie Kendall, with dauby cheeks and lifted skirt smiled daubily from her poster" (*U* 10.1220–21).

Even if Miss Dunne is critical of Marie Kendall's appearance, in particular "the way she's holding up her bit of a skirt," she starts thinking of how to get "a concertina skirt like Susy Nagle's" which had such a telling effect on "Shannon and all the boatclub swells" (*U* 10.382–85). This little vignette says something about the way in which music hall stars served as fashion leaders and about the attraction of their revealing costumes at a time when skirts still swept the ground. On posters announcing stars like Marie Lloyd, emphasis was given to the fact that "new songs and new gowns" would be presented.[47] During their performance the singers made sure that their costumes were not overlooked. Thus Marie Lloyd in "When I Take My Morning Promenade" coquettishly drew the attention of her audience to the way in which she was dressed:

> Do you think my dress is a little bit,
> Just a little bit—
> Well—not much of it,
> Tho' it shows my shape just a little bit
> That's the little bit the boys admire.[48]

Even Gerty MacDowell might have learned "one of love's little ruses" (*U* 13.757) indirectly from music hall singers like Lottie Collins, who with her high kicks in "Ta-ra-ra Boom-der-é" allowed an eyeful of her lace petticoats, or who like Marie Lloyd in a similar performance revealed, as the young Compton MacKenzie was pleasantly shocked to find out, "a great display of amber silk petticoats, and long amber silk drawers frilled below her knees."[49] Pictures of these highkicking music hall artistes found their way into the spicier magazines of the day. Bertha Supple had told Gerty "in dead secret . . . about the gentleman lodger . . . that had pictures cut out of papers of those skirtdancers and highkickers and she said he used to do something not very nice you could imagine sometimes in the bed" (*U* 13.701–6). Gerty is convinced that her own performance will have the same effect on Bloom, "because he couldn't resist the sight of the wondrous revealment half offered like those skirtdancers behaving so immodest before gentlemen looking" (*U* 13.731–33).

Thus, as probably in Gerty's case, one could be exposed to the pervasive influence of the music hall without ever having seen one from inside. Its stars were shown in illustrated magazines and on posters, its songs distributed as sheet music, sung at home and at the pub, played by street-organs and brass bands. On the way to Paddy Dignam's funeral the carriage is followed by the sounds of a street organ playing "a rollicking, rattling song of the halls. Has anybody here seen Kelly? Kay ee double ell wy. Dead March from *Saul*. He's as bad as old Antonio. He left me on my ownio" (*U* 6.373–75). The song "Has Anybody Here Seen Kelly?" tells the story of "Kelly and his sweetheart . . . bent upon a holiday." In London they get separated in the crowd "up Piccadilly way" and the young woman starts searching for her Kelly all over London, asking everyone she meets:

> Has anybody here seen Kelly?
> K E double L Y.
> Has anybody here seen Kelly
> Find him if you can.
> He's as bad as old Antonio,
> Left me on my own-i-o
> Has anybody here seen Kelly.
> Kelly from the Isle of Man?[50]

Many music hall songs told stories of young couples being lost in the big city, or of a young man or woman being ditched, sometimes, as in Vesta Victoria's "Waiting at the Church,"[51] at the very last moment. "Has Anybody Here Seen Kelly" was sung by Florrie Forde and alludes to one of her earlier hits, "Oh! Oh! Antonio," which tells the story of an "Italian maid" betrayed by her young man, an Italian ice cream vendor. She keeps crying:

> Oh! Oh! Antonio.
> He's gone away,
> Left me alone-i-o,
> All on my own-i-o,

I want to meet him with
His new sweet heart,
Then up will go Antonio
And his ice-cream cart.[52]

Antonio's ice cream cart could also be found in Dublin, in fact not far from where the Blooms live. In "Wandering Rocks" it is called "Rabaiotti's icecream car" (*U* 10.229), but in "Circe" we get the full name of the ice cream vendor, Antonio Rabaiotti (*U* 15.150). But the song has other than topographical connections. In "Hades" Kelly's sudden disappearance is charged with some gloomier overtones of a metaphysical nature and linked with the sudden disappearance of the mysterious man in the mackintosh: "Where has he disappeared to? Not a sign. Well of all the. Has anybody here seen? Kay ee double ell. Become invisible. Good Lord, what became of him?" (*U* 6.899–901).

Florrie Forde, as Roy Busby's *British Music Hall: An Illustrated Who's Who* tells us, "was a great favourite on the Isle of Man, where for 36 consecutive years she wooed generations of holiday-makers with 'Flanagan' and 'Has Anybody here Seen Kelly?'"[53] We know from Stanislaus Joyce that his brother liked female music hall singers to be "sizable"[54] and Florrie Forde would certainly have qualified in this respect.

Of course, Bloom has reasons of his own to be particularly interested in a song associated with the Isle of Man. He explains the advertisement for Keyes to the printer: "The idea . . . is the house of keys. You know, councillor, the Manx parliament. Innuendo of home rule. Tourists, you know, from the isle of Man. Catches the eye, you see" (*U* 7.149–51).

In "Eumaeus" Murphy exhibits a tattoo on his chest done, as he explains to his listeners, by a Greek fellow with the name of Antonio, which, as the narrator adds, has "no relation to the dramatic personage of identical name who sprang from the pen of our national poet" (*U* 16.839–40). Murphy tops off his story of Antonio's end ("ate by sharks" *U* 16.691) with the lines:

—*As bad as old Antonio,*
For he left me on my ownio.
(U 16.702–3)

Our "*soi-disant* sailor" (*U* 16.620), incidentally, shares his name with the writer of the song, C. W. Murphy; but, as between the two Antonios, "no relation" seems to exist, Murphy being, after all, a common

Florrie Forde on the cover of one of the Boer War songs. The text of the chorus is more domestic than Miss Forde's costume suggests. Collection of Ulrich Schneider.

name ("Shakespeares were as common as Murphies. What's in a name?"
U 16.364). In a chapter full of mistaken identities, however, the coincidence is appropriate.[55]

In "Wandering Rocks" a band at Trinity College plays "My Girl's a Yorkshire Girl," a music hall song that was actually written in 1908:[56]

Unseen brazen highland laddies blared and drumthumped after the cortège:

> *But though she's a factory lass*
> *And wears no fancy clothes.*
> *Baraabum.*
> *Yet I've a sort of a*
> *Yorkshire relish for*
> *My little Yorkshire rose.*
> *Baraabum.*
>
> *(U* 10.1249–57)

Among the many Dubliners who are accompanied on their way through the city is Boylan, "stepping in tan shoes and socks with sky-blue clocks to the refrain of *My girl's a Yorkshire girl*" (*U* 10.1241–42). The rhythm is catchy and the song particularly significant in a situation in which Boylan is looking forward to his rendezvous even if the lady in question is neither from Yorkshire nor a factory lass. But Molly is also associated with roses and, like the Yorkshire girl, entangled in a tricky situation. While Bloom goes out of his way, however, not to return too early to his unfaithful Penelope, the two admirers of the Yorkshire girl get a bad surprise when they want to find out whom she prefers:

> To a cottage in Yorkshire they hied
> To Rose, Rose, Rose,
> Meanwhile to make it clear
> Which was the boy most dear.
> Rose, their Rose didn't answer the bell,
> But her husband did instead.
> Loudly he sang to them
> As off, off they fled:
>
> CHORUS:
> My girl's a Yorkshire girl,
> Yorkshire through and through
> My girl's a Yorkshire girl,
> Eh! by gum, she's a champion!

Though she's a fact'ry lass,
And wears no fancy clothes
I've a sort of a Yorkshire Relish
For my little Yorkshire Rose.

It is typical of many music hall songs that the words of the chorus apply to different situations or characters with comic effect. Joyce's leit-motifs usually achieve a comic effect too by using the same words in different contexts. In "Circe" the song turns up again, this time bawled out by the two drunken English soldiers. Zoe, who is actually a Yorkshire girl, wants to dance to the song and drops two pennies into the pianola. In a letter to Frank Budgen Joyce talks about the "whirligig movement of Circe" (*Letters 1* 151) that culminates in this scene. For this movement "My Girl's a Yorkshire Girl," with its waltzing rhythm, is quite appropriate. At the beginning of the nineteenth century the waltz could still count as "that intoxicating, inflammatory, and whirligig dance" (*OED*), whereas toward the fin de siècle it could be turned into a *valse triste* just as the ecstatic dancing of Zoe and Stephen ends in a dance of death with the apparition of Stephen's mother. The song was also played in the afternoon at the Mirus bazaar by a whirligig, as Kitty remembers, which now adds its noise to the scene as "groangrousegurgling Toft's cumbersome whirligig" (*U* 15.4112–13).

The music hall added many catch phrases to the language as it was spoken, not only in England but also in Dublin. These phrases were not necessarily coined by the songwriters of the music hall, but in any case they were given wide currency in the halls until they became part and parcel of colloquial speech. Many of them are used, often to comic effect, by the Dubliners in *Ulysses:* "Tommy, make room for your uncle" (*U* 7.264–65), "not for Joe" (*U* 8.344), "winking the other eye" (*U* 11.148), "you're not the only pebble on the beach" (*U* 11.310), "a little bit off the top" (*U* 12.20), "there's hair" (*U* 12.1176), "the whole hog" (*U* 13.882), "what ho! she bumps" (*U* 15.2345), "slap bang, here we are again" (*U* 15.2366–67), "chase me, Charley" (*U* 15.2426–27). When the chauvinistic Citizen wants to express his contempt for Bloom, one of the first epithets he calls to mind is the sobriquet of the black-face singer G. H. Chirgwin, "The White-Eyed Kaffir," used derisively of Bloom (*U* 12.1552). Charles Coborn's "The Man That Broke the Bank at Monte Carlo" is so well known in Dublin that he can be included among the "many Irish heroes and heroines of antiquity" in the same chapter (*U* 12.185–86).

When Molly addresses her Poldy in "Circe" as "a poor old stick in the mud" (*U* 15.329–30), she uses a phrase much older than the music hall. When we read, however, in one of the labyrinthine sentences in "Eumaeus," "that the man in the street . . . was debarred from seeing more of the world they lived in instead of being always and ever cooped up since my old stick-in-the-mud took me for a wife" (*U* 16.540–44), we begin to suspect that a more specific reference might be involved. In "At My Time of Life," the music hall singer Herbert Campbell sang the role of an old-fashioned "dame" who is scandalized by the "new woman" and her latest fads:

> There was none o' yer "Highty Flighty" girls,
> yer "Hi-Tiddley Hity" girls,
> When my old "Stick-in-the-mud" took me for a wife,
> Now fancy me a-smoking "fags,"
> riding bikes and wearin' bags,
> A-leaving off my bits o' rags,
> At *my* time of life.[57]

The enormous Herbert Campbell and the fragile Dan Leno played together in Christmas pantomimes for fourteen years and became a legend after they both died in 1904. Even Gerty MacDowell seems to remember Herbert Campbell's song when she sees herself ideally suited as a wife: "She was a womanly woman not like other flighty girls unfeminine he had known, those cyclists showing off what they hadn't got" (*U* 13.435–37).

Has Bloom ever been inside a music hall? There is no clear evidence in the text, as far as I can see, but it seems unlikely for a man of his universal curiosity not to have been to one. Once he had been commissioned by Michael Gunn to write a topical song for a Christmas pantomime at the Gaiety Theatre, perhaps along the line of Herbert Campbell's song, but nothing came of it. Writing a song for the Gaiety is one thing, his daughter becoming a music hall singer another; this he considers as one of the worst choices she could make: "Still she might do worse. Musichall stage" (*U* 4.425–26). Nevertheless he is familiar with music hall entertainment and with subjects related to the music hall. In his library we find *"Physical Strength and How to Obtain It* by Eugen Sandow (red cloth)" (*U* 17.1397) and in earlier days he used a "Sandow-Whiteley's pulley exerciser" (*U* 17.1817). He starts his day with resolutions to "begin again those Sandow's exercises" (*U* 4.234). Sandow was the strong man of the music hall who "topped bills

throughout the UK and . . . [whose] name was used to advertise everything from corsets to cocoa."[58] Bloom is also familiar with "Pepper's
ghost idea" (*U* 8.20), a device by which ghosts like Hamlet's father can
be brought upon the stage. It was never widely adopted for the theater,
but frequently shown at fairs and in the music halls of the 1860s as the
latest sensation. Another ghost returning from the dead is the famous
Tichbourne claimant, who is included among the avatars of the returning Odysseus in "Eumaeus." In a sensational trial the claimant was
found guilty of being an impostor and sentenced to penal servitude.
After his release he had a comeback in the music halls and also turned
up at Dan Lowrey's. In the words of Watters and Murtagh: "Of all the
Mystagogues who appeared at Dan's he was the most mysterious."[59]
Bloom remembers some details of the lawsuit quite well and takes it as
an illustration of the hazards of an unexpected return. Bloom also
knows at least the titles of music hall songs such as "O Please, Mr
P'liceman" (*U* 4.179), "Tommy, Make Room for Your Uncle" (*U*
7.264–65), "His Funeral's Tomorrow" (*U* 8.221), and "The Wild Man
of Borneo Has Just Come to Town" (*U* 13.1223), all listed by Hodgart
and Worthington.

One song not yet identified sets the pattern to the lines that occur to
Bloom when he considers the possibility that Gerty might have been a
false name:

> Her maiden name was Jemima Brown
> And she lived with her mother in Irishtown
> (*U* 13.947–48)

In his *Idols of the Halls,* H. Chance Newton remembers the Moore and
Burgess Minstrels (the former Christy Minstrels) and quotes their song
"Hunkey Dorum, We Are the Boys" as "perhaps the drollest and most
popular of these ditties":

> I went out one day for a lark—
> Hunkey Dorum, we am the boys
> I met with a lubly gal in de park—
> Hunkey Dorum doodle dum dey.
> Her hair it was frizzed all over her head—
> Hunkey Dorum, we am the boys.
> She nearly killed dis darkie dead
> Hunkey Dorum doodle dum dey!

Cover of "The Wild Man of Borneo." Collection of Ulrich Schneider.

CHORUS:
Her hair was frizzed all over her head,
She nearly killed dis darkie dead—
Her maiden name she said it was Brown,
And she lived wid her mudder in Camden Town.[60]

Although the minstrel shows had, as we have seen, a better reputation than the music halls, the two were closely interconnected, the one appropriating the latest hits of the other. In this case, the minstrel song follows Harry Clifton's "Jemima Brown, or the Queen of the Sewing Machine," one of the many music hall songs that tells of the infatuation with a woman, very often an attractive widow, who freely spends the cash of her admirer and then "skedaddles" with another one. Harry Clifton exploited this pattern in many of his songs. While the minstrel song has a happy ending ("We got married one day in Camden Town"), the music hall song typically concludes in a tragicomic vein:

From that very day I miss'd her,
Tho' she said she'd be my bride.
From Kennington to Chester,
I sought her far and wide.
Years after that, when passing by
A shop in Camden Town,
'Midst heaps of green, and kidney beans
There stood Jemima Brown.

She was weighing out potatoes,
Throwing coppers in the till.
Three lovely children by her side,
The image of brother Bill.
Her broken vow, I see it now,
But not my fifty pounds.
That shop was *bought* and I was *sold*
By naughty Jemima Brown.[61]

Earlier in the day Bloom thinks of Corny Kelleher "singing with his eyes shut. Corny. Met her once in the park. In the dark. What a lark. . . . Her name and address she then told with my tooraloom tooraloom tay. . . . With my tooraloom, tooraloom, tooraloom, tooraloom" (*U* 5.13–16). The source of this song is still unknown, but its rhyme words and its theme, in particular the concern about the "name and address" of the female, connect it with the minstrel song in "Nausicaa."

Many of these songs deal not with romantic love, but with love as a commodity; many of them are set in an urban environment that offers more opportunities for striking up an acquaintance in the park, in a shop, in a train or on a bus, but also more opportunities for being frustrated and disappointed. Young girls are left on their "ownio" or they are taken to Crewe instead of Birmingham, meeting in the train some "dear old chappie" as in "Oh, Mr. Porter, What Shall I Do?"[62] Another common story is about a young girl from the provinces losing her innocence in London and developing "a naughty little twinkle in her eye," as in "Her Golden Hair Was Hanging down Her Back,"[63] or about a servant striking up an acquaintance with a policeman. In *They Were Singing* Christopher Pulling has a whole chapter about music hall songs on policemen.[64] Since Bloom's encounter with the "nextdoor girl" at the porkbutcher has all the ingredients for a spicy music hall song, it is not surprising that, when she ignores him, he immediately assumes that she must have a liaison with a policeman: "The sting of disregard glowed to weak pleasure within his breast. For another: a constable off duty cuddling her in Eccles lane. They like them sizeable. Prime sausage. O please, Mr Policeman, I'm lost in the wood" (*U* 4.176–79). As Gifford and Seidman point out, Bloom combines *Babes in the Wood,* fairy tale as well as Christmas pantomime, with the music hall song "Oh Please, Mr. P'liceman, Oh! Oh! Oh!" sung by the Tillie Sisters:

> Oh, please, Mr. P'liceman, do be good to us;
> We've not been long in London,
> And we want to take a 'bus
> They told us we could go by 'bus to Pimlico,
> Oh, what a wicked place is London—
> Oh! Oh! Oh![65]

All things considered, Bloom is too much of "a cultured allround-man" to give the music hall more than its due in the complex cultural situation of his day. There is one particular music hall song, however, that occurs to Bloom again and again throughout the day for obvious reasons. Early in the morning he receives Milly's letter in which she mentions Boylan's "song about those seaside girls" (*U* 4.408–9) and he remembers vividly a pleasure cruise around Dublin Bay with Boylan as a "friend of the family." At Kingstown pier a band played the music hall song "Those Girls, Those Girls, Those Lovely Seaside Girls" and

Boylan must have sung along with his "hands stuck in his trousers' pockets" (*U* 4.439). This was one of Vesta Tilley's many songs in which she took the role of a young "swell," "masher" or "toff"—Burlington Bertie, Algy, the Piccadilly Johnny, the Seaside Sultan—singing about the pleasures of a spree in the West End or a holiday at the seaside. In a song like "Sidney's Holidays Are in September" she appeared to one of her many admirers as the "quintessence of seaside dandyism":

> she tells us of Bertie, the thirty bob clerk, who sweats in a London office for fifty-one weeks of the year, and for this one blessed week is lording it on the Brighton promenade as the mashaw (and she shoots off her cuffs)—er—Claude de Vere. Exquisite caricature! Every gesture is right; every tone is right. . . . These are not quite the gestures a dandy clerk would make; they are better than that—they explain him, laugh at him, justify him. They have all the deep truth of uncynical humour. . . . And the gestures moving to rhythm—the strut, the cocking of the hat, the dusting of the clothes and boots with the purple handkerchief, the throwing of stones into the water from the pier—pier—pier, all the ironic melody controls. Is it a dainty, flitting butterfly you are looking at or an affected fop? Perhaps seen from this proper distance, they are the same.[66]

Vesta Tilley's latest styles in men's clothing were the talk of the day, and just as she imitated the mashers in her performance, so they imitated her. Thus Blazes Boylan, hands in his pockets and with a white straw hat as well as "socks with skyblue clocks" (*U* 10.1241–42), seems to be the spitting image of Vesta Tilley.

A song about seaside girls is of course perfectly suited for being included among the songs in "Sirens" where, in fact, it turns up repeatedly. When Bloom is trying to break the spell of music, the song occurs to him for the last time in this chapter: "Want to keep your weathereye open. Those girls, those lovely. By the sad seawaves. Chorusgirl's romance" (*U* 11.1077–78). The tag "By the sad seawaves" is usually traced back to a song in Julius Benedict's opera *The Bride of Venice,* but as so often in *Ulysses,* such phrases have been used more than once and, in this context, another well-known song from Vesta Tilley's repertoire, "By the Sad Sea Waves," seems to be closer to Bloom's mind:

> In the glorious summer season
> Everybody takes a trip,
> To the seaside for enjoyment
> On the sands they gaily ship;

Vesta Tilley cross-dressed as "The Seaside Sultan," and almost a fashion model for Blazes Boylan's appearance. Collection of Ulrich Schneider.

Married men with wives and children,
Single Johnnies on the mash,
Pretty girls who seek for husbands
Who have pockets full of cash!

CHORUS:
By the sad seawaves,
Where the ladies look so charming
By the sad seawaves in the glorious summer time;
With their fetching smiles and dresses,
Rosy lips and golden tresses,
Shady nooks and sly caresses,
By the sad sea waves, by the waves.

Fetching smiles and dresses and, above all, golden hair, if not golden tresses, are in abundance in this chapter; moreover, the two barmaids, like the girls in the song, would certainly not reject a husband with "pockets full of cash."

Without having exhausted the material included in Joyce's earlier works and without having dipped into *Finnegans Wake,* enough examples have been assembled here to demonstrate how much the music hall adds to the polyphony of Joyce's works. Among the many dissonant voices of the city around the turn of the century, the "rollicking rattling song of the halls" (*U* 6.373) makes itself heard quite distinctly.

Notes

1. Stanislaus Joyce, *The Dublin Diary,* ed. George H. Healey (London: Faber and Faber, 1962), 38.

2. For general background on music halls, see Ulrich Schneider, *Die Londoner Music Hall und ihre Songs, 1850–1920.* Tübingen: Niemeyer, 1984; and for a bibliography on music hall, see Laurence Senelick, David F. Cheshire, and Ulrich Schneider, eds., *British Music Hall 1840–1923: A Bibliography and Guide to Sources* (Hamden, Conn.: Archon Books, 1981).

3. Elizabeth Robins Pennell, "The Pedigree of the Music-Hall," *The Contemporary Review* 63 (1893): 575–83.

4. Stanislaus Joyce, *My Brother's Keeper* (London: Faber and Faber, 1958), 110.

5. J. A. Hobson, *The Psychology of Jingoism* (London: Grant Richards, 1901), 3.

6. Walter Macqueen-Pope, *Twenty Shillings in the Pound* (Rpt. London: Hutchinson, 1949), 322.

7. "Mafeking and the Music Halls," *Music Hall and Theatre Review,* 25 May 1900, 329.

8. Quoted in Cheryl Herr, *Joyce's Anatomy of Culture* (Urbana: University of Illinois Press, 1986), 203–4.

9. W. B. Yeats, *The Letters of W. B. Yeats,* ed. Allan Wade (London: Macmillan, 1954), 534.

10. See David Hayman. "Language of/as gesture in Joyce," *"Ulysses" Cinquante Ans Après,* ed. Louis Bonnerot (Paris: Didier, 1974), 209–21.

11. Eugene Watters and Matthew Murtagh, *Infinite Variety: Dan Lowrey's Music Hall, 1879–97* (Dublin: Gill and Macmillan, 1975). See also Richard M. Kain, "'The music hall, not poetry, is a criticism of life'—A Note on Dan Lowrey's Star of Erin," *James Joyce Quarterly* 14 (Fall 1976): 96–99.

12. Max Beerbohm, "At the Tivoli," *Saturday Review,* 3 December 1898, 730–31. Reprinted in Beerbohm, *Around Theatres* (London: Hart-Davis, 1953), 11–14, at p. 11.

13. Max Beerbohm, "The Triumph of the 'Variety Show,'" *Saturday Review,* 18 November 1902, 487–88, at p. 488.

14. Arthur Symons, "A Spanish Music Hall," *The Fortnightly Review* (1892): 716–22, at p. 716.

15. Rudyard Kipling, *Something of Myself* (London: Macmillan, 1951), 79.

16. George Moore, *Confessions of a Young Man,* ed. Susan Dick (Montreal: McGill-Queen's University Press, 1972), 144–47.

17. Linda Dowling, *Language and Decadence in the Victorian Fin de Siècle* (Princeton: Princeton University Press, 1986), 175–243. I also draw upon Ulrich Schneider, "'That Exquisite Sense of the Frivolous,'" *Die 'Nineties: Das englische Fin de siècle zwischen Dekadenz und Sozialkritik,* ed. Manfred Pfister and Bernd Schulte-Middelich (Munich: Francke, 1983), 341–57; and Ulrich Schneider, "Joyce und die Music Hall," *Erlanger Anglistik und Amerikanistik in Vergangenheit und Gegenwart,* ed. Ulrich Bertram and Dieter Petzold (Erlangen: Erlanger Forschungen, 1990), 295–309.

18. Filippo Tomaso Marinetti, "The Variety Theatre," *The Mask* (January 1914): 188–89.

19. R. B. Kershner, *Joyce, Bakhtin, and Popular Literature* (Chapel Hill: University of North Carolina Press, 1989).

20. F. S. L. Lyons, *Culture and Anarchy in Ireland, 1890–1939* (Oxford: Oxford University Press, 1979), 2.

21. Other music hall songs for *Dubliners* and *Ulysses* are listed in Matthew J. C. Hodgart and Mabel Worthington, *Song in the Works of James Joyce* (New York: Columbia University Press for Temple University Publications, 1959); Weldon Thornton, *Allusions in "Ulysses,"* (Chapel Hill: University of North Carolina Press, 1968); Zack Bowen, *Musical Allusions in the Works of James Joyce: Early Poetry through "Ulysses"* (Albany: State University of New York Press, 1974); Don Gifford, *Joyce Annotated: Notes for "Dubliners" and "A Portrait of the*

Artist as a Young Man," 2d rev. ed. (Berkeley: University of California Press, 1982).

22. Watters and Murtagh, 37–38.

23. Jacqueline C. Bratton, "English Ethiopians: British Audiences and Black-Face Acts, 1835–1865," *Literature and Its Audience. The Yearbook of English Studies* 11 (1981): 127–42, at p. 139.

24. H. R. Haweis, *Music and Morals,* 14th ed. (London: Allen, [n.d.]), 551–52.

25. Tighe Hopkins, "Music Halls," *Dublin University Magazine* 92 (1878): 192–206.

26. Hopkins, 195–96.

27. Peter Davison, *Songs of the British Music Hall* (New York: Oak Publications, 1971), 135.

28. *Francis and Day's Community Book of Music Hall Songs,* Book 2 (London: Francis, Day and Hunter, n.d.) 26–27.

29. Clarkson Rose, *Beside the Seaside* (London: Museum Press, 1960), 25. The music of this song was written by C. W. Murphy, one of the most prolific songwriters around the turn of the century, who also composed "My Girl's a Yorkshire Girl," "Has Anybody Here Seen Kelly?" and "Oh! Oh! Antonio." All of these songs were written after 1904. See Ruth Bauerle, *The James Joyce Songbook* (New York: Garland, 1982, 1984), 276, and Introduction, above.

30. On "The Boarding House," see also Ulrich Schneider, "Eine irische Heirat: James Joyces 'The Boarding House,'" *Englisch-Amerikanische Studien* 2 (1980): 99–105.

31. Walter Macqueen-Pope, *The Melodies Linger On: The Story of the Music Hall* (London: Allen, 1950), 346.

32. Quoted in Macqueen-Pope, *The Melodies Linger On,* 557.

33. Macqueen-Pope, *Twenty Shillings in the Pound,* 316.

34. *Marie Lloyd* (London: EMI Music Publishing, 1977).

35. See T. S. Eliot, "In Memoriam: Marie Lloyd," *Criterion* (January 1923), 192–93. Reprint. "Marie Lloyd," *Selected Essays,* 3d enlarged ed. (London: Faber and Faber, 1951; New York: Harcourt Brace Jovanovich, 1964).

36. Frank Budgen, *James Joyce and the Making of "Ulysses"* (Rpt. Bloomington: Indiana University Press, 1961), 191.

37. H. Baumann, *Londonismen (Slang und Cant). Wörterbuch der Londoner Volkssprache* (Berlin: Langenscheidt, 1902), xciv-xcv.

38. Walter Matthews, *Cockney Past and Present* (London: Routledge, 1938), 82–104.

39. William Archer, "The Music Hall: Past and Future," *The Fortnightly Review,* New series (1916): 253–62, at p. 257.

40. Matthews, 101. The truth of this was brought home to me at the workshops of the Zurich James Joyce Foundation in 1985 and 1987 when

Charles Peake could still remember not only the chorus but whole stanzas from old music hall songs which, as he told me, his mother sang to him as lullabies. Many of these "folksongs" can be found in Charles Keeping, *Cockney Ding Dong* (London: Kestrel-EMI, 1975).

41. Daniel Joseph Kirwan, *Palace and Hovel; or Phases of London Life* (1870; rpt. London: Abelard-Schuman, 1963), 76.

42. This is the narrator's derisive version of a tale given by Christopher Pulling as follows: "Queen Victoria, much taken by a melody which a military band was playing on the terrace at Windsor, sent a Court official to ask Dan Godfrey, the bandmaster, for the name of the piece. Only a lifelong habit of discipline enabled the embarrassed man to report that the title was *Come Where the Booze is Cheaper*" (Christopher Pulling, *They Were Singing and What They Sang About* [London: Harrap, 1951], 133). See Fritz Senn, "Where the Booze is Cheaper," in "Trivia Ulysseana II," *James Joyce Quarterly* 13 (Winter 1976): 242–46.

43. Macqueen-Pope, *Twenty Shillings in the Pound,* 331.

44. Quoted in Angus Wilson, *The Strange Ride of Rudyard Kipling* (New York: Viking, 1977), 215.

45. Quoted in L. C. B. Seaman, *Victorian England: Aspects of English and Imperial History, 1837–1901* (London: Methuen, 1973), 332.

46. For the Freemasonic signs in this passage, see Ulrich Schneider, "Freemasonic Signs and Passwords in the 'Circe' Episode," *James Joyce Quarterly* 5 (Summer 1968): 303–11.

47. Quoted in Harold Scott, *The Early Doors: Origins of the Music Hall* (London: Nicholson and Watson, 1946), 183.

48. *Marie Lloyd,* 61.

49. Compton MacKenzie, *My Life and Times: Octave Two, 1891–1900* (London: Chatto and Windus, 1967), 34.

50. Bauerle, *James Joyce Songbook,* 276.

51. Davison, 140–41.

52. Bauerle, *James Joyce Songbook,* 278.

53. Roy Busby, *British Music Hall: An Illustrated Who's Who from 1850 to the Present Day* (London: Elek, 1976), 59. The first song was about a young woman who turns down a holiday at fancy places like Ostend and insists on going to the Isle of Man. Again Florrie Forde alludes to her earlier hit also associated, as we have seen, with the Isle of Man:

> CHORUS:
> Flanagan, Flanagan,
> Take me to the Isle of Man again.
> Take me where the folks all cry,
> "K - E - double L - Y!"
> Flanagan, Flanagan,

> If you love your Mary Ann,
> Oh! Flanagan, Take me to the Isle of Man!
>
> (*Francis and Day's Community Book of Music
> Hall Songs*, 1:20–21).

54. S. Joyce, *My Brother's Keeper*, 125.
55. Bauerle, *James Joyce Songbook*, 276.
56. Ibid., 349–51.
57. For complete words and music of this song see "Words and Music" chapter in this collection.
58. Busby, 158.
59. Watters and Murtagh, 81.
60. H. Chance Newton, *Idols of the "Halls"* (1928; Rpt. East Ardesley: EP Publishing, 1975), 130. The printed version I found in the British Library differs slightly from the version quoted in Newton and follows the call-and-response pattern of many minstrel songs:

> SOLO: I was out one day for a lark,
> CHORUS: Hunkey Dorum we am de boys,
> SOLO: I met with a lovely girl in the Park.
> CHORUS: Hunkey Dorum doodle dum da;
> SOLO: Her hair was frizz'd all over her head,
> CHORUS: Hunkey Dorum we am de boys,
> SOLO: She nearly kill'd this darkey dead,
> CHORUS: Hunkey Dorum doodle dum da.
> Her hair was frizz'd all over her head
> She nearly kill'd dis darkey dead.
> And her maiden name it was Brown,
> She liv'd with her mother in Camden Town.

61. See Jane Traies, "Jones and the Working Girl: Class Marginality in Music-Hall Song, 1860–1900," *Music Hall: Performance and Style,* ed. Jacqueline S. Bratton (Milton Keynes: Open University Press, 1986), 23–48, at pp. 39–40.
62. *Marie Lloyd,* 62.
63. Davison, 85.
64. Pulling, 87–105.
65. Don Gifford with Robert J. Seidman, *"Ulysses" Annotated,* rev. ed. (Berkeley: University of California Press, 1988), 73–74.
66. W. R. Titterton, *From Theatre to Music Hall* (London: Swift, 1912), 148–49.

Joyce, Wagner, and Literary Wagnerism

Timothy Martin

Considered as an artistic force, Wagner is something almost without parallel, probably the most formidable talent in the entire history of art.

—Thomas Mann, "Wagner and the Present Age," 1931

As a singer and operagoer, James Joyce was often asked his opinion of Richard Wagner's operas. His reviews were mixed at best. It was characteristic of the Irish writer to denigrate Wagner when others had praised him, as if the proud artist in Joyce resented the tremendous influence that Wagner had exerted in nearly every corner of turn-of-the-century European culture. When Nora and Lucia admired Wagner's music, Joyce objected to its sensuality;[1] when his friend Ottocaro Weiss preferred the music of *Die Walküre* to that of "Sirens," Joyce left the theater (*JJ2* 460). In Zurich, Richard Ellmann writes, Joyce "had no patience with the current adulation of Wagner, objecting that '*Wagner puzza di sesso*' (stinks of sex); Bellini, he said, was far better" (*JJ2* 382). The *Ring,* he claimed on one occasion, was mere "operetta music."[2] At a performance of *Götterdämmerung* in Rome, Brünnhilde's horse, as Joyce put it to Stanislaus, "being unable to sing, evacuated"; this deflation of the sublime by the ridiculous must have delighted the eventual writer of *Ulysses* and *Finnegans Wake* (*Letters 2* 214, 217–18). Indeed, Wagner's mythic method must have seemed almost unrelentingly serious to the wry sensibility that had detected the shy gentleman and the draft-dodger in Odysseus.[3]

But Joyce did have a consistent favorite among Wagner's works—*Die Meistersinger von Nürnberg.* We know that in Trieste in 1909 he performed in a concert version of the famous quintet in act 3 (*Letters 1* 67), probably taking, between the two tenor parts, that of the apprentice Meistersinger David, since the part of Walther, the lead, would have demanded a higher range and stronger voice than Joyce apparently had. Frank Budgen found that Joyce "was not a great admirer of Wagner, except for *Die Meistersinger,*" and the impression of Louis Gillet, who knew Joyce in Paris, was the same: "He could not stand modern music and except for *Die Meistersinger* and some arias from *The Flying Dutchman* he had a dislike for Wagner."[4] In 1919 Joyce told his language student Georges Borach that *Meistersinger* was "my favorite Wagnerian opera" (*JJ2* 459), and according to Herbert Gorman, Joyce "never missed a performance" of this work.[5] But even this favorite, when first praised by others, might provoke the iconoclast in Joyce: "Do you understand the infatuation of people for this opera?" he wrote composer G. Molyneux Palmer from Trieste. "I think it is pretentious stuff" (*Letters 1* 67).

The exception that Joyce apparently made for *Die Meistersinger* can perhaps be explained by the fact that this opera is in many ways the most "un-Wagnerian" of Wagner's works. With its historical setting in sixteenth-century Nuremberg, *Meistersinger* is the only mature opera that is not based on myth or legend. Its characters are common burghers and guildsmen, not the mythic figures who occupy the stage in *Lohengrin,* the *Ring,* and *Parsifal,* where the art of Wagner speaks, as Thomas Mann put it, in "a language without tense."[6] Its central character, the cobbler, poet, and singer Hans Sachs, combines irascibility, good humor, and generosity in altogether human proportions. It is Wagner's only comic opera, with mistaken identities, a chastised villain, and a love plot with the usual obstacles. Moreover, when measured against the composer's own standards, *Meistersinger* is stylistically retrograde, with ensembles and large final choruses, both of which the reformer in Wagner had once banned from his stage as "operatic." There is a good deal of four-bar melodic writing, and the harmonies are less consistently radical than those, for example, of *Meistersinger*'s immediate predecessor in Wagner's canon, *Tristan und Isolde.* In conceiving the opera, Wagner, according to "A Communication to My Friends," was taking the advice of associates who thought a "lighter" style might get his demanding works into the German opera houses more readily.[7] If Joyce's favorite opera, as is generally believed, was in the *bel canto* tradition, if, as Gillet reports, he "doted upon singing, adoring Rossini,

Meyerbeer, Verdi,"[8] then *Meistersinger* would have found a place in his operatic affections more readily than any other Wagnerian opera. Indeed, it may have been the only one with a tenor part available for Joyce himself.

As we turn from the aficionado of opera to the writer of literature, where do we find *Die Meistersinger* in Joyce's work? The first place to search would be "Sirens," Joyce's most concentrated attempt to make his work "musical," and, indeed, Wagner, the composer who had done more than any other to make opera "literary," is linked to "Sirens" in several tantalizing ways. Stuart Gilbert, whose collaboration with Joyce in the writing of Gilbert's guide to *Ulysses* gives him special authority, uses Walther's *Preislied* from act 3 to explain how the literary "leitmotif" works in "Sirens."[9] In fact, Joyce himself seems to have authorized such a search: in 1919 he told Georges Borach, "I finished the Sirens chapter during the last few days. A big job. I wrote this chapter with the technical resources of music . . . *piano, forte, rallentando,* and so on. A quintet occurs in it, too, as in *Die Meistersinger,* my favorite Wagnerian opera" (*JJ2* 459). Finally, the chapter's introduction resembles the table of leitmotifs often found at the beginning of Wagner's piano-vocal scores.[10]

Joyce's characters in *Ulysses,* like those in *Die Meistersinger,* are common people in a city rich in musical tradition, and in "Sirens" Joyce treats his old-fashioned singers with the same mixture of irony and affection that one finds in the opera. Both *Meistersinger* and "Sirens" culminate in a tournament of song with two main performers. In act 3 a bass and a tenor, Sixtus Beckmesser and Walther von Stolzing, compete for Eva's hand and sing the praises of love; in "Sirens," a "bass barreltone," Ben Dollard, and a tenor, Simon Dedalus, both sing love songs, "Love and War," and *M'appari,* respectively. Does a quintet "occur" in this chapter, as Joyce suggested? *Meistersinger*'s quintet, though it does draw on the traditional operatic ensemble, is nonetheless highly "Wagnerian." The characters do not sing "in harmony": each has his own text and expresses his own thoughts, and each vocal line in Wagner's contrapuntal writing goes its own way. One critic calls the quintet "five simultaneous soliloquies."[11] What "Sirens" and Wagner's quintet share, therefore, is the attempt (which Joyce pursued more fully in "Wandering Rocks") to depict simultaneous but independent thought or action, what might in the case of Joyce be called "narrative counterpoint." Five characters in "Sirens" have what amount to their own leitmotifs: Bloom's "Bloowho," Boylan's "jingle," the piano tuner's "tap," Miss Kennedy's "gold," and Miss Douce's "bronze." They form a quintet of three men and two women who move independently through the chapter (in several locations) and pursue their own thoughts (the same configuration found in *Meistersinger*). But Wagner's dramatic situation, which involves two couples and a lone man, suggests another possibility. The quintet's couples—Eva and Walther, David and Magdalene—have recently seen prospects for their love grow, while the single man and oldest character—Hans Sachs—has just come to acknowledge the futility of his love for Eva. In "Sirens" a similar quintet may be discovered in the two couples who are coming together—Boylan and Molly (offstage), George Lidwell and Lydia Douce—and Bloom, who, like the sympathetic Hans Sachs, stands aside from love and submits to the desire of his woman for a more vigorous man: "Woman," he thinks. "As easy stop the sea. Yes: all is lost" (*U* 11.641). Like Wagner's quintet, "Sirens" is a complex expression of ardent love and renunciation.

If the presence of *Meistersinger* in "Sirens" is a matter of parallels rather than direct allusions and is therefore elusive, references to the opera elsewhere in Joyce's work are relatively infrequent. The *"Silentium"* in the confusion of the last few pages of "Oxen of the Sun" may echo the cry of the Apprentices in act 3, before the prize-singing begins: *"Silentium! Silentium! Macht kein Reden und kein Gesumm'."* [12] Several contexts in *Finnegans Wake* link the mastersinger Beckmesser, town clerk of Nuremberg, with Ibsen's master builder "Bygmester Solness," and thus to the fallen Tim Finnegan and HCE. The phrase "Bigmesser's conversions" in "Haveth Childers Everywhere" (*FW* 530.32) might refer to Beckmesser's comic attempt to pirate Walther's *Preislied* in act 3, an attempt that ends in the same ridicule and disgrace that HCE endures. A few allusions in the *Wake* align Wagner's mastersingers with the Four Masters of Ireland and, thus, the Four Evangelists. At one point, for example, the *Wake*'s annalists are described as "mastersinging always with that consecutive fifth of theirs" (*FW* 513.34–35); the "fifth" is apparently the ass that trails along after one of the masters, and all students of harmony know parallel fifths (called "consecutive fifths" in British usage) are *verboten*. [13] Finally, Joyce's thematically important *taufen* motif may draw on the baptismal theme that is introduced in the opera's opening chorus and emphasized in the opera's setting on Midsummer Day, the feast of John the Baptist. *Meistersinger* is palpable in Joyce, but it is not pervasive or central.

In assessing Wagner's presence in Joyce's work, it may be better to follow Joyce's literary interests rather than his musical ones, to trace the path of the writer rather than that of the musician and lover of opera. Joyce's first important encounters with Wagner, in fact, were not in the opera house; for in Dublin the scale and, in Joyce's time, the dubious morality of the operas would have limited opportunities to hear the composer to excerpts played in concerts. By the time Joyce left in 1904, full-scale productions of only two of the operas—*The Flying Dutchman* and *Lohengrin*—had been attempted in that city known for its love of opera and the musical theater.[14] But as a student at University College, Joyce read contemporary writing voraciously, and in the Continental literature in which he was especially interested Wagner was ubiquitous. In Gabriele D'Annunzio's *Il fuoco,* for example, which the young Joyce thought "the highest achievement of the novel to date,"[15] Wagner's operas and aesthetic theories are a constant theme in the artistic circle of the protagonist Stelio Effrena, and Wagner's own personage helps constitute the novel's Venetian background. The time span of *Il fuoco,* from September of 1882 to February of 1883, covers the months Wagner actually spent in Venice before his death on February 13, and the book's final chapter gives an account of Wagner's funeral procession to the railway station. In Arthur Symons's influential *Symbolist Movement in Literature,* which Joyce read enthusiastically shortly after it was published in 1899, Wagner is numbered, all too readily, among "Symbolist" writers like Mallarmé, Huysman, Laforgue, Villiers, and Verlaine, who had pursued their own interests in Wagner during their association with Edouard Dujardin's *Revue wagnérienne* in Paris from 1885 to 1888. Joyce would also have found Wagner in the writings of Yeats and other Irishmen who looked to his achievements at Bayreuth, as they did to Ibsen's in the Norwegian theater movement, in their own efforts to establish a national theater based on Irish myth. In "The Celtic Element in Literature," Yeats writes: "In our own time Scandinavian tradition, because of the imagination of Richard Wagner and of William Morris and of the earlier and, as I think, greater Henrik Ibsen, has created a new romance, and, through the imagination of Richard Wagner, become all but the most passionate element in the arts of the modern world."[16] It may, in fact, have been this frequent conjunction with Ibsen that first led Joyce to Wagner. "To like Ibsen's plays in the eighties," George Moore wrote, "was equivalent to liking Wagner's music. Both were regarded with oblique looks, and few were quite sure that the new music and the new drama were not an immorality, which it was perhaps the duty of the state to stamp out." [17] In defying the philistines at the Paris Opera, challenging conventional operatic and musical tastes, creating a revolutionary "music drama," and founding his own operatic temple at Bayreuth, Wagner the "total artist" had combined ambition with achievement in a way that seemed to epitomize the romantic idea of genius. Thomas Mann's contention that the composer was "probably the most formidable talent in the entire history of art" [18] may have struck many of Joyce's contemporaries as hyperbolic; nonetheless, for the man or woman of letters at the turn of the century, Wagner was a looming presence.

Joyce's own Wagnerism, apparent by the time he was seventeen, reflects the composer's status in literary circles rather than musical ones. In his early critical writings Joyce frequently invokes Wagner as a dramatist and maker of myth and carefully chooses Wagner's own preferred term—not "opera" but "drama"—in identifying his work. The artistic manifesto "Drama and Life," which Joyce presented at University College in 1900, cites Wagner three times. Joyce writes that the "author" of *Parsifal* has drawn on the resources of myth and made his work "solid as a rock" (*CW* 43); and he creates his own conjunction of Wagner and Ibsen in describing *Lohengrin* and *Ghosts* as "world drama[s] . . . of universal import" (*CW* 45). A distinction between the "musical" Wagner and the "literary" Wagner who composed his own librettos and wrote prolifically on art, music, and culture, a distinction that Shaw's popular *Perfect Wagnerite* might have encouraged in Joyce, is evident in "Drama and Life": "Even the least part of Wagner—his music—is beyond Bellini. Spite of the outcry of these lovers of the past, the masons are building for Drama, an ampler and loftier home, where there shall be light for gloom, and wide porches for drawbridge and keep" (*CW* 40–41). The reader may be pardoned if he or she finds Wagner's Bayreuth and Wotan's Valhalla in this rhetorical flourish. In Dublin Joyce followed the examples of Symons, Moore, and Dujardin in playing the literary Wagnerite: pleasing a French professor at University College with "idée-mère" as a translation of "leitmotif" (*JJ2* 60); writing, after the tradition of Dujardin's *Revue,* a poem on the "Valkyrie"; [19] and, during a brief stay in Paris in 1903, following the libretto at what was probably his first experience of Wagner on the operatic stage. "Tell Stannie," he wrote his mother urgently, "to send me *at once* (so that I may have it by Thursday night) my copy of

Wagner's operas" (*Letters 2* 25). This orthodox Wagnerism did not survive Joyce's move to the Continent, where, so widely performed and so much better known, the composer did not cut, for Joyce, the same exotic figure he did in turn-of-the-century Dublin. In a letter written to Stanislaus in 1906 about Moore's Wagnerian *The Lake,* Joyce would lump Wagner, the *Ring,* and Bayreuth with Oliver Gogarty among the "memories of my youth" (*Letters 2* 154).

But if the youthful enthusiasm that was Wagnerism did not persist, a genuine interest in Wagner's work did. Despite his many complaints about the music, Joyce's letters and conversation show that, living in European cities with resident opera companies, he saw all the mature operas performed, many of them frequently. Especially telling evidence of a persistent interest in the composer may be found among Joyce's books. Joyce began acquiring works by Wagner in his late teens, when he was preparing the Wagnerian "Drama and Life"; by 1920, when he left his library behind him in Trieste, it included some fifteen books by or about Wagner and many more in which Wagner is a significant presence. Among these were the first volume of the *Prose Works,* which contains most of the influential theoretical essays written from 1849 to 1851; the well-known *Letters to August Roeckel,* Wagner's unlucky associate in the Dresden uprising of 1849; a two-volume collection of letters to Wagner's first wife Minna; the infamous *Judaism in Music;* and five studies of Wagner, including, most importantly, Shaw's *Perfect Wagnerite* and Nietzsche's *Case of Wagner* and *Nietzsche contra Wagner.* The Trieste library includes four librettos to Wagner's operas but no piano-vocal scores. Not surprisingly, the only musical score Joyce is known to have owned was to *Meistersinger;* neither this copy, which Joyce used for the performance of the quintet in Trieste, nor the collection of librettos that Joyce had sent to him in Paris has survived.[20] A comment Joyce made in 1918 shows, again, that the *writer* in Joyce applied the language of the literary critic, not the enthusiasm of the operagoer, to Wagnerian opera: "There are . . . hardly more than a dozen original themes in world literature," he told Georges Borach. "*Tristan und Isolde* is an example of an original theme. Richard Wagner kept on modifying it, often unconsciously, in *Lohengrin,* in *Tannhäuser;* and he thought he was treating something entirely new when he wrote *Parsifal.*"[21]

It is important to emphasize, however, that Joyce's Wagnerism was not exclusively literary and that the Irish writer brought his well-trained ear to his experience of the composer. When Joyce told his brother after the performance of *Götterdämmerung* in 1907 that he had heard members of the audience humming "correctly and incorrectly the nine notes of the funeral motive," he was thinking of the "Helden" motif in E-flat major, one of the most distinctive motifs in the entire *Ring*. "I have heard the funeral music often before," he wrote Stanislaus (*Letters 2* 214). When Robert Hand "strums" Wolfram's "*O du, mein holder Abendstern*" in act 2 of *Exiles* (*E* 73), the reader may forget that Robert is playing the piano and remember, instead, the harp and pizzicato strings that accompany the Minnesinger's aria in act 3 of *Tannhäuser*. And when Joyce, in his public letter to tenor John Sullivan, wrote that Rossini had saved "Kamerad Wagner . . . the annoyance of finding flauts for his *Feuerzauber*" (*CW* 263), he was probably thinking of the flutes in the memorable conclusion of *Die Walküre*. The essays of the tone-deaf Yeats that call Wagner a "Symbolist" cannot boast this sort of detail. Though Joyce may not have possessed Shaw's acumen as a music critic, he would not require, as George Moore did, someone to check his books for musical howlers.

Joyce's mature attitude toward Wagner and his work may be best expressed in his complex treatment of the composer in *Exiles*. In this revealing play, Wagner is explicitly linked with the overblown Robert Hand, who speaks what Richard Rowan (echoing Joyce's own denigration of Moore's *The Lake,* quoted above) dismisses as "the language of my youth" (*E* 89) and who, in anticipation of his tryst with Bertha at the beginning of act 2, plays on the piano "*O du, mein holder Abendstern*" (popularized as "O Evening Star"). Surprised by Richard's appearance, Robert covers his embarrassment by saying, "I was just strumming out Wagner when you came" (*E* 73). It is tempting to count Wagner, on the basis of his association with Robert Hand, among the youthful enthusiasms that, as David Hayman suggests, Joyce may be exorcising in this play.[22] Nonetheless, *Exiles* betrays an influence by as many as five of the operas: *The Flying Dutchman,* in Robert's maudlin death-wish in act 1 (*E* 41); *Tannhäuser,* in Wolfram's aria from act 3 (*E* 73); *Tristan,* in the play's published notes (*E* 157); the *Ring,* in a parallel drawn in the notes between Robert and Richard, and Wotan and Siegfried (*E* 152); and *Parsifal,* in the allusion, at the final curtain, to the wound of Amfortas that will not heal (*E* 146–47). It is probable, too, that Joyce borrowed details for the setting of act 2 from a popular book by May Byron that he owned in Trieste, a writer to whom, Ellmann has shown,

Joyce would also turn for material on Shakespeare for "Aeolus" and "Scylla and Charybdis." [23] Among the models for Robert Hand may be the Arthur Symons whom Joyce and Yeats met in London in 1902, and whom Joyce, afterward, would call "ninetyish" (*JJ2* 112):

> During this meeting . . . Symons told stories of the poets and artists he had known, of Verlaine and Dowson, of Lionel Johnson and Beardsley, and, hearing that my brother was interested in music, he sat down at the piano and played the Good Friday music from *Parsifal*.
>
> —When I play Wagner, he murmured, closing the piano and standing up, I am in another world. [24]

Exiles expresses, through the character of Robert Hand, a good deal of detachment from the Wagnerism that Joyce had come to see as a youthful fling—from "Boyrut season," as the *Wake* would put it (*FW* 229.34). But the fascination with Wagner's work is undeniable. Significantly, Joyce is careful to reserve Wagner's celebrated role as artist-exile as well as the composer's first name for his alter ego, Richard Rowan.

For more substantial contributions to Joyce's art than his operatic favorite *Die Meistersinger* apparently offered him, we must turn to works that, as "opera," Joyce may have considered "oversexed" and "in poor taste"—works, however, that were a good deal more influential than was *Meistersinger* among the contemporary writers whom the young Joyce had studied. [25] Of all the Wagnerian connections, one of the best known is between Siegfried, the hero of the *Ring*, and Stephen Dedalus. [26] This association is clearly established in chapter 5 of *A Portrait*, when Stephen passes through the college quadrangle and hears his friend Dixon whistle the "birdcall from *Siegfried*" (P 237). In act 2.2 of this opera, before Siegfried faces the first serious test of his heroic mettle, the song of the bird among the forest murmurs is a simple tune, meaningless to him. But after he slays the dragon Fafner and accidentally tastes his blood, he suddenly understands the bird; that is, a soprano provides words for the pentatonic tune. The changing birdcall reflects, therefore, Siegfried's growth as a hero, and it is perfectly positioned in *A Portrait*. The whistling of the birdcall near the novel's end asserts Stephen's promise as an "artist-hero," through the association with the quintessentially heroic Siegfried; however, the fact that Dixon's birdcall is whistled, not sung (with words), emphasizes Stephen's distance, at this point in his development, from the heroic standard Siegfried represents.

The connection with the *Ring* is carried, with Stephen, into *Ulysses*. The ashplant that Joyce's artist picks up late in *A Portrait* and manipulates nervously throughout *Ulysses* is not clearly identified at first, though the student of the *Ring* may remember the sword that Wotan once "planted" in an "ash" tree for his son Siegmund, the sword that Siegfried would be compelled to reforge from its broken pieces as part of his heroic apprenticeship in *Siegfried*. But in the climax of "Circe"— the climax of *Ulysses* itself—the sword's identity is made clear when Stephen, attacking Bella Cohen's lampshade, shouts its Wagnerian name: "Nothung!" (*U* 15.4242). In the *Ring* the sword represents masculine creative power and, once Siegfried has reforged it, independence from the authority of its original owner Wotan, who is god and the state in one. When, in imitation of the memorable forging scene in act 1 of *Siegfried,* Stephen brandishes the ashplant and shouts its Wagnerian name, he makes an assertion of independent will that is the basis of the unselfconscious Siegfried's character: "Break my spirit, all of you, if you can. I'll bring you all to heel!" (*U* 15.4235–36). The association with Siegfried had been emphasized earlier, in the episode's palmreading scene (*U* 15.3648–61), as Stephen "extends his hand" to Zoe and "chants to the air of the bloodoath in *The Dusk of the Gods:* Hangende Hunger, / Fragende Frau, / Macht uns alle kaputt." Stephen's chanting follows the rhythm of the oath of blood-brotherhood that Siegfried and Gunther swear in *Götterdämmerung* 1.2, and the phrase "Fragende Frau" derives, as Ellmann has shown (*JJ2* 460), from material in *Die Walküre* 1.2. In the ensuing reading, Zoe finds "courage" in Stephen's palm, and Lynch remarks, "Sheet lightning courage. The youth who could not shiver and shake." Lynch's comment recalls the fact that, among mythic heroes, Siegfried's distinguishing mark is his inability to experience fear. But it reminds us, ironically, of Stephen's many sources of fear—dogs, thunder, water, the image of his dead mother—and of his self-assessment, articulated in "Telemachus," that "I'm not a hero, however" (*U* 1.62). In the grandiloquence of the climax of "Circe," Stephen will only damage the chimney of Bella Cohen's lamp, "not sixpenceworth of damage," as Bloom insists when he settles with the whoremistress (*U* 15.4290–91). If the comparison to Siegfried inflates our image of Stephen in *A Portrait,* it begins to deflate it in *Ulysses,* to work subtly against Stephen as he continues to founder in Dublin and to fall far short of the artistic heroism that *A Portrait* seemed to promise.

The powerful Wagnerian presence in the climax (or anticlimax) of *Ulysses* shows the importance of Stephen's association with Siegfried. In linking these two figures, in fact, Joyce was drawing on a literary tradition that made Wagner's hero a type of the revolutionary artist, destined to rejuvenate his culture. The tradition begins in *The Birth of Tragedy,* where, in a catalog of Siegfried's heroic achievements, Wagner and his operas represent, for Nietzsche, the embodiment of the spirit of Greek tragedy in modern Germany: "Let no one believe that the German spirit has for ever lost its mythical home when it still understands so obviously the voices of the birds which tell of that home. Some day it will find itself awake in all the morning freshness of a deep sleep: then it will slay the dragons, destroy the malignant dwarfs, and waken Brünnhilde—and Wotan's spear itself will be unable to obstruct its course!"[27] The tradition continues in *Il fuoco,* which identifies Wagner's own artistic heroism with that of Siegfried; in George Moore's autobiographical *Hail and Farewell,* where Moore considers whether he might be destined to wake Ireland from its centuries of cultural slumber; and in the early essays of Yeats, where references to Wagner and to Siegfried and his sword link the movement for an Irish national theater and Wagner's own Bayreuth: "We were to forge in Ireland a new sword on our old traditional anvil for that great battle that must in the end re-establish the old, confident, joyous world."[28] Thus, when Stephen resolves at the end of *A Portrait* "to forge in the smithy of my soul the uncreated conscience of my race," and evokes, in so doing, the forging scene in *Siegfried,* he aligns himself with this tradition of the artist-revolutionary who redeems his nation's art and culture. Indeed, a reading of the essays gathered in the first volume of Wagner's *Prose Works* shows the close compatibility of Stephen's artistic principles and Wagner's own: the acceptance of a Greek model of artistic fullness or perfection, the embracing of an idealized "life" as the material of art, the emphasis on the purity of the artist's "soul," the idea of a collective "conscience," and the social function of art. And an examination of Joyce's own copy of the *Prose Works* shows a clear pencil marking in the margin of the following passage from "Art and Revolution":

[Art] lives . . . and has ever lived in the individual conscience, as the one, fair, indivisible Art. Thus the only difference is this: with the Greeks it lived in the public conscience, whereas to-day it lives alone in the conscience of private persons, the public *un*-conscience recking nothing of it. Therefore in its flowering time the Grecian Art was *con-*

servative, because it was a worthy and adequate expression of the public conscience: with us, true Art is *revolutionary,* because its very existence is opposed to the ruling spirit of the community.[29]

The consistency of Joyce's association of Siegfried with the figure of the artist is suggested by a passage in the published notes to *Exiles,* where Joyce writes of Robert's equivocal role as Richard's advocate and adversary. Robert's "position" in helping Richard reestablish himself in Ireland, Joyce writes, "is like that of Wotan who in willing the birth and growth of Siegfried longs for his own destruction" (*E* 152).

One of the most striking parallels between Joyce and Wagner is that each, in the midst of creating what is arguably his most influential work, shifted his primary interest from the figure of the young revolutionary to the passive victim of the vicissitudes of experience. The *Ring,* by the time of its completion in 1874, had become the psychological drama of the watchful bystander Wotan instead of the tragedy of Siegfried that had been envisioned at the outset in 1848. The sympathies of *Ulysses,* likewise, are more firmly invested in Bloom than they are in the artist figure who shows evidence of ossification as early as "Telemachus." Evidently, as a note for *Exiles* suggests, Joyce saw the emphasis on passive, equivocal heroes at the expense of active, heroic ones as characteristic of modern literature. "Since the publication of the lost pages of *Madame Bovary,*" he writes, "the centre of sympathy appears to have been esthetically shifted from the lover or fancyman to the husband or cuckold" (*E* 150). The presence of the *Ring* in Joyce's work reflects this shifting sympathy. "Circe" represents the apogee of Siegfried's position in Joyce's work; for in the *Wake,* where the artist is a "low sham" (*FW* 170.25) who carries "nothung up my sleeve" (*FW* 295.18), he simply takes his place among the numberless gods, heroes, and men who constitute Shem and Shaun. But as Siegfried gradually fades from Joyce's books, Wotan grows more palpable and important.

There is no indication that Joyce found a role for Wotan in *Ulysses.* In fact, in combining elements of Odysseus and the Wandering Jew, as "Circe" and "Eumaeus" suggest, Bloom is more Flying Dutchman than he is any other Wagnerian figure.[30] But in *Finnegans Wake* Wotan makes an excellent counterpart to HCE, who, in all his manifestations, is a figure of authority: father, lawgiver, builder of civilization, founder of church and state. Both Wotan and HCE have undermined their positions with a crime or an indiscretion—a "fall"—that brings mortality on themselves and upon their society. The offense, in both cases, involves the exploitation of "female" nature for the sake of "male" culture or civilization. Wotan's crime is to have taken the gold ring from Alberich and to have used it to pay for the building of Valhalla, instead of returning it to its pristine home in the bed of the maternal Rhine; the result is the fallen world of *Die Walküre* and the doom of the *Götterdämmerung*. HCE's crime is not clearly identified, but its effect is apparent in the squalor and congestion of the modern urban landscape, summarized, in I.1, as "wallhall's horrors" (*FW* 5.30—cf. "Valhalla's heroes"). As Adaline Glasheen has put it, "HCE builds, therefore he falls."[31] The "Butt and Taff" episode in II.3 articulates the plight of the *Wake*'s postlapsarian man: "We all, for whole men is lepers, have been nobbut wonterers in that chill childerness which is our true name after the allfaulters" (*FW* 355.33–35).[32] The coinage "wonterer" suggests "Wanderer," the name the doomed Wotan takes in *Siegfried*, and "allfaulter" includes "Allfather," one of Wotan's many names in Germanic myth. Joyce's alteration of the latter name reinforces the idea that HCE, like Wotan, is not only the first father but the original sinner as well, "fafafather of all schemes for to bother us" (*FW* 45.13). Both HCE and Wotan, that is, combine features of God and Adam.

In the *Wake*, Valhalla, the great symbol of Wotan's rule, is counted among the phallic landmarks of power and ambition that spring up nearly everywhere: the towers of Babel and of Halvard Solness, Howth Castle, the house that Jack built, and Wall Street, to name just a few. In "Haveth Childers Everywhere," when Joyce's Allfather boasts of the "Megalopolis" that he has created (*FW* 128.3), a nameless antagonist interrupts him with a sardonic reference to Wotan's own creation: "Wallpurgies! And it's this's your deified city?" (*FW* 530.31). HCE recalls the founding of his *"Urbs in Rure"* (*FW* 551.24), in one sense Dublin itself, with the particular help of *Das Rheingold:* "and I fenced it about with huge Chesterfield elms . . . and pons for aguaducks . . . the hallaw vall" (*FW* 553.18–22). "Hallaw vall" is an easy reversal of "Valhalla," and the "pons" mentioned in close proximity to Valhalla evokes the rainbow bridge of *Rheingold*'s stirring conclusion. Built by Donner and "[F]roh, the frothy freshener" (*FW* 553.27) as the gods' thoroughfare to their newly built home, the rainbow bridge helps HCE describe the occasion on which ALP—the river Liffey and maternal nature as well as the archetypal woman—was first "bridged": "and I abridged with domfine norsemanship till I had done abate her maidan

race, my baresark bride, and knew her fleshly when with all my bawdy
did I her whorship, min bryllupswibe: Heaven, he hallthundered;
Heydays, he flung blissforhers. And I cast my tenspan joys on her . . .
from back of call to echobank . . . and to ringstresse I thumbed her
with iern of Erin" (*FW* 547.26–33). "Heydays" recalls Donner's thun-
dering "Heda! Heda! Hedo!" in the last measures of *Das Rheingold*,[33]
and "tenspan joys . . . from bank of call to echobank" describes the
bridge itself, the *"Ring*-Strasse" to Valhalla. Here Donner's thunder
takes on special significance, for the recurring sound of thunder in the
Wake is HCE's stuttering confession of guilt. Joyce must have been
delighted that thunder, which punctuates the score of the *Ring* a dozen
or more times, should have marked the famous "Gods' Entry into
Valhalla."[34]

In *Ulysses,* for all the importance of Telemachus to Stephen, Odysseus to Bloom, and Penelope to Molly, the most significant juxtaposi-
tion is that of the *Odyssey,* considered as a whole, to *Ulysses.* The same is
true of the relation between the *Ring* and *Finnegans Wake.* In the *Ring*
Joyce encountered the most powerful contemporary analogy, expressed
in Germanic myth, to the story that had preoccupied him since his days
in Dublin, that of Genesis. In creating his four-part drama Wagner had
taken the legend of Siegfried from his mythic sources and spliced it to
that of the Germanic Twilight of the Gods. The result was a philosoph-
ical drama about the nature of evil, the vulnerability of innocence, and
the sources of redemption in a postlapsarian world. The *Ring* and the
Wake, taken as whole works, invite immediate comparison. Both in
four parts, the *Ring* comprises three substantial operas with a shorter
prelude, the *Wake* three substantial books with a short postscript. Both
are structured on the model of the circle, with the principle of return
represented in the idea of nature and symbolized in a river, Rhine or
Liffey, which appears at the end and at the beginning of each work. The
Ring, in fact, merits space on Atherton's shelf of "structural books" for
the *Wake.*[35] In 1904 Joyce told John Eglinton that he intended to re-
write *Paradise Lost,*[36] a vow he commemorates in "Scylla and Charybdis," when Eglinton and the group gathered to hear Stephen speak on
Hamlet enjoy a smile at the expense of Stephen's youthful ambition (*U*
9.18–35). In the *Wake* Joyce would ultimately honor that vow to
Eglinton. Indeed, the simple fact of Wagner's existence, instilling ambition in the Faustian Irish writer who had determined that his work

would be "great"—in manner, in scale, and in subject—may represent the most important Wagnerian influence of all.

In tracing the presence of the *Ring* in Joyce, we have treated Wagner as a dramatist and have discussed his librettos, characters, and themes. To what extent can we speak of the importance of Wagner the *musician* to Joyce, of the influence of his musical language, his harmony, orchestration, counterpoint, and melody? The interest in music as the "art of arts" has been a recurring theme in modern literature, beginning with the Romantic movement and continuing well into our own century. The Symbolists in France, many of whom were associated with Dujardin's *Revue wagnérienne* in the 1880s, made a vaguely defined "musicality" their poetic ideal, and in "The School of Giorgione" Walter Pater went so far as to argue that all art be evaluated by its adherence to "musical law." [37] Pater, whose *Renaissance* gave us the lapidary phrase "all art constantly aspires towards the condition of music," may have inspired a remark Joyce made to Arthur Power in the early days of *Work in Progress*. "[J]udging from modern trends," Joyce told Power, "it seems that all the arts are tending towards the abstraction of music; and what I am writing at present is entirely governed by that purpose." [38] In the *Revue,* editor Teodor de Wyzewa wrote a series of essays on "L'Art wagnérien," taking up several arts—painting, literature, and music—in turn. "Literature only becomes art," Wyzewa wrote, "by grafting upon itself a musicality quite alien to its essential, intellectual, nature." [39] As Wyzewa's series would suggest, Wagner's role in this discussion was crucial. As the "total artist" who had melded the disparate arts into a single *Gesamtkunstwerk,* Wagner justified the claim for the artistic integrity of opera and appeared to redeem the genre from its historical status as mere entertainment. Though his idea of a synthesis of arts in drama was not completely original—Wagner himself pointed to Greek drama as his forerunner and inspiration—his "total artwork" gave the attraction to music already evident in nineteenth-century aesthetics emphasis and credibility. For if a composer could harness the expressive potential of all the arts in an inclusive "music drama," if in particular a musician could make opera "literary," could poet and novelist not make their work "musical"?

The attraction to music was especially powerful among writers of fiction, who saw analogies between the score and the narrative, both of which must be realized in time, and to whom Wagner's music in particular seemed to embody, as Arthur Symons put it, "the whole expression of the subconscious life."[40] In the age of the psychological novel, writers found their model in Wagner's "continuous melody": the *arioso* that, with its irregular phrasing, had freed the vocal part to depict the full subtlety of the poetic text, and that, with the use of leitmotifs, had enabled the orchestra to provide a musical commentary on the dramatic action. George Moore wrote of efforts among novelists of the period to create what he called a "melody of narration" in which distinctions between description, dialogue, and character analysis would be muted much in the same way Wagner's continuous melody had muted those between aria and recitative; Thomas Mann acknowledged his own attempt to bring the Wagnerian leitmotif into his novels, "not mechanically, but in the symbolic style of music"; and Edouard Dujardin, after Joyce had identified his novel *Les Lauriers sont coupés* as the inspiration for the interior monologue in *Ulysses,* confessed that he had gotten the idea from Wagner's continuous melody.[41] In their search for analogies to music, these writers fixed on the leitmotif, the brief musical phrase that becomes associated with a particular character, theme, or symbol and that reappears, often somewhat altered, in appropriate contexts. Thus, if one category of "Wagnerian" novel would, like *Il fuoco* and Moore's *The Lake,* comprise those that borrowed Wagner's characters and themes, another would include those that attempted to develop a literary leitmotif.[42]

Joyce criticism has traditionally granted the leitmotif an important position in Joyce's later work. Following the lead of Stuart Gilbert, whose book on *Ulysses,* published in 1930, describes major themes like "omphalos" and "paternity" as leitmotifs,[43] Joyce's critics have defined the term loosely—so much so, however, that it has begun to lose its link to music. Recurring literary and musical allusions (to *Là ci darem,* for example), reappearing characters (like Denis Breen, Tom Kernan), phrases associated with particular characters ("Jingle" with Blazes Boylan), and, as in Gilbert's case, major themes: all have been described as leitmotifs. A stricter, more Wagnerian definition would emphasize the distinctive verbal phrase that has a counterpart in the musical score and that retains some independent value as a signifier; it should form, as it does in Wagnerian opera, part of the stream of narration, or melody; it should recur and draw its various contexts together.[44]

From *Ulysses,* "agenbite of inwit" makes an excellent leitmotif according to this definition.[45] Its distinctiveness gives it special quality as a signifier, a "musicality" like that of the phrase that Stephen draws from his "treasure" near the end of *A Portrait* (P 166–67, discussed below); its unfamiliarity enables it to function as a musical symbol does, establishing its meanings within the contexts provided by *Ulysses* itself. These contexts define "agenbite of inwit" as the particular form of guilt Stephen feels when he is reminded, generally by a woman, of his cruelty to his mother. In "Telemachus," for example, Stephen's encounter with the milkwoman as he talks with Mulligan and Haines prompts the first appearance of the phrase: "Speaking to me. They wash and tub and scrub. Agenbite of inwit. Conscience. Yet here's a spot" (*U* 1.481–82). The motif recurs in "Scylla and Charybdis" (twice) and, finally, in "Wandering Rocks," when Stephen runs across his sister Dilly:

> She is drowning. Agenbite. Save her. Agenbite. All against us. She will drown me with her, eyes and hair. Lank coils of seaweed hair around me, my heart, my soul. Salt green death.
>   We.
>   Agenbite of inwit. Inwit's agenbite. (*U* 10.875–89)

The drowning woman is of course Dilly, doomed by the fecklessness of the men in her family, but she is also the image of May Dedalus, whose grasp on Stephen's conscience this passage vividly describes. Among the many leitmotifs in *Ulysses,* "met him pike hoses," "the incertitude of the void," and "a kind of retrospective arrangement"—to cite just a few—share with "agenbite of inwit" the lapidary quality and relative unfamiliarity that make them seem "musical." The *Wake*'s most important leitmotifs are connected with the central mythic theme of repetition and variation and, altered from context to context, they approximate Wagner's leitmotifs, which are themselves subject to alteration in key or orchestration, even more closely than do the leitmotifs of *Ulysses.* "The seim anew," the baptismal motif *taufen,* the rhythmic "beside the rivering waters of," and the "O felix culpa" only begin to represent the many hundreds of repeated words and phrases that feed the stream of narration in the *Wake.*[46]

Though the leitmotif may be the most "Wagnerian" of Joyce's musical analogies, it does not exhaust the musical character of his work. But the more pervasive musicality that Joyce is widely conceded is, in part, a Wagnerian inheritance as well, since, as has been suggested, much of the attraction to music in literature may be traced to the influence of

Wagner's synthesis of arts in music drama. The huge number of musical allusions in Joyce provides a subtext that, for some readers, keeps
musical phrases constantly in the ear. What lover of opera, for example, does not "hear" *M'appari* during a reading of "Sirens" or "Dido's
Lament" in the last few lines of the *Wake?* The chapters of *Ulysses,* with
their individual styles and techniques, acquire the distinctive quality
we associate with musical pieces. With what novelist but Joyce may we
detach and describe the individual chapter so neatly? The multiple
meanings of the *Wake* make a good analogy to musical counterpoint or
"polyphony," especially when the book is read aloud. In fact, the most
important musical quality of Joyce's work is found in the attention to
tone and rhythm that makes Joyce's writing as satisfying to read aloud
as that of any writer.

The place of music in Joyce's work is best articulated in *A Portrait,*
where Joyce's young man reflects on his fascination for the expressive
powers of language:

> He drew forth a phrase from his treasure and spoke it softly to
> himself:
> —A day of dappled seaborne clouds.
> The phrase and the day and the scene harmonised in a chord. Words.
> Was it their colours? He allowed them to glow and fade, hue after hue:
> sunrise gold, the russet and green of apple orchards, azure of waves, the
> greyfringed fleece of clouds. No, it was not their colours: it was the
> poise and balance of the period itself. Did he then love the rhythmic rise
> and fall of words better than their associations of legend and colour? Or
> was it that, being as weak of sight as he was shy of mind, he drew less
> pleasure from the reflection of the glowing sensible world through the
> prism of a language manycoloured and richly storied than from the con-
> templation of an inner world of individual emotions mirrored perfectly
> in a lucid supple periodic prose? (*P* 166–67)

In Stephen's devotion to the "sound" of language before its "sense" may
be found the two chief sources of the power of music in nineteenth- and
twentieth-century literary circles: its "pure" existence outside mimetic
reference and its capacity to express feeling. We might ascribe Stephen's use of the musical idiom at this point in his development to his
Ninetyishness and to his distance from the implied author of *A Portrait*
itself if Joyce's own commitment to musical expression had not endured
for his entire career.

In the complex relationship between "this most musical of writers"
and "that most literary of composers" are many lessons for the student

of interdisciplinary connections.[47] René Wellek and Austin Warren, in their influential *Theory of Literature,* offer a skeptical assessment of the impact of music, *qua* music, on literature. Many of the qualities we call "musical"—"tone" and "rhythm," for example—are themselves inherent in language, while others—the principle, for instance, of repetition and variation—are not exclusively musical.[48] The most specific and tangible "musical" influence of Wagner on literature—that of the leitmotif—turns out not to be especially musical at all. Thomas Mann saw a relationship between these repeated musical phrases and Homeric epithets like "wine-dark sea" and "grey-eyed goddess," and Wagner himself felt that leitmotifs made his orchestra the equivalent of the Greek chorus, "supporting and elucidating on every hand."[49] The "inexpressibility" of music, its theoretical inaccessibility to verbal expression, its emotional and mimetic "purity," inspired literary artists who were attempting to depict the emotional realm of experience and to assert the integrity of their art; but in practical terms, novelists like Joyce were able to draw on the leitmotif as a "musical" model precisely because of its "literary" qualities. To assign Wagner—and indeed, opera—along with "tone" and "rhythm" to the realm of music is itself a convention, a simple matter of convenience, and if Richard Wagner were not a good deal more than a musician, an investigation like this one could scarcely have been attempted. Joyce's relationship with Wagner testifies far more to his immersion in literary culture than it does to his affection for music, deep as the latter certainly was. *Die Meistersinger,* the anomaly in Wagner's canon, appealed to Joyce as "opera"; but it had little to say to the writer in Joyce. The *Ring,* the *Dutchman,* and *Tristan,* as "opera," may have struck Joyce as oversexed and esoteric; but these works, far more resonant in the realm of literature and, indeed, far more "Wagnerian," spoke volumes to Joyce the creator.

Notes

1. August Suter, "Some Reminiscences of James Joyce," trans. Fritz Senn, in *Portraits of the Artist in Exile,* ed. Willard Potts (Seattle: University of Washington Press, 1979), 64.

2. Louis Gillet, "Farewell to Joyce," trans. Georges Markow-Totevy, in Potts, 168.

3. See Frank Budgen, *James Joyce and the Making of "Ulysses"* (Bloomington: Indiana University Press, 1960), 16–17.

Among the articles and book chapters in which Joyce's relationship to Wagner has received more than glancing treatment, I am especially indebted to the following: David Hayman, "Tristan and Isolde in *Finnegans Wake:* A Study of the Sources and Evolution of a Theme," *Comparative Literature Studies* 1 (1964): 93–112; William Blissett, "James Joyce in the Smithy of His Soul," in *James Joyce Today,* ed. Thomas F. Staley (Bloomington: Indiana University Press, 1966), 96–134; Matthew Hodgart, "Music and the Mime of Mick, Nick and the Maggies," in *A Conceptual Guide to "Finnegans Wake,"* ed. Michael H. Begnal and Fritz Senn (University Park: Pennsylvania State University Press, 1974), 83–92; and Hodgart, *James Joyce: A Student's Guide* (London: Routledge, 1978), especially 130–88.

My own published work on the subject is as follows: "Wagner's *Tannhäuser* in *Exiles:* A Further Source," *James Joyce Quarterly* 19 (Fall 1981): 73–76; "Joyce, Wagner, and the Artist-Hero," *Journal of Modern Literature* 11 (1984): 66–88; "Joyce and Wagner's Pale Vampire," *James Joyce Quarterly* 23 (Summer 1986): 491–96; and "Joyce, Wagner, and the Wandering Jew," *Comparative Literature* 42 (1990): 49–72. See also Timothy Martin, *Joyce and Wagner: A Study of Influence* (Cambridge: Cambridge University Press, 1991).

4. Budgen, 182–83, and Gillet, 168.

5. Herbert Gorman, *James Joyce* (New York: Rinehart, 1948), 239.

6. Thomas Mann, *Pro and contra Wagner,* trans. Allan Blunden (Chicago: University of Chicago Press, 1985), 100.

7. Richard Wagner, *Prose Works,* 8 vols., trans. William Ashton Ellis (1892–99; rpt. New York: Broude, 1966), 1:328–29.

8. Gillet, 168.

9. Stuart Gilbert, *James Joyce's "Ulysses": A Study* (New York: Random House, 1955), 243.

10. Hodgart, *James Joyce: A Student's Guide,* 99.

11. Carl Dahlhaus, *Richard Wagner's Music Dramas,* trans. Mary Whittall (Cambridge: Cambridge University Press, 1979), 75.

12. Richard Wagner, *The Mastersingers of Nuremberg,* trans. Frederick Jameson, rev. Norman Feasey and Gordon Kember, Opera Guide 19 (New York: Riverrun, 1983), 118.

13. Grove's *Dictionary of Music* defines consecutive or parallel fifths as "the simultaneous duplication of the melodic line of one part by another at the interval of a perfect 5th."

14. *Lohengrin* was first produced in Dublin, in Italian, in 1875; *The Flying Dutchman,* also in Italian, in 1877. See Alfred Loewenberg, *Annals of Opera: 1597–1940,* 3d ed. (Totowa, N.J.: Rowman and Littlefield, 1978), cols. 826, 885. In "Eumaeus," Bloom recalls the "stupendous success" of "Ludwig, *alias* Ledwidge, when he occupied the boards of the Gaiety . . . in the *Flying Dutchman*" (U 16.859–61). Bloom's recollection is corroborated by Weldon Thornton, who links the Dublin-born baritone William Ledwidge with the

1877 production of the *Dutchman* cited in Loewenberg. See *Allusions in "Ulysses"* (Chapel Hill: University of North Carolina Press, 1968), 439–40.

15. Stanislaus Joyce, *My Brother's Keeper*, ed. Richard Ellmann (New York: Viking, 1969), 147.

16. W. B. Yeats, *Essays and Introductions* (New York: Macmillan, 1968), 186.

17. George Moore, Introduction, *The Heather Field and Maeve*, by Edward Martyn (London: Duckworth, 1899), ix.

18. Mann, *Pro and contra Wagner*, 88.

19. S. Joyce, 86.

20. For my knowledge of Joyce's Trieste library, I am indebted to Richard Ellmann, *The Consciousness of Joyce* (New York: Oxford University Press, 1977), 97–134; and especially to Michael Patrick Gillespie with Erik Bradford Stocker, *James Joyce's Trieste Library* (Austin: Harry Ransom Humanities Research Center, 1986). For information on the extant books mentioned in this paragraph, see Gillespie and Stocker, nos. 93, 194, 351, 405, 448, and 527–34. Ellmann's list in *Consciousness* erroneously identifies the pocket librettos now at Texas as piano-vocal scores.

21. Borach, "Conversations with James Joyce," trans. Joseph Prescott, in Potts, 71.

22. See Hayman, 111 n. 18.

23. For a discussion of Joyce's use of *A Day with Richard Wagner* (New York: Hodder and Stoughton, [1911]), see Martin, "Wagner's *Tannhäuser* in *Exiles.*" Ellmann treats Joyce's use of Byron's *A Day with William Shakespeare* in *The Consciousness of Joyce*, 59–61. Byron's books are listed by Gillespie and Stocker as nos. 93–94.

24. S. Joyce, 197.

25. These more influential operas include *Der Ring des Nibelungen, Tristan und Isolde, The Flying Dutchman, Parsifal*, and *Tannhäuser*, all of which figure prominently in Joyce's work. For reasons of space, the remainder of this essay concentrates on just one of Wagner's works, the *Ring*.

26. Stephen's association with Siegfried has received more than brief mention in the following: Blissett, 96–102; Edmund L. Epstein, *The Ordeal of Stephen Dedalus* (Carbondale: Southern Illinois University Press, 1971), 102, 111–12, 145, 163–67; John Louis DiGaetani, *Richard Wagner and the Modern British Novel* (Rutherford, N.J.: Fairleigh Dickinson University Press, 1978), 136–44; Stoddard Martin, *Wagner to "The Waste Land"* (Totowa, N.J.: Barnes, 1982), 143–46; and Timothy Martin, "Joyce, Wagner, and the Artist-Hero."

27. Friedrich Nietzsche, *The Birth of Tragedy*, trans. Wm. A. Haussman, in *The Complete Works of Friedrich Nietzsche*, ed. Oscar Levy (1909; rpt. New York: Russell, 1964), 1:185.

28. D'Annunzio, *The Flame*, trans. Dora Knowlton Ranous ([New York]:

National Alumni, 1907), 118–21; Moore, *Hail and Farewell,* 3 vols. (New York: Appleton, 1917–19), 3:306; Yeats, *Essays and Introductions,* 249.

29. Wagner, *Prose Works,* 1:51–52, emphasis Wagner's. See Gillespie and Stocker, no. 531.

30. The presence of *The Flying Dutchman* in Joyce's work receives full treatment in chapter 3 of Timothy Martin, *Joyce and Wagner.*

31. Adaline Glasheen, *Third Census of "Finnegans Wake"* (Berkeley: University of California Press, 1977), lxv.

32. Wotan is identified as "Allfather" in Wolfgang Golther's *Richard Wagner as Poet,* trans. Jessie Haynes (New York: McClure, 1907), 65, a copy of which Joyce owned in Trieste. See Gillespie and Stocker, no. 194. For reasons of accessibility, the edition I cite here is slightly later than the book now at Texas.

33. Hodgart identifies this allusion in *James Joyce: A Student's Guide,* 181.

34. The allusions to the *Ring* traced in the previous two paragraphs only begin to represent the multiplicity of borrowings in the *Wake,* in which I count roughly two hundred references to the four-part cycle.

35. James S. Atherton, *The Books at the Wake* (New York: Viking, 1960), 25–55.

36. This anecdote is reported by Herbert Howarth, in *The Irish Writers: 1880–1940* (London: Rockcliff, 1958), 274.

37. "The School of Giorgione," in *Victorian Poetry and Prose,* 2d ed., ed. Walter Houghton and G. Robert Stange (Boston: Houghton Mifflin, 1968), 734.

38. Arthur Power, *Conversations with James Joyce,* ed. Clive Hart (Chicago: University of Chicago Press, 1974), 106.

39. Paraphrased by A. G. Lehmann, *The Symbolist Aesthetic in France,* 2d ed. (1968; rpt. Folcroft, Pa.: Folcroft Library, 1974), 200.

40. Arthur Symons, *Plays, Acting, and Music* (New York: Dutton, 1909), 311.

41. Moore, *Confessions of a Young Man,* ed. Susan Dick (Montreal: McGill-Queen's University Press, 1972), 158; Mann, quoted in Peter Egri, *Avant-gardism and Modernity,* trans. Paul Aston (Tulsa: University of Tulsa, 1972), 77; Dujardin, *Les Lauriers sont coupé suivi de le Monologue intérieur* (1931; rpt. Rome: Bulzoni, 1977), 258.

42. On the tradition of the literary leitmotif, see Calvin Brown, *Music and Literature* (Athens: University of Georgia Press, 1948), 208–18; Melvin Friedman, *Stream of Consciousness: A Study in Literary Method* (New Haven: Yale University Press, 1955), 14–16, 128–31; and Clive Hart, *Structure and Motif in "Finnegans Wake"* (Evanston: Northwestern University Press, 1962), 161–81.

43. Gilbert, 33–64.

44. This definition of the literary leitmotif is most like those of Hart, 164–67, and Brown, 211.

45. Friedman identifies "agenbite of inwit" as a leitmotif without discussing its use.

46. See "An Index of Motifs in *Finnegans Wake*," in Hart, 211–47.

47. The phrases are Blissett's, 109.

48. René Wellek and Austin Warren, *Theory of Literature,* 3d ed. (New York: Harcourt, Brace, 1956), 126–27.

49. Mann, *Pro and contra Wagner,* 25–26; Wagner, *Prose Works,* 2:335–36.

American Popular Music in *Finnegans Wake*

Ruth Bauerle

Though all his writing was nourished by his Irish roots, James Joyce composed *Finnegans Wake* within a cultural milieu very different from that which shaped his earlier books. Consequently, the final achievement was more international in content than any of Joyce's previous works. Particularly, *Finnegans Wake* became his most American book, though Joyce never visited the United States.

Chamber Music, Dubliners, and *Stephen Hero* were begun or completed in Dublin. *A Portrait of the Artist as a Young Man,* though completed away from Ireland, yet drew on the *Stephen Hero* manuscript and events, all of them Irish in setting. *Exiles,* Joyce's postexilic play, is set in Dublin; and Richard Rowan, the chief among the exiles, is named after an Irish tree and an Irish hero. Even finishing *Dubliners* and *A Portrait* or writing *Exiles* in Trieste, Joyce was still working in a city that, like Dublin, was a port on the edge of an ancient empire. If the two cities drew a measure of cosmopolitanism from their empires, their locations on the geographical edges of power left them provincial.

Joyce not only wrote these early books in Ireland, or immediately after leaving Ireland. He also wrote them, or parts of them, while he was still considering plans to return himself and his family to Ireland— as cinema owner, woolen trader, or perhaps (as Richard Rowan seems to have hoped) as artist. He was, to modulate the British phrase, a semidetached exile.

Ulysses, too, was begun in the Triestine milieu as a story for *Dubliners.* Its writing was continued during World War I in Zurich—a city that, despite its continental flavor, was isolated by the war—and finished in a Paris still recovering from that war. In the process of these geographical moves, *Ulysses* outgrew its framework, so that its center became not only Bloom but Dublin itself. For even in Zurich, as Carola Giedion-Welcker has pointed out, Joyce was envisioning "Dublin, *la cité suprême,* . . . in eternal transformation and eternal beauty."[1] Limmat was Liffey. As much as a tale of a modern Odysseus, *Ulysses* is a love song to Dublin, the first city of Joycedom.

Finnegans Wake was a different affair. Joyce began it in 1922, three and a half years after World War I, in a Paris that was again a center of world power in politics and banking. It was also a giant tourist center where Joyce, after the fame brought him by *Ulysses*'s publication in 1922, was one of the sights to see. In addition to tourists, Paris of the twenties and thirties was flooded with expatriates from England, the United States, Canada, Russia, Spain, and Germany: Ford Madox Ford, Nancy Cunard, Morley Callahan, Ernest Hemingway, Gertrude Stein, Samuel Beckett, Robert M. Coates, James Thurber, Elliot Paul, John Dos Passos, e. e. cummings, Malcolm Cowley, Stuart Davis, Matthew Josephson, Pablo Picasso, Sara and Gerald Murphy, Constantin Brancusi, Vladimir Nabokov, Henry Miller, and more. It was even a city with three American newspapers—the *Tribune,* the *Herald,* and the *Paris Times*—a distinction envied by many American cities today.

Joyce's personal circle of friends included many of these expatriates. Americans, as Nino Frank remarked, "were very well received."[2] There were Sylvia Beach, Ezra Pound, Eugene and Maria Jolas, Archibald and Ada MacLeish, George Antheil, Robert McAlmon, Kay Boyle, Myron Nutting, Richard Wallace, and of course Joyce's daughter-in-law, Helen Fleischman Joyce and the son of her first marriage, David Fleischman. Lucia Joyce, too, had American friends such as Albert Hubbell visiting the Joyce apartment.[3] Most important, after 1932 Joyce had a grandchild, Stephen James Joyce, who was half-American.

Irish friends and acquaintances were traveling or living in the United States, and reporting to Joyce from America by the time he began work on *Finnegans Wake.* Oliver Gogarty and John McCormack settled there, and though Joyce had little direct contact with either, he followed their careers with interest. Padraic and Mary Colum traveled and taught in the States, and returned to Paris to recount their experiences. Joyce's younger brother, Charles, lived for a time in Boston, and sent his own "letters from Boston" to the writer in Paris. John Quinn, born in Ohio of Irish parentage, tended to Joyce's legal affairs in New York City, bought Joyce's manuscripts and visited the writer in Paris. Joyce's son, George, crossed the Atlantic to sing on American radio.

The importance of a writer's milieu has been well stated by Cheryl Herr, in the introduction to *Joyce's Anatomy of Culture*. She demonstrates that Joyce's numerous allusions, beyond reflecting one man's "obsessions," indicate his acute sensitivity to "the force of culture on the writer," so that "what we conceive to be a continuous individual consciousness is composed of materials derived from sources outside the mind."[4] Having made this point, Herr limits her excellent study to the Irish culture of the press, the stage, and the pulpit in Joyce's Dublin years. Yet the "force of culture" does not cease to act upon a writer— not even Joyce—after age twenty-two. And whereas his years from 1904 to 1920 were divided among the cultures of Trieste, Pola, Rome, and Zurich, the two decades from 1920 to 1940 were as "settled" in Paris as the first two decades of his life were "settled" in Dublin.[5]

Little wonder, then, that *Finnegans Wake,* more than any other of Joyce's works, reaches out to the world beyond Ireland—by its multiple languages and multilinguistic puns; by its geographical and historical references; and by its inclusion of an international music as none of his previous works had done. Most particularly, Joyce, living in the midst of an expatriate "Little America," produced in *Finnegans Wake* a book suffused with the New World. There is an American counterpart to the legend of Finn McCool in that literary giant, Huckleberry Finn. There is the geography of Laurens County, Georgia, introduced as a parallel to that of Dublin and Howth. But then, the outline of Howth invites an American comparison since it has the form of a "Little America," where Doldrum Bay overlays the Gulf of Mexico, Lion's Head marks New Orleans; the Bailey Lighthouse, Miami; Piper's Gut, Washington, D.C.. The village of Howth lies along the north coast from Chicago to Cleveland, the Ben of Howth rises a little east of Pike's Peak, and the route for Howth's 31A bus follows U.S. Highway 101 along the Oregon and California coastline.[6]

In no way is *Finnegans Wake* more American than in its incorporation of the titles and lyrics, the melodies and rhythms, of American music. These songs appear, moreover, throughout the book, from the title song (the American-Irish stage ballad, "Tim Finnegan's Wake") and its first citation (4.18) to the book's last page, where Fritz Senn has noted "White Wings" at 628.9–10.[7] Manifestly, Joyce has included a New World of song in the *Wake.*

Statistical analyses do little to explain how Joyce's imagination functioned; yet numbers do suggest the proportions of his interests. By rough count—and all counts of allusions in his work are rough—we have thought there were some 1,500 individual songs alluded to in all of Joyce's fiction, poetry and drama.[8] About two-thirds of the songs originally identified—a thousand in all—are in *Finnegans Wake;* of these, about a quarter (250) were opera and light opera.[9] Of the non-operatic songs, some three hundred, or 40 percent, are American. By contrast, only about twenty-six American songs (less than 7 per cent) may be found among the 397 listed by Zack Bowen for all of Joyce's work through *Ulysses.*[10]

If we count not individual songs, but the total number of allusions, a similar picture emerges. Since some songs are alluded to more than once, there are at least 5,500 musical references in the entire body of Joyce's writing;[11] *Finnegans Wake* alone has nearly seven hundred allusions to American music, representing one-eighth of the musical allusions in all of Joyce's books together.

This multitude of American music incorporated by Joyce falls into natural (and sometimes overlapping) groups. There is a large number of nineteenth-century songs, popular on both sides of the Atlantic, and sung regularly among the Joyces as family entertainment and at social gatherings. Such songs would include many by popular American composers and writers such as Stephen Foster, James A. Bland, or John Howard Payne (whose "Home, Sweet Home," to Henry Bishop's melody, appears thirteen times). Probably because so many Irish-Americans fought for North or South, a number of Civil War songs mark the *Wake:* "Just before the Battle, Mother," "John Brown's Body," "Tramp, Tramp, Tramp, the Boys Are Marching" (adapted by T. D. Sullivan as the Irish "God Save Ireland"), and "When Johnny Comes Marching Home Again" (which emigrated in the other direction, from Ireland, where it was called "Johnny, I Hardly Knew Ye," to the United States).

A smaller group is that of the romantic ballads of the turn of the century. They have little to recommend them as exceptional, barring their singable sentimentality. For Joyce, that was often recommendation enough.[12] Nor can we identify where Joyce learned such songs, unless, again, their melodious quality led his American friends to sing and hum these popular favorites. So "After the Ball Was Over," "And the Band Played On," "By the Light of the Silvery Moon," "Girl of My Dreams," and "Waltz Me Around Again, Willie" found their way into *Finnegans Wake.* It was indeed, just such a song that brought the American novelist Theodore Dreiser into Joyce's wake. Dreiser's brother, Paul Dresser (born Dreiser), wrote the melody and part of the lyrics for "On the Banks of the Wabash"; but Theodore, whose unsentimental, realistic fiction would, like Joyce's, encounter censorship problems, claimed to have contributed the idea and to have written some of the lyrics of the song.[13] Joyce incorporates it twice in the "Anna Livia Plurabelle" chapter, and again in the final pages as the river moves toward the sea: *FW* 202.22–23 ("such a loon waybashwards to row!"), 210.1 ("in her culdee sacco of wabbash"), and 615.25–26 ("backed in paladays last, on the brinks of the wobblish").[14]

Another song type in *Finnegans Wake* is the American-Irish ballad— sometimes comic and full of pratfalls and braggadocio, but often mawkishly sentimental about Ireland and things Irish, even though composed by Americans.[15] This would include such favorites as

> The Ballad of Finnegan's Wake
> Bedelia
> The Daughter of Rosie O'Grady
> Eileen Alannah*
> Harrigan, That's Me
> A Little Bit of Heaven*
> Little Mother of Mine*
> Mister Dooley
> Mother Machree*
> My Wild Irish Rose*
> Peg o' My Heart
> Pretty Kitty Kelly
> Roderick O'Dwyer
> Smilin' Thru'*
> Song o' My Heart*
> Sweet Peggy O'Neil*
> Sweet Rosie O'Grady
> That Old Irish Mother of Mine
> Toora Loora Loora
> When Irish Eyes Are Smiling*
> Where the River Shannon Flows*

As Carole Brown and Leo Knuth have pointed out,[16] Joyce introduced many of these (indicated above by an *) into the *Wake* because they had been recorded by John McCormack. Others Joyce picked up from Sigmund Spaeth's *Read 'Em and Weep*. Whether Joyce conceived of them as Irish or as American one cannot tell, but certainly, despite their Irish themes, they are as American as the naturalized McCormack himself, or as their authors and composers—men and women like Harry von Tilzer, William Jerome, J. Keirn Brennan, Maud Nugent, Jean Schwartz, Ernest R. Ball, and Chauncey Olcott—immigrant or native-born Americans who often reached success by playing to the prevailing sentimentality about Ireland.

Three substantial groups of American songs in *Finnegans Wake* are of particular interest either because we can identify Joyce's sources for them with some certainty, or because we can infer his sources from what we know of his habits of working and living.

Read 'Em and Wake: The Songs Joyce Wants to Remember

The first such group is constituted of songs Joyce drew from Sigmund Spaeth's volume of popular music history, *Read 'Em and Weep: The Songs You Forgot to Remember*. Spaeth's volume appeared in 1927, fairly early in Joyce's composition of the *Wake*.[17] It was not limited to American music; nevertheless, most of the songs are characteristically American, permeated by the history, slang, and special dialects of the United States. Those English songs included by Spaeth had enjoyed enormous American popularity, and some of these, such as "The Man That Broke the Bank at Monte Carlo" or "Kafoozalem," were already known to Joyce and used by him in his own writings long before Spaeth's volume appeared.

In transcribing and annotating the notes Joyce made from *Read 'Em and Weep*,[18] Danis Rose observed that entries were to be found in two notebooks: VI.B.46 (which he was transcribing) and VI.B.45 (whose Spaeth notes Rose included with the VI.B.46 transcription for completeness' sake). Comparing Joyce's notebook entries to the songs in *Read 'Em and Weep*, Rose concluded Joyce had copied titles of eleven songs; both title and phrases or unusual words from seven others; and appealing words, without titles, from yet another eighteen.[19] The *Notebooks* also record nine unusual phrases from Spaeth's commentary that find their way into the *Wake*—terms such as "stein song," "rathskeller," "songdom," "piker," or "Poor Rube." Four songs that Spaeth names without providing either words or music also find their way into the *Notebooks* and thence into the *Wake*. The titles Joyce entered in his notebooks tend to have a distinctly American flavor, as do the words Joyce noted from the songs themselves: "fixings," "redhot cook," "waterboy," "locofoco," "slavocrat," "de bobtail nag," "hopjoint," or "he was my man & he done me wrong."

An examination of the text of *Finnegans Wake* indicates, however, that the songs from which Joyce entered phrases in *Notebooks* VI.B.45 and VI.B.46 constitute less than half the Spaeth songs referred to in the *Wake*.[20] Of 164 songs in Spaeth's volume, Joyce uses 83, or more than twice the 36 Rose has identified from the VI.B.46 and VI.B.45 workbooks. Similarly, in addition to the four song titles copied into the notebooks, Joyce also picks up titles or parts of titles from five other songs Spaeth mentions without providing either words or music. It is clear that Joyce mined *Read 'Em and Weep* for American melodies and words to add to his own monumental work.[21]

Of what use were these songs to Joyce? Primarily, one must remember his passion for song itself. Philippe Soupault, recalling Joyce's fondness for Paris, remarked, "He knew and loved Paris like a song and God knows that he loved songs."[22] Louis Gillet, writing of the same period in Joyce's life, remarks repeatedly on this same musical passion, concluding, "For Joyce, if there was no song, there was no joy."[23] One might emend that to read, "If there was no song, there was no Joyce."

In a general sense, the musical allusions contribute to the encyclopedic quality of *Finnegans Wake;* that quality, as Walton Litz has pointed out, when achieved through the "overwhelming accretion" of detail, effects a kind of realism in the *Wake*'s evanescent dream-world.[24] Stuart Gilbert recorded with some pain Joyce's method of searching through volumes of *Encyclopaedia Britannica* for information on the world's cities to include in *Work in Progress*.[25] Joyce's listings in *The Index Manuscript* confirm a similar way of working with songs from Spaeth, or from the *1916 Songbook*.[26] Like the cities, the rivers, the battles, or the multiple languages, songs were to augment St. James's *Summa Joyceana,* a compilation of his interests and those of his century. Such bits of music and fact are not merely informational, of course. Gilbert also recorded his own sense of punishment in waiting while Joyce pondered how to convert each "queer name" from *Britannica* into a pun.[27] The song titles, too, were intended for pleasurable comic effect, a part of the "funnaminal world" of the *Wake*.[28]

It is important to remember, too, Joyce's remark to a friend that *Finnegans Wake* was not merely trivial but quadrivial. Like the medieval quadrivium, it included arithmetic, geometry, astronomy, and *music.* In this sense Joyce included musical allusion not only by textual elements of the songs (title, lyrics, or themes), but also by those musical elements that could be embedded in his text: rhythm and the sounds of the words. Literary scholars, being people of the word, tend to focus on the texts of songs.[29] Yet it is most common to refer to songs by the composer's, rather than the lyricist's, name. Who speaks of Robert Cameron Rogers's "The Rosary"? Or Otto Harbach's and Oscar Hammerstein's "Indian Love Call"? Or Arthur Jackson's and Buddy DeSylva's "Nobody But You"? Rather, we associate these compositions with Ethelbert Nevin, Rudolf Friml, and George Gershwin.[30] And Joyce was a musician; to him, rhythm, melody—all of sound—were important.

Songs from different lands probably also were intended to make *Finnegans Wake* appeal to a wider audience. A friend recalls Joyce promising that a musical allusion would spark memories in "every English reader." Just as Catholics of any country would recognize the elements of the mass, or cricket fans the vocabulary from that sport, so each song in the *Wake* might be expected to sound its own overtones among the book's readers.[31] In this sense, national music contributed to the international plurabilities of the book. As was pointed out in *The James Joyce Songbook,* "Little Brown Jug" becomes, for Joyce, an American version of two Irish songs, "Cruiskeen Lawn" and "Drimin Dhown Deelish."[32] Both the American song and the "Cruiskeen Lawn" refer to pottery drinking jugs. "Drimin Dhown Deelish" is about a cow, however, a "white-backed, brown, beloved cow," the "Silk of the Kine." Such lines, as well as the fact that "the branded cow" was an Irish term for a private still to make poteen, lead the Irish song easily into the American, whose second stanza compares the jug of whisky to a cow: "If I had a cow that gave such milk, I'd dress her in the finest silk." "Silk of the kine" is of course also one of the "secret names" for Ireland. By alluding to two Irish songs and one American song, then, Joyce is able to move allusively among his themes of whisky as water of life, Ireland, and America almost simultaneously.[33]

In a similar fashion, by using the American songs "Polly Wolly Doodle" and "Yankee Doodle" in association with Oliver Cromwell (see "Thematics" below), Joyce assists the process of making everybody into somebody else in his portrayal of multiple personalities with dual or triple nationality.

There are visible patterns in Joyce's handling of specific allusions to the songs from *Read 'Em and Weep.*[34] These are, in approximate order of frequency:

1. a semantic play upon the sound of the words;
2. an allusion to the name of the song or air;
3. an allusion varying the sound of the lyrics within the song, without semantic change of (1) above;
4. an allusion to distinctive words or sounds within the song;
5. an allusion to the rhythm of the song;
6. an allusion to the theme of the song's lyrics, often fitting a theme in *Finnegans Wake;*
7. a purely archival use (rare);
8. a reference to the composer or lyricist (very rare).

What seems noteworthy about such a listing is the emphasis Joyce gives, in his musical allusions, to musical elements of the lyrics such as sound and rhythm (categories 1, 3, 4, and 5). The other musical elements, melody and harmony, cannot be represented with words, of course—except insofar as recognition of a song recalls these to the reader's mind. These musical elements have had little attention from scholars, for Joyce's language draws us initially, mesmerizes us, and keeps us in thrall. Musical analysis, in any case, requires different critical skills operating upon a different sort of composition. Because Joyce's *Wake* is not just "any case" of musical composition, but a merging of words and music, the present study will focus upon the musical elements in the words of his allusions. In this it differs from the chief previous analysis of how Joyce used American music, which considered principally the songs' association with themes in the *Wake.*[35]

Musical Word Play (1 and 3 above)

Not surprisingly, Joyce's preferred form of allusion to Spaeth's songs seems to be word play. Most frequently this takes the form of a play upon the sound of the words, usually making a pun to achieve a semantic change (1 above); or varying the sound within the song's lyrics as a musician might invert a harmonic pattern (3). Thus at *FW* 33.28 the "Little Brown Jug" becomes the "little old joq"; shifting from voiced "g" to unvoiced "k" turns the jug into a joke. A similar change, coupled with the rhythm of the song, turns the refrain of "Oh ho ho, you and me" into a reminiscence of Latin pronoun declensions as "hay, hay, hay, hoq, hoq, hoq!"

The same g/k shift from voiced to unvoiced achieves a sex-change pun at *FW* 234.7–8, where "the kerl he left behind him?" substitutes German "Kerl" for "Girl."[36] Other puns shifting from voiced to voiceless consonants occur at *FW* 250.31 (bride/pride) and *FW* 288.17 (Barnum/Publikum). Sometimes the pun moves from unvoiced *k* to voiced *g,* as at *FW* 431.35 (Erie Canal/erigenal).[37] Occasionally the pun simply translates into a different language (*FW* 240.9–10), though in this instance Joyce is also negating the semantics of the song's line from "singing . . . all the day" to "No more singing all the dags."

Joyce emphasized to Jacques Mercanton that although in a few lines or pages he effected changes that took hundreds of years in the language itself, as "his only guarantee of truth" he followed both the semantics and the phonetics of the languages he used.[38] Though Joyce does not identify which laws of language history appear in *Finnegans Wake,* nor which language historians influenced him, he was doubtless aware of the work of the great Danish writer, Otto Jespersen, whose *Growth and Structure of the English Language* first appeared in 1905, and went through nine editions in Joyce's lifetime.[39] Jespersen pointed out, for instance, that in early English, similar noun and verb pairs of the same word were distinguished by an unvoiced consonant in the noun, and a voiced consonant in the verb, as in such surviving pairs as life/live, calf/calve, grief/grieve, cloth/clothe.[40] Similarly Joyce has changed the voiced ending of "jug" to the unvoiced (noun) "joq"; the voiced "girl" to the unvoiced (noun) "kerl," and similarly produced unvoiced consonants in the nouns "pride" (for "bride"), or "Publikum" (for "Barnum").[41]

Other substitutions are of vowels, not consonants, as at *FW* 250.31, where "Voolykin" for "vilikin" suggests the wooly sheepskin worn by Brian O'Linn in another song. At *FW* 368.29 the same vowel shift is applied to "Willie the Weeper" to produce "Whooley the Whooper," with an additional phonetic change of the alliteration from *w* to *hw.*

Another kind of pun changes both vowel and initial consonant, as at *FW* 317.14, where the "son of a son of a son of a son of a son of a gambolier" loses its central schwas for three other vowels, and its initial *s* for *dan, fin,* and *ven*—all sounding more Scandinavian—to become "For a dan of a ven of a fin of a son of a gun of a gombolier." Additionally, "son of a son" becomes the slangier American "son of a gun," itself a euphemism for a coarser term. A similar trick with "Son of a Gambolier" occurs at *FW* 323.23, where the change of initial consonant from *s* to *h* remains steady, while the vowels change like the internal notes of chords, until everything concludes with a double pun on "hill" in two languages—"camel[h]ump" and the Danish "*bakk*[en]": "that hell of a hull of a hill of a camelump bakk."[42] This rephrasing, and that found at *FW* 229.14 (where in "A Wondering Wreck" Joyce modulates from "rambling" to "wandering" and then, by a vowel change, to "wondering") show that Joyce was familiar with Georgia Tech's popular parody of this song,[43] as well as with the version given in Spaeth.

Joyce's puns have yet another function. It is essential that a pun surprise, by substituting an unexpected word that nevertheless fits the context in some new way. The pun produces laughter in the classic way of comedy, the shock of laugh–ignition. A fine example of this occurs at *FW* 328.11, where "the clonk in his stumble strikes warn" keeps both the sound of the original (the clo–k in the st——le strikes –n–) and its essential meaning, but makes it far funnier. (The p/b is, of course, another unvoiced/voiced change, this time from the noun *steeple* to the verb *stumble*.)

Another kind of complex Joycean pun is both anagrammatic and mnemonic. "Two Little Girls in Blue" is transformed into "two legglegels in blooms." Here, by memory inspired, "blue" yields to "blooms" to recall the "blue bloom is on the rye" of "Sirens" (*U* 11.6, *U* 11.230–31, *U* 11.1126–27). At the same time Joyce makes a transformation similar in nature to his cork frame for the picture of Cork (*JJ2* 551). "Little" becomes "leggle," and "leggle" is two legs—*leg,* and (anagrammed) *gle.* "Girls" also becomes an anagrammed plural for "leg," as "gels." The whole has an almost mathematical grammar to it: *leg* + *gle* [=] *gels* (leg + leg = legs). Two legs make a gel (girl), and gels thrust their legs into bloom[er]s. All of this brings us, by a commodius vicus of recirculation, back to Joyce's interest in women's underclothes. At the same time it is a kind of musical inversion, a chord now played l-e-g, then g-l-e, and finally g-e-l.

Similar word play appears in Joyce's many versions of the refrain of "Little Brown Jug." Spaeth's original proclaims,

> Ha, ha, ha! 'Tis you and me,
> Little brown jug don't I love thee?
> Ha, ha, ha! 'Tis you and me,
> Little brown jug, don't I love thee?[44]

Joyce renders this as "Hay, hay, hay! Hoq, hoq, hoq!" (*FW* 33.27); "*Ik dik dopedope et tu mihimihi*" (*FW* 104.10–11); "*My, my, my! Me and me! Little down dream don't I love thee!*" (*FW* 153.7–8); "*O! O! O! Par la pluie!*" (*FW* 158.23–24); "*Why, why, why! Weh, O Weh! I'se so silly to be flowing but I no canna stay!*" (*FW* 159.17–18); "*O I you O you me*" (*FW* 584.34); "Mees is thees knees. Thi is Mi" (*FW* 607.19). Such variations seem, often, mere wordplay; yet they, too, have a musical function in a compositional sense: Joyce as composer is reintroducing his theme with variation. By using American songs in these word and sound games, Joyce achieved two goals: he extended his history of language to the New World; and he emphasized the song lyrics as music.

Rhythmania (5 above)

Not surprisingly, a favorite form of Joycean allusion is to the rhythm of songs, for rhythm is the musical element that carries over most directly into prose. Certain rhythms in particular seemed to appeal, like that of "Yankee Doodle." At *FW* 71.32 it appears as "*Flunkey Beadle Vamps the Tune Letting on He's Loney,*" a version that also incorporates rhymes and off-rhymes of the original: flunkey/yankee, beadle/doodle, town/tune, letting/riding, he's/his, loney/pony. At *FW* 418.2–3, "Flunkey Footle furloughed foul, writing off his phoney" again preserves the rhythm with rhymes and slant rhymes linking to the original; and the same thing happens at *FW* 464.21–22 ("and yunker doodler wanked to wall awriting off his phoney").

"The Man That Broke the Bank at Monte Carlo," though not an American song, and known to Joyce long before he was mining Spaeth's work, also lent its rhythms to the *Wake:* "Like the crack that bruck the bank in Multifarnham" (*FW* 90.24); "For the mauwe that blinks you blank is mostly Carbo" (*FW* 232.2–3); "The man what shocked his shanks at contey Carlow's" (*FW* 538.28–29); or "For the man that broke the ranks on Monte Sijon" (*FW* 274.1–2).

Another distinctive beat in *Finnegans Wake* is "Camptown Races," with "We haul minymony on that piebold nig. Will any dubble dabble on the bay?" at *FW* 250.36–251.1. "The Mermaid" not only provided rhythm for Joyce's text, but offered an opportunity for the p/k change he loved at *FW* 267.F5 with "but I thinks more of my pottles and ketts [than I care for the bottom of the sea]."

Another lively rhythm derived from "The Cat Came Back." Joyce rendered this as "*hereis cant came back saying he codant steal no lunger, yessis, catz come buck beques he caudant stail awake*" (*FW* 349.36–350.1), which also uses multiple sound shifts from the original: cat/cant/catz; came back/come buck; couldn't/codant/caudant; stay/steal/stail. This rhythm reappears at *FW* 427.15–16, but the action is reversed from coming to going: "And the lamp went out as it couldn't glow on burning, yep the lmp wnt out for it couldn't stay alight." As part of the fun, Joyce omits vowels to indicate the snuffed-out flame.

Borrowed rhythms are sometimes sonorous, rather than lively. Thus bombastic Fourth of July sentiments about George Washington from "Adams and Liberty" are transferred to William III, "who repulsed from his burst the bombolts of Ostenton and falchioned each flash downsaduck in the deep" at *FW* 135.24–26. (These sentiments also allow him to be a genuine Joycean hero by confronting thunder, of course.)

Another sober rhythm comes from a spiritual, "Were You There When They Crucified My Lord," at *FW* 506.11–15:

—Were you there, eh Hehr? Were you there when they lagged um through the coombe?
—Wo wo! Who who! Psalmtimes it grauws on me to ramble, ramble, ramble.
—Woe! Woe! So that was how he became the foerst of our treefellers?

Joyce's source for these and other spirituals will be discussed in the next section, but this one obviously carries over the rhythm of the original, plus the repeated "O-O-O" and "tremble, tremble, tremble." There are also bilingual puns (Lord/Hehr) and slant rhymes (sometimes/Psalmtimes, laid/lagged, and tomb/coombe).

Title and Archival Allusion (2 and 7 above)

Joyce's allusions to the name of a song or to the air to which it is sung are often the easiest to identify. Thus "P. T. Barnum's Show" becomes, at *FW* 29.4–5, "showm! . . . Phineas Barnum." Likewise "Woodman, Spare That Tree" appears at *FW* 42.20 as "spare, woodmann, spare!" "The Sorrow of Marriage" is sounded by Joyce at *FW* 135.22 as "O sorrow, the . . . Mairie." Two songs named in Stephen Foster's "The Song of All Songs" (Spaeth 48–49) appear in *FW* 228.30–31's "on the raging canal, for othersites of Jorden."[45] At *FW* 317.13–14 Joyce mentions "One fishball with fixings," alluding to the title of the song ("The Lone Fish-Ball") and to the "Moral" as stated in Spaeth:

Who would have bread with his Fish-ball,
Must get it first, or not at all.
Who would Fish-ball with fixin's eat,
Must get some friend to stand a treat.

(Spaeth 85)

On occasion, Joyce alludes only to the title, but with a pun, as when he converts "Major Gilfeather" to "major guiltfeather" (*FW* 355.12). At other times he puns on the title but adds the rhythm of the song itself, as when he returns the name of famed engineer Casey Jones to its presumed original (K.C., for Kansas City), but elaborates: "K.C. jowls, they're sodden in the secret. K.C. jowls, they sure are wise. K.C. jowls, the justicestjobbers, for they'll find another faller if their ruse won't rise" (*FW* 368.27–29).

Now and then Joyce inverts a title's meaning by dropping or adding a word, as he changes "Waste Not, Want Not" to *"We are Wastenot with Want"* (*FW* 418.30). At other times he inverts the title just for fun, as with "No kidd, captn" at *FW* 587.5 for "Captain Kidd," or he varies the title only slightly as with "Elsies from Chelsies" at *FW* 587.26.

Some of these title allusions are so little changed from the original that Joyce's purpose seems (as with "Captain Kidd" or "Elsie from Chelsea") chiefly that of being all-inclusive of the music of his day. In fact, his motives were somewhat more complex. As he explained to Jacques Mercanton, he was seeking, "the richest, the most intense concentration of multiple significations" to unite in one phrase or word "all of the space and duration of great and of slight events." [46] These allusions directly to titles of American songs are perhaps one of Joyce's most obvious efforts to provide American significations in *Finnegans Wake*.

Laughing Words (4 above)

Joyce is said to have told one questioner, who asked whether there were not enough words for him in English, that they were numerous enough, but they were not the "right" words. Little wonder, then, that in addition to his own coinages, he seized so happily upon new or different expressions from all languages. Musical titles and lyrics were as much sources for such collections as any scrap of overheard conversation. The baby talk of "Only a 'ittle Dirly Dirl" went into *Finnegans Wake,* both from the song's title (*FW* 601.17–18) and in the w/r switch in the lyrics, which Joyce echoes at *FW* 61.6–7 with "Have you evew thought, wepowtew, that sheew gweatness was his twadgedy?" (These "vowelthreaded syllabelles" continue for three more lines.) Other words he collected from Spaeth included "'tarnal" (for "eternal") from "Yankee Doodle," at *FW* 177.2–3; "hopjoint" at *FW* 231.31; "locofoco" and "redhot" at *FW* 231.32; "shoo" and "flutterbye" at *FW* 262.13 as "shoo, his flutterby"; "fairy fay" from "Polly Wolly Doodle" at *FW* 328.3; "donochs" [mugs] at *FW* 328.10; "the volumed smoke" at *FW* 328.11 from "My Last Cigar"; "Hyededye, kittyls, and howdeddoh, pan!" from Cab Calloway's version of "Minnie the Moocher" (*FW* 340.31), which also echoes a favorite Joycean line in "The Mermaid" about "I care more for my kettles and my pots"; "polcat" from "P. T. Barnum's Show" at *FW* 513.13; and "cubarola" from "Cubanola Glide" at *FW* 618.22. These examples of American diction were added to others Joyce used in the *Wake*.[47]

Another song from Spaeth, "Polly Wolly Doodle," appealed through its rhyming nonsense title, and also because it helped Americanize the "Doodle Family" for the *Wake* (see "Thematics," below). The title is echoed repeatedly, as in "For you've jollywelly dawdled all the day" (*FW* 250.12–13); "pollyfool fiansees" (*FW* 15.14); "Puellywally" (*FW* 61.25); "pollynooties" (*FW* 209.31); "pollyvoulley foncey" (*FW* 346.18); "volleyholleydoodlem!" (*FW* 379.12); "Polldoody" (*FW* 479.6); or "pollywollies" (*FW* 508.19).

Occasionally the appeal was not in an individual word, but in the turn of phrase; in this way "Polly Wolly Doodle's" line about "curly eyes and laughing hair" becomes the *Wake's* "wiry eyes and winky hair" (*FW* 328.5). The lines from the little-known third stanza, "I came to a river, and I couldn't get across, An' I jump'd upon a nigger, and I tho't he was a hoss" are transformed into "a psumpship doodly show whereat he was looking for fight niggers with whilde roarses" (*FW* 40.12–13). Mabel Worthington also identified the passage, "I ahear of a hopper behidin the door slappin his feet in a pool of bran" (*FW* 486.30–31) as "Polly Wolly Doodle,"[48] though the closest phrase in Spaeth's version has the singer "Behind de barn, down on my knees."

Not only American words in Spaeth were culled for Joyce's use. *Read 'Em and Weep* includes a Dutch reapers' song, describing their being paid all the buttermilk they could drink and one-tenth of the harvest:

> Yanker, dudel, doodle down,
> Diddle, dudel, lanther,

> Yanke viver, voover vown,
> Botermilk und tanther.
>   (Spaeth 4)

Joyce makes this "their bowl of brown shackle and milky and boterham clots" (*FW* 397.17–18), and also varies "Yanker" at *FW* 464.21–22 in "yunker doodler."

Thematics

The most complete analysis of how Joyce used American music to develop themes in *Finnegans Wake* has been Mabel Worthington's "American Folk Songs in Joyce's *Finnegans Wake*." As Worthington acknowledged, it was a study limited in scope and in details.[49] Of the forty-nine songs she lists there, about half (twenty-two) were drawn by Joyce from Spaeth's work. When we extend Worthington's study to include all of the songs Joyce used from *Read 'Em and Weep*, we realize that a Joycean principle is at work. Ireland, he said, was important because it belonged to him. The themes, as Worthington analyzed them, belong to Joyce, not to America: the Viconian cycles; birth, death, and resurrection; the female temptress; the communion service. When Joyce drew on the themes in the Spaeth songs' lyric narratives, it was because those narratives supported concepts he had already begun to develop in *Finnegans Wake*. Possibly for this reason the allusions seem to have thematic significance only about a quarter as often as they contribute patterns of sound and rhythm. Nevertheless, their use helped universalize the themes in Joyce's book.[50]

The present study of Spaeth's songs suggests additions to the themes adduced in the Worthington essay. "Little Brown Jug" adds its bit to the theme of dismemberment identified by Worthington, for instance, when the refrain becomes a confusion of body parts: "Mees is thees knees. Thi is Mi" (*FW* 607.19). Similarly, when the little girls in blue become two legs (*FW* 587.26), Joyce is dismembering as well as synecdochizing the lasses.

HCE's unnamed (and perhaps unnamable) misconduct in the Phoenix Park is supported, too, by American lyrics, as Frankie and Johnnie's refrain becomes "Why was that man for he's doin her wrong!" (*FW* 231.34; by *FW* 624.35, and from a woman's perspective, this becomes "Howsomendeavour, you done me fine!"). The sexual reversals of the *Wake* appear in Joyce's rephrasing of "The Gipsy's Warning" as "*Gettle*

Nettie, Thrust him not" (*FW* 104.24), where the song's trust becomes thrust and its "Gentle lady" acquires overtones of a prickly nettle.

"Old Rosin the Beau," (originally Irish, but treated as American by Spaeth) is sung by a hero who asks to be laid out on the counter after death, and "sprinkled with whiskey and water," rather like Finnegan, though without the latter's resurrection. Old Rosin also asks for two "donochs" or drinking mugs to be placed in his coffin, one at his head and one at his toe; and, finally, for his six pallbearers to drink to Old Rosin from the "big bellied bottle." [51] Joyce refers to the donochs and the laying-out on the counter at *FW* 328.10, 12, and at *FW* 526.21–22 to Rosin's having "wandered the wide world over."

The most frequent thematic uses occur for two old American favorites already cited for rhythm and nonsense vocabulary: "Yankee Doodle" and "Polly Wolly Doodle" supported Joyce's concept of his "Doodles" family. Worthington attributes to "Yankee Doodle" the added role of "expressing a critical or contemptuous attitude" toward Shem or toward HCE's Shem aspect. [52] Its use, and that of "Polly Wolly Doodle," were probably suggested to Joyce by Spaeth's note on "Yankee Doodle's" origins: the English version began as a quatrain ridiculing Oliver Cromwell's appearance as he rode into Oxford, during England's Civil War. [53] Spaeth goes on to suggest that when General Braddock's officers saw the disreputable state of the uniforms worn by colonial soldiers who were to aid in attacking the French and Indians at Niagara and Frontenac in 1755, they were reminded of the Cavalier doggerel, and Dr. Richard Shuckburg, a surgeon with Braddock's forces, wrote the parody now known as "Yankee Doodle." The song's metamorphosis from an attack on Cromwell, to one on the colonists, and its final turn back upon its monarchist originators as a rallying cry against the English crown, fitted it neatly into Joyce's historical cycles. So some eighteen or more allusions in *Finnegans Wake* associate "Yankee Doodle" and "Polly Wolly Doodle" with Cromwell, as where *"Remove that Bible"* (*FW* 71.16) and the Grunt Owl (Cromwell) precede *"Flunkey Beadle"* (*FW* 71.31–32); or where an inversion of a line from "Polly Wolly Doodle" ("no more singing all the dags," *FW* 240.9), is inserted among Cromwell references: "Hymserf, munchaowl, maden, born of thug tribe into brood blackmail, dooly redecant allbigenesis henesies" (*FW* 240.11–12) and "big dumm crumm . . . with pruriest pollygameous inatentions" (*FW* 241.1, 5). Other associations of these songs with Cromwell include:

FW 15.14: "pollyfool fiansees." With Cromwellian associations at *FW* 15.11: "on the eve of Killallwho."

FW 40.11–13: "when lavinias had her mens lease to sea in a psumpship doodly show whereat he was looking for fight niggers with whilde roarses." With Cromwellian associations at *FW* 39.7–8: "Bold Boy Cromwell."

FW 61.25: "Puellywally." With Cromwellian associations at *FW* 64.10: "allower" and *FW* 61.25: "by the siege of his trousers."

FW 206.36: "jellybelly." With Cromwellian associations at *FW* 206.35: "allover."

FW 209.31: "pollynooties." With Cromwellian associations at *FW* 209.30: "glashaboys."

FW 244.33: "cockeedoodle." With Cromwellian associations at *FW* 244.27 as "lolling ears."

FW 250.12–13: "For you've jollywelly dawdled all the day." With Cromwellian associations at *FW* 250.16–18, discussing regicide in Macbeth; and *FW* 250.5, "a shorn stile" (short hair of roundheads).

FW 258.5: "buncskleydoodle!" With Cromwellian associations at *FW* 258.1 as "roguesreckning reigns."

FW 299.n.4: "Hoodle doodle, fam.?" With Cromwellian associations at *FW* 299.9 as "Ollover Krumwall."

FW 323.7: "voyaging after maidens, belly jonah hunting the polly joans." With Cromwellian associations at *FW* 322.33–34: "from the millestones of Ovlergroamlius," and at *FW* 323.8 "hurss." (As in song "I went . . . for to see my gal, singing, etc." plus "curse" of Cromwell, plus reference to horse in stanza 3 of "Polly Wolly Doodle").

FW 346.18: "*pollyvoulley foncey.*" With Cromwellian associations at *FW* 346.16 "lumbs"; *FW* 347.10 "Crimealian Wall," and *FW* 347.32 "Crummwiliam wall."

FW 368.31–32: "Peaky booky nose over a lousiany shirt." With Cromwellian associations at *FW* 368.29 to "Whooley the Whooper" (Cromwell's "lambs" and an earlier Cromwell's association with Cardinal Woolsey).

FW 376.24–25: "Scaldhead pursue! Before you bunkledoodle down." With Cromwellian associations at *FW* 376.24 "Scaldhead" (roundhead).

FW 379.12: "volleyholleydoodlem!" With Cromwellian associations at *FW* 379.8: "Saxolooter for congesters are salders' prey," and at *FW* 379.20–21: "He'll be the deaf of us pappappoppopcuddle, samblind daiyrudder. Yus, sord, fathe, you woll, putty our wraughther!" (Saxon looters, soldiers' prey, sword, faith, [noll], death, wrath.)

FW 397.17–18: "their bowl of brown shackle and milky and boterham clots, a potion a peace" (Dutch Yankee Doodle version); *FW* 397.24 "phlegmish hoopicough" (Polly Wolly Doodle stanza 7, "He sneezed so hard wid de hoopin' cough" + Dutch [Flemish] Yankee Doodle). With Cromwellian associations at *FW* 396.25–26: "a lally a lolly a dither a duther one lelly two dather three lilly four dother"; *FW* 397.9 "all"; *FW* 397.12 "follies"; *FW* 397.14 "crowning themselves"; *FW* 397.21 "xmell"; *FW* 397.22 "skillet"; *FW* 397.23 "all"; *FW* 397.34 "Lally". This is extremely tenuous were it not that throughout *Finnegans Wake* "allover" has stood for "Oliver," as have "Noll," "Knoll," and "Poll," so these double-l words may also refer to him; likewise, "crowning themselves" may refer to the government of the Protectorate, even though Cromwell rejected the mace (which he called a "bauble") as a symbol of royal power (*FW* 579.10: "Renove that bible"; *FW* 71.16: *"Remove that Bible"*).

FW 404.28: "a starspangled zephyr with a decidedly surpliced crinklydoodle front." With Cromwellian associations at *FW* 404.28, surplice suggesting cleric.

FW 443.14 "federal in my cup." With Cromwellian associations at *FW* 443.18: "Charley you're my darling"; *FW* 443.21 with "Rollo the Gunger," and *FW* 443.30's "Olaf Stout"; previous page refers to "Blonderboss" (blunderbuss) at *FW* 442.27.

FW 454.27–28: "Fare thee well, fairy well!" With Cromwellian associations at *FW* 455.8: "Iereny allover irelands."

FW 464.21–22: "and yunker doodler wanked to wall awriting off his phoney." With Cromwellian associations at *FW* 464.13 as "Tulliver" (for "Oliver").

FW 479.6: "Polldoody." With Cromwellian associations at *FW* 479.13: "Dood and I dood" in a discussion of County Mayo; and *FW* 479.15 "Wooluvs" (Cromwell's lambs).

FW 622.5: "sookadoodling." With Cromwellian associations at *FW* 621.18 "nolly," *FW* 622.2 "poll", and *FW* 622.31 "poll."

Another song that fitted neatly into Joyce's scheme was the now-forgotten "Call Me Pet Names," with lyrics by Frances Sargent Locke Osgood. Joyce apparently used the song only twice (*FW* 232.9–13, 531.36), but it illustrates both that he noted material he did not use, and that he used material he did not note down. Spaeth introduces the song with the suggestion that "if a gentleman and a lady are available simultaneously for the performance of this song, she should do the first verse, and he the second, with the third in close harmony." Spaeth then provides three stanzas and music. The words italicized here are those used by Joyce:

Call me *pet names,* dearest! Call me a *bird*
That flies to thy breast at one cherishing word;
That folds its wild wings there, n'er dreaming of flight,
That tenderly sings there in loving delight.
Oh my sad heart is pining for one fond word.
Call me *pet names,* dearest! Call me a *bird!*

Call me *pet names,* dearest! *Call* me a *star*
Whose smile's beaming welcome thou feel'st from afar;
Whose light is the clearest, the truest to thee,
When the night-time of sorrow steals over life's sea.
Oh, trust thy rich bark where its warm rays are.
Call me *pet names,* dearest! *Call* me a *star!*

Call me sweet *names, darling! Call* me thine own.
Speak to me always in love's low tone;
Let not thy look nor thy voice grow cold.
Let my fond worship thy being enfold;
Love me for ever, and love me alone,
Call me *pet names, darling! Call* me thine own![54]

Joyce entered Spaeth's singing instructions in his notebook as
"W. 1.M 2 M & W 3" (woman first verse, man second, man and woman
third)[55] along with the song's title, but apparently did not use the instructions in the *Wake*. The title itself was somewhat scrambled, in a
passage including words from all the song's stanzas, though the stanzas
themselves were *not* entered in the VI.B.56 index workbook: "When
(pip!) a message interfering intermitting interskips from them (pet!) on
herzian waves, (call her venicey names! call her a stell!) a butterfly from
her zipclasped handbag, a wounded dove astarted from, escaping out
her forecotes. Isle wail for yews, O doherlynt! The poetesser" (*FW*
232.9–13). "Call me a star" swiftly fits in with the themes of Astarte
[a star] and Stella and Vanessa, of course. The bird becomes one of the
Wake's doves; and "darling" metamorphoses to "doherlynt" in a squinting reference to poet Kevin Isod O'Doherty, whose middle name also
echoed a Wakean theme.

Composers and Lyricists

Not many of the composers whose work appears in Spaeth seem themselves to have been memorialized in *Finnegans Wake*. Bob Farrell, who
possibly wrote "Turkey in the Straw," may be encompassed in "Pat Far-

rel" at *FW* 176.17, coming just three lines after a reference to "Zip Coon" (sung to the "Turkey in the Straw" melody). Stephen Foster may similarly have a slanting allusion at *FW* 280.17 as part of "Poppa Vere Foster," coming soon after a free recasting of Foster's themes in "Way down upon the Swanee River" and "My Old Kentucky Home" at *FW* 280.4–7: "in the now woodwordings of our sweet plantation where the branchings then will singingsing tomorrows gone and yesters outcome." [56] A "Rosengorge" (whom Adaline Glasheen identifies with Rosencrantz) appears at *FW* 563.31 with the admonition, "Weeping shouldst not thou be when man falls but that divine scheming ever adoring be." To read this as an allusion to Monroe Rosenfeld, who wrote words and music for "With All Her Faults I Love Her Still," seems to be straining at naughts. Likewise, though a clear allusion to "Woodman Spare That Tree!" lies in "wouldmanspare!" (*FW* 77.16), its composer, Henry Russell, is hardly included in the reference to "aerial" at *FW* 77.7 (read by Glasheen as referring to George Russell). But "soptimost" (*FW* 234.13 and listed by Glasheen as unidentified) may refer to Septimus Winner, composer and lyricist for "Listen to the Mocking-Bird" (*FW* 251.35).

Given the importance Joyce placed on the role of the creator-artist in his own life and work, this subordination of composers and lyricists to the words and musical rhythms is puzzling. It may be explained in part by Joyce's recorded indifference to many other creators—the coolness with which he met Gertrude Stein, his bland meeting with Proust, or his declining to write an introduction to the English translation of Italo Svevo's *Senilità* (*JJ2* 529n, 635), particularly when compared to his enthusiasm for a performing artist such as the tenor John Sullivan. Another key may lie in the lectoral quality of these songs in *Read 'Em and Weep;* rather than sung in his own voice, or heard as music, they were songs read (or read aloud by a friend), intriguing or lovely shells collected on the beach, not stone sculpted by his own hand.

Spirituals in *Finnegans Wake*

Just as it is possible to trace a large number of American songs in *Finnegans Wake* to Joyce's ownership of Sigmund Spaeth's *Read 'Em and Weep: The Songs You Forgot to Remember,* it is also feasible to identify the sources for the sixteen Negro spirituals he included. In a general way, of course, these may be traced to the particular craze for black music in the Paris of the twenties and thirties. Josephine Baker, Marian Anderson, Alberta Hunter, Louis "Satchmo" Armstrong, Fletcher Henderson, Coleman Hawkins, Duke Ellington, Adalaide Hall, Ada Ward, Tim Moore, Paul Robeson, Bob Cole, and Rosamund Johnson (brother of James Weldon Johnson, who collaborated on some of the Cole-Johnson songs) all worked in Paris during these years. A hugely popular stage production, *The Black Birds of 1928,* appeared in Paris in summer, 1929, with a cast of over a hundred and the all-black jazz band from the Plantation Club in New York.[57] The French gave the experience their own name: *Le Tumulte Noir,* a title later attached to a volume of lithographs about the experience by Paul Colin, with an introduction by Josephine Baker herself.[58]

Fortunately Joyce's experience of spirituals can be identified even more explicitly in three cases.[59] He twice heard Paul Robeson sing. The first performance came at a "port and sandwich" party arranged by Sylvia Beach at Shakespeare and Company in 1925.[60] Then in October 1927, Robeson appeared at the Salle Gaveau in concert. This time his wife, Eslanda, had written ahead from the United States to invite the Joyces to the recital.[61] With his deep baritone voice, Robeson was, unknowingly, at a disadvantage in singing for Joyce, who much preferred the tenor. The Joyces did attend, however, and copies of Robeson's program have survived to tell us part of what they heard.[62] Selections included a dozen spirituals and four folksongs. (Robeson's encores, which with applause occupied a full hour, are regrettably not identified in accounts of the recital.) Five of the songs we know Robeson sang do appear in the *Wake,* three of them multiple times. "Water Boy," which Robeson sang, was also in Spaeth's book, so Joyce could have encountered it that same year or later in its printed form before archiving it as "heave a hevy, waterboy!" (*FW* 228.31). The other Robeson songs that found their way into *Finnegans Wake* were "Go Down, Moses"; "O! Didn't It Rain!"; "Swing Low, Sweet Chariot"; and "Were You There."[63] (See appendix 2 for specific citations of these songs.)

Two songs—perhaps three—that Robeson recorded also found their way into *Finnegans Wake.* The first he possibly sang at Shakespeare and Company, or as an encore at the 1927 concert: "My Curly-Headed Baby" lends its characteristic refrain at *FW* 333.30: "hush lillabilla lullaby." The second was "Old Man River," which Robeson was to popularize in the first London production of the Kern and Hammerstein musical, *Showboat,* in May 1928. Finally, there is probably the labor song, "Joe Hill," included in Joyce's "Sam Hill" at *FW* 185.8.[64]

Between Robeson's concert of 1927 and the next reported occasion when Joyce heard spirituals sung, more than a decade elapsed. In the interim other recitals of spirituals, such as Marian Anderson's at the Salle Gaveau in 1935,[65] had occurred in Paris. By the time Maria Jolas is remembered as singing these melodies, they may have become for Joyce, as for the slaves who first composed them, a part of an escape to a safer, happier existence. As Jacques Mercanton remembered it later, the Joyce family had returned to Paris after a visit to Nantes during the Munich crisis of 1938. Worry engulfed them: the coming war; Lucia's illness; how to move Lucia from her French sanitarium to safety if/when war came; Joyce's deteriorating eyesight. In an evening gathering Maria Jolas sang spirituals; then, as the group hummed along, Joyce sang Irish and Scots melodies "in . . . an almost interior voice, his face illuminated by the grace of the moment."[66]

Though Joyce has been the subject of more biographical research than any other modern writer, parts of his life are still lost in a Beckettian silence. We do not know, for example, how many times Joyce may have heard, or heard of, spirituals in the intervening years as he worked on *Finnegans Wake.* Did Maria Jolas sing them only once? Was Robeson's the only recital Joyce attended where he heard spirituals? Did he never encounter James Weldon Johnson's influential two-volume collection of Negro spirituals?[67]

In the absence of concrete evidence, we can only examine the milieu. Musicologists and sociologists in the United States had been collecting spirituals since the decade after the Civil War,[68] and the songs had been performed not only in America, but in concerts across Europe by choirs such as the Fisk Jubilee Singers, whose first tour of Europe in 1870 was a major force in acquainting the continent with Negro music.[69] They were followed by soloists like Roland Hayes, Robeson, or Anderson. The songs and their singers were written about in the press, and doubtless discussed by Joyce's friends in conversations with him, or with one another, but overheard by Joyce. The music was a major portion of the "black tumult" of the 1920s and 1930s.

American Dance Music, 1913–38

The interest in black spirituals in Joyce's Paris was but a small aspect of a much larger change in the culture of Paris and, indeed, of all Europe in the 1920s and after. Not only spirituals but all American popular music became the European fashion.[70]

In part this resulted from the technological revolution of the early twentieth century. In the Dublin of Joyce's youth, music had meant attending live performances at concert or music halls. Often these singers came from England or the continent. Music also meant home performance, by family members or guests, around the parlor piano. Though Edison had invented the phonograph in 1877, it did not achieve wide use immediately. By the 1920s, however, phonographs had become relatively less expensive and even portable. Joyce's friends recall that in his workroom he had a phonograph always near, on which he played his own reading from *Work in Progress,* or records by Caruso;[71] and he told friends how the maid tended to confuse his records of John McCormack with his own singing voice.[72] Sometimes, too, Joyce danced to music from the phonograph, as Nino Frank recalled.[73] Neighbors also had record players, sometimes distracting to Joyce, as he complained in his letters.

Like the phonograph, radio surged in popularity and accessibility after World War I, bringing with it "American-derived dance music" that was "firmly established" on the continent by the mid–1920s.[74] The most popular French radio orchestra was Ray Ventura's Collegians, which performed in France and other countries before crossing the channel to play in England in 1931,[75] and was one of several continental dance bands to play over the BBC at various times (Joyce mentions "Bona ventura" at *FW* 207.26 and "collegians" at 385.8 and 388.35, as well as "collegions" at 228.32). Another popular orchestra that broadcast both on the BBC and from Hilversum (for Netherlands radio) was the Ramblers, who invited American players like saxophonist Coleman Hawkins or trumpeter Louis Armstrong to sit in.[76] And the popular Jack Hylton led one of his English bands in a performance at the Paris Opéra on 16 February 1931,[77] as well as playing on BBC.

Cinema, too, brought American dance music to Joyce's Paris. Even before talkies, movies appeared with a soundtrack recorded on a disc to be played as the film was shown. Erno Rapee's and Lew Pollack's song "Charmaine" was featured on the Vitaphone soundtrack for the 1926 silent film *What Price Glory?* Joyce did not have the song in the section of *Work in Progress* that appeared in *transition 1* in 1927; but he later inserted the title (as "his cousing charmian") into his revision of the *transition 1* pages.[78] When talkies arrived, they were in fact "singies," with Al Jolson holding forth in the very first "talkie" as *The Jazz Singer.*

It is characteristic of Joyce, as of most of us, that in his letters he did not normally remark on the movies he attended; then as now, going to the movies was not an "event" like attending the theater or opera. Yet he was interested in the cinema, and attended movies with friends.[79] Philippe Soupault has recalled Joyce's passionate attention in theaters, and his pleasure in "even the crudest vaudeville."[80]

Two other sources of familiarity with popular dance music existed for Joyce: the humming, singing, records, or radio choices of his children George and Lucia (who were in their late teens and early twenties and enjoying social life in Paris); and the orchestras that in the period between the wars played routinely—all too routinely, oftentimes—in Europe's hotels and restaurants.[81] Lucia's friend Albert Hubbell has recalled how much Lucia enjoyed going dancing, and that the big hotels and restaurants regularly held tea dances. Hubbell also names Louis Armstrong as a favorite of Lucia and Hubbell himself.[82]

Being a Joyce, could Lucia have liked dancing and not sung the music around home? And in his well-documented evenings at Paris restaurants like Les Trianons, could Joyce have escaped hearing the inevitable background music to his conversations? Such evenings were an opportunity, as Ellmann has noted, to fill his "mind with the way people talked and behaved" (*JJ2* 680), but also with the people's music. For Joyce had a Charybdian ear, drawing in for his own possible use everything that came within hearing.

What technology did not bring Joyce's way, tourism did. The general American invasion of Paris was especially an American musicians' presence, not only in Paris, but in other European theater and resort centers. In addition to the performers listed earlier, composers such as Aaron Copland, Virgil Thomson, Jerome Kern, Irving Berlin, George Gershwin, or Cole Porter were in Paris, and some became continental celebrities—Kern as early as 1912. Porter was a frequent guest of the Gerald Murphys in Paris and on the Riviera (Mabel Worthington thought him memorialized at *FW* 221.3 as "coldporters")[83] and his wife attended the Robeson concert at the Salle Gaveau (see n. 61). But perhaps the best illustration of this phenomenon is the reception accorded Gershwin and his music in Paris. He visited the City of Light in 1928, where he called in at Shakespeare and Co. to buy a copy of *Ulysses*.[84] Frances Gershwin, George's sister, had a week's singing engagement at Les Ambassadeurs, and George accompanied her first evening's performance.[85] Ira Gershwin, who frequently wrote the lyrics for

George's melodies, was also in the group, and Sylvia Beach recalled being invited to a party for the three of them where Frances sang and George accompanied.[86] Gershwin was celebrity enough to be interviewed by the Paris *Tribune,* to whose reporter he confided plans to write *Americans [sic] in Paris* out of his response to the excitement of the city.[87] In fact, he composed the blues section of that opus at Paris's Hotel Majestic.[88] Moreover, Gershwin's music was being heard among Joyce's friends and discussed in Paris, for as Nino Frank remembered in recalling the period, "our phonographs still played *The Rite of Spring,* but more often *Rhapsody in Blue,* which had just been released and seemed sad to us."[89] The same work was given a two-piano performance at the Théâtre Mogador on 31 March 1928 and a single-piano performance on 16 April that same year at the Théâtre des Champs Élysées. Gershwin's *Concerto in F* had its European premiere at the Opéra on 29 May 1928.[90]

As Frank's recollection indicates, not only Gershwin, but also his music was crossing the Atlantic. The adventure of "The Man I Love" is instructive. Though the Gershwin brothers had written the song for Adele Astaire in *Lady, Be Good!* (1924), it was dropped from the production during rehearsals. Then at a private party in Derby, Connecticut, Lady Edwina Mountbatten was so delighted when she heard Gershwin playing it that she carried an autographed copy of the song to London, where it became a big success for the Berkeley Square Orchestra. Thereafter it crossed to Paris, and returned to New York as Gershwin's Paris hit![91]

Not only composers but performers were in Paris, of course. In addition to those already mentioned, early jazz orchestras had toured Europe very successfully: James Reese Europe's "Tennessee Students" appeared in Paris and other capitals as early as 1905. During World War I, an American army jazz band received considerable attention; and after the war, Will Marion Cook's "New York Syncopated Orchestra" introduced Sidney Bechet's jazz clarinet to London.[92] Paul Whiteman brought his orchestra to Paris in June 1926,[93] to great applause, and they performed, among other pieces, Gershwin's *Rhapsody in Blue.* Of the many American musical artists mentioned above, it was Louis "Satchmo" Armstrong "who really turned Europe on," according to jazz historian Bruce Cook. Armstrong's initial trip to England in 1932 had a "fabulously successful two-week engagement" with a "pick-up band from Paris, mixed French and expatriate black." Pleased by his success,

Armstrong returned to the continent in 1933 for eighteen months to tour England, Scandinavia, France, Belgium, Switzerland, and Italy, and also did a radio broadcast from the Netherlands (probably with The Ramblers). During Armstrong's stay Duke Ellington and Fats Waller also performed in Europe. Europe had become "jazz-conscious."[94]

"Serious" musicians were also talking about jazz. A German critic, "Herr Doktor Siemens" was reported by George Seldes to have equated "jazz, booze, and bolshevism."[95] And one of those writing about jazz for the Paris *Tribune* was Joyce's close friend, Eugene Jolas, who interviewed both Stravinsky and Koussevitsky on the subject.[96]

Joyce never was much impressed by mere fame or celebrity, however. He was distinguished from Marcel Proust, he said, by the Frenchman's preoccupation with duchesses and his own interest in duchesses' maids.[97] But his proximity to jazz occurred in other ways. McAlmon relates a period when he, Joyce, and Wyndham Lewis met nightly to drink and talk, often at the Gypsy Bar. Regular patrons of the bar gathered often at Joyce's table, where even—or especially—late at night he would quote from his own work or from Dante, to a constant background of "jazz music badly played by a French orchestra."[98]

Other bars and restaurants also had orchestras, and one observer complained that after the Rotonde expanded into the next-door restaurant, redecorated, and added an upstairs jazz band, in 1923, it tripled the prices of its drinks. Bricktop, the famous Left Bank bistro owner who had married an American jazz musician, installed a jazz band of black musicians in her bar in 1923 and herself sang songs that McAlmon identified as "something banal by Berlin or Porter."[99] Nor was music necessarily indoors: McAlmon also recalled Bastille Day, 1923, with street orchestras playing outside the Stryx and other cafes on the Left Bank.[100]

In sum, the aural sources of American jazz, dance, and blues music lay all around Joyce. Given his pattern of drawing to himself everything in his environment that might be useful in *Finnegans Wake*, it is little wonder that he included at least 195 allusions to the new music, including 114 different songs by 79 composers, plus a few anonymous musicians. Appearing most often is Vincent Youmans, whose "Tea for Two" (nineteen allusions) had a particular Joycean theme to it. But only three of Youmans's songs were incorporated in *Finnegans Wake*, whereas thirteen of George Gershwin's melodies are named, with a single allusion for each. Irving Berlin ranked just after Gershwin, with seven songs and ten allusions. The most popular individual songs, after "Tea for Two," were John Schonberger's "Whispering" (another Wakean theme, used eight times); Erno Rapee's "Charmaine" (seven); and Eddie Leonard's "O! Didn't It Rain!" (six).

The titles of American popular music provided other appeals. There were many songs honoring both city sirens and home-town sweethearts; Joyce included almost enough of these to name a set of rainbow girls: "Cecelia," "Charmaine," "Chloe," "The Daughter of Rosie O'Grady," "Dinah," "Eileen Alannah," "Liza," "Margie," "Mercenary Mary," "Minnie the Moocher," "Nannette," "Katharina," "Peg o' My Heart," "Rose Marie," "Pretty Kitty Kelly," sweet "Peggy O'Neil," "Tootsie," "Wild Rose," and the "Mademoiselle from Armentières" all populate the *Wake*. Only three men from American music appear, however: "Dapper Dan, the Sheik of Alabam'," "The Sheik of Araby," and "Sonny Boy." Maternal presence is equally reduced, with only "My Mammy," "That Old Irish Mother of Mine," and "Little Mother of Mine" included.

Songs of water, rain, and clouds were naturals for inclusion. "Between the Devil and the Deep Blue Sea," "Look for the Silver Lining," "There's a Rainbow Round My Shoulder," "Till the Clouds Roll By," and "O! Didn't It Rain!" fit naturally enough with songs naming American rivers ("Mississippi Mud," "Old Man River," "Swanee," and the "Missouri Waltz") or with boating songs like "Ciribiribin," "My Little Canoe," and "Drifting with the Tide." These river songs provided some American geography to Joyce, as did songs naming states: "Dapper Dan, the Sheik of Alabam'," "You're in Kentucky," and "Carolina in the Morning." Joyce even created a state song of his own: "Indiana Blues" (*FW* 285.F6) seems not to exist as a real song. There are several other references to blues in general, but only "Wang, Wang Blues," "Mood Indigo," and "Blue Monday Blues" are named individually.

In other ways the application Joyce made of these popular songs of the quarter century from 1913 to 1938 differs somewhat from his treatment of songs in Spaeth. His most frequent method of allusion is to the title, a form of reference applied twice as often as his puns or semantic plays upon the words in the song. The emphasis on titles results in part from repeated reference to a few titles: "Tea for Two"; "Whispering"; "Charmaine"; "Dapper Dan, the Sheik of Alabam'"; "Dinah"; "Remember," and "O! Didn't It Rain!" Other titles appear only once, like Dorothy Donnelly's and Sigmund Romberg's 1921 musical *Blossom*

Time (*FW* 64.36, "blossomtime"); "Black Bottom" (*FW* 78.31–32, "Bellona's Black Bottom"); Gershwin's "Lady, Be Good" (coupled with Ibsen's *The Lady from the Sea* at *FW* 208.30–31 as "Missus, be good and don't fol in the say"); or "Love Walked In," whose chorus is altered to "when love walks in" (*FW* 618.18).

A master of assemblage art, Joyce seldom employed a text fragment only one way if he could give it three layers of meaning. So "Charmaine" becomes one of his chord-words, modulated into "charmian" (*FW* 20.3); "Charmeuses" and "charmeuse" (*FW* 236.1; *FW* 271.n.5); "charmhim" (*FW* 288.10); "charmaunt" (*FW* 384.30); "sharming" and "sharmeng" (*FW* 427.14); and "charmeen" (*FW* 527.18). Similar alterations occur for "Yes, We Have No Bananas," which unfolds as "writress of Havvah-ban-Annah" (*FW* 38.30); "*Yass We've Had His Badannas*" (*FW* 71.11–12); "halve a bannan in two" (*FW* 145.35–36); or "yea, he hath no mananas" (*FW* 170.20). The "Wang Wang Blues" metamorphoses to produce "Lang Wang Wurm" (*FW* 270.n.2). Another blues song, "Blue Monday Blues," appears as "a bluemoondag" (*FW* 453.13). "Ballin' the Jack" acquires an extra American slang quality as "bawling the whowle hamshack" (*FW* 309.22) with an accompanying nod to amateur radio operators (hams) in their radio "shacks." The "Daughter of Rosie O'Grady" is treated none too kindly as "Roseoogreedy (mite's)" (*FW* 133.7); and another Irish lass is given uneven treatment as "Sweet Peck-at-my-Heart" (*FW* 143.1–2), "the peg-of-my-heart" (*FW* 290.3), "What though it be for the sow of his heart? If even she were a good pool Pegeen?" (*FW* 490.31–32); and "peg of his claim and pride of her heart" (*FW* 577.16). "I Cried for You" is transcribed as "Isle wail for yews" at *FW* 232.13. And "Song of My Heart," which was the title melody of a movie starring John McCormack, becomes not only the "sow of his heart" cited above, but, at *FW* 224.35, "thong off his art."

Songs are alluded to in a thematic way about two-thirds as often as by semantic changes, and most of these are also used as title-allusions, as noted above. Notable are "Whispering," "Tea for Two," and "O! Didn't It Rain!"; and "Old Man River" is echoed frequently, as "They jest keeps rosing. He jumps leaps rizing. Howlong!" (*FW* 363.10–11), "his shool comes merging along!" (*FW* 364.9–10), "he, to don't say nothing" (*FW* 288.5–6) and "they don't say nothings" (*FW* 599.35).

Uncommon phrases in these songs appealed to Joyce as had phrases in earlier music. Black composer George Clutsam's "My Curly-Headed Baby" included the refrain "So lulla, lulla, lulla, lulla, bye bye," and a concluding phrase, "So lulla, lulla, lulla, lulla, bye," represented by Joyce as "hush lillabilla lullaby" at *FW* 333.30. (Paul Robeson was associated with this song, as already noted.) Joyce also picked up Cab Calloway's interpolation in "Minnie the Moocher" (Hi di Hi, Hi de Ho), to introduce it at *FW* 340.31 ("Hyededye, kittyls, and howdeddoh, pan!") and *FW* 455.14 ("one finel howdiedow"). Ira Gershwin's "Maybe I shall meet him Sunday, Maybe Monday, maybe not; Still I'm sure to meet him one day, Maybe Tuesday will be my good news day" appears at *FW* 457.19–20: "Someday duly, oneday truly, twosday newly, till whensday."

As with the songs from Spaeth's *Read 'Em and Weep*, the songs of the twenties and thirties were useful sources for American slang, as Joyce incorporated "Becky, Do the Bombashay," "Fine and Dandy," "Fit as a Fiddle," "Making Whoopee," "Yes Sir, That's My Baby," and the mooching Minnie.

Sound variations also appealed, of course. Al Jolson's famous "Mammy" undergoes vowel shifts in "Mammy was, Mimmy is" (*FW* 226.14). "Fit As a Fiddle and Ready for Love" also has its vowels shifted, to become "fat as a fuddle" (*FW* 603.4). The title and final line of "Music, Maestro, Please" becomes "Music, me ouldstrow, please!" (*FW* 617.15–16). Similarly, the "No, No," of "No, No, Nannette" is changed into an aspect of her character, as she becomes "nozzy Nanette" (*FW* 117.16).[101] Some of the spelling variants convey changes into another language, as when "Sonny Boy" gains a Gaelic lilt as "Shonny Bhoy" (Seón Buidhe: "Yellow John" or John Bull, according to O Hehir) at *FW* 377.27.

Surprisingly, considering the highly rhythmic nature of popular music in the 1920s and 1930s, Joyce made relatively less use of these songs for rhythmic purposes than for any other. The four references to "Mademoiselle from Armentières" are all unmistakably in the song's rhythm ("puddywhackback to Pamintul" at *FW* 64.25; "Marmarazalles from Marmeniere" at *FW* 75.3; "Mademoisselle from Armentières" at *FW* 230.15; "Parley vows the Askinwhose?" at *FW* 276.n.4). Likewise "You're the Cream in My Coffee" at *FW* 106.2–3 is evident in *"He's the Hue to Me Cry, I'm the Stitch in his Baskside You'd be Nought Without Mom."* Equally strong is the rhythm of "Bye, Bye, Blackbird" at *FW* 273.7–10: where Mort Dixon and Ray Henderson wrote, "Pack up all my care and woe, here I go, singing low, Bye, Bye, Blackbird," Joyce gives us "So wrap up your worries in your woe (wumpumtum!) and shake down the shuffle for the throw." Both rhythm and rhyme give us the echo of "Sweetie Pie" at *FW* 436.33–34: "Lay your lilylike long his shoulder but buck back if he buts bolder," a strong recall of the original's "Lay your little head on my shoulder, Wait until you get a little bit older." Both the rhythm and the syntactic pattern of "Thou Swell!" appear at *FW* 454.16–18 as "Thou pure! Our virgin! Thou holy! Our health! Thou strong! Our victory! O salutary!"

Joyce's virtuoso performance of popular music came with "Tea for Two," however. As mentioned earlier, the song's emphasis on tea lent itself to a *Wake* theme.[102] He also loved to vary the sound of the lyrics, as in "elazilee him on her knee" (*FW* 232.35–36) or as a puzzle at *FW* 247.15's "Teapotty. Teapotty" (Two teapots = tea for two). The teapot merged into the "Little Brown Jug" to become a statement of the platonic coalescing of lovers at *FW* 607.19: "Mees is thees knees, Thi is Mi." At other times Joyce modulated the words as if they were chords: "Teaseforhim. Toesforhim. Tossforhim. Two" (*FW* 246.34–35). And he surpassed even his own previous ingenuity in handling the rhythm; for he captured the chorus's opening lilt ("Three for two will do for me and he for thee and she for you" at *FW* 584.10–11); yet he also made the long whole note at the end of the first part of the chorus sing out; in the original's "you for me a-LONE," "lone" gets a whole measure plus the first beat of the next measure to itself. Joyce substitutes "A tear or two in time is all there's toot" (*FW* 457.21), letting the long vowel of "toot" hold as the long *o* of "lone" had in the original. He even manages to capture Vincent Youmans's rhythmic shift within the chorus, from dotted quarter notes followed by eighths, to quarter notes followed by dotted eighths plus sixteenth notes. Joyce achieves this syncopation at *FW* 603, where "shay for shee and sloo for slee" (lines 12–13) is followed by "Tyro a tora" (line 34).

Summary

As much as the happenstance knock on the door that found its way into *Finnegans Wake,* the American popular songs permeating the Parisian atmosphere in the twenties and thirties were ideally suited to Joyce's methods in "writing" his last work. He denied to Jacques Mercanton that he had any talent, adding, "I write with such difficulty, so slowly.

Chance furnishes me what I need. I am like a man who stumbles along; my foot strikes something, I bend over, and it is exactly what I want." [103]

In the Paris years when he was assembling *Finnegans Wake* from the rag and bone shop of the world's heart, it was not always his foot striking something he might include; sometimes he was "pricking up ears to my phono on the ground and picking up airs from th'other over th'ether" (*FW* 452.11–12). These songs formed an incidental music in the background of his life, but we cannot doubt their importance to him. It is significant that Mercanton's memories of Joyce begin and almost end with Joyce listening to radio music, first Purcell, then "a high, thin voice singing . . . 'Take Love When You Can Get It.'" [104]

At one of their last meetings, on a day in 1938 in Lausanne, James and Nora Joyce recalled for Mercanton a dancer in a bar they had visited the previous night. Joyce had dreamed of the dancer, whom Nora compared to her Jim in one of his holiday-drinking moods. The man who had given the world *A Portrait of the Artist as a Young Man, Dubliners, Ulysses,* and was just concluding seventeen years' work on *Finnegans Wake,* measured his life against the dancer and, with a sigh, wondered whether he could not better make a living as a radio singer. "I could have made a fortune with my voice. And what have I done?" After further discussion, he returned to the dancer and to his own work: "After all, [*Finnegans Wake*] is nothing but a game, or a dance, like the one the little Negro did at the bar. That's what I was made for, a little Negro dance." [105] In his despair Joyce wrongly impugned his last work as "only" a game. It is that; but in its compelling accretion of picked-up airs and melodies, puns and plays, *Finnegans Wake* is Joyce's voice, his song, his dance.

Notes

1. Carola Giedion-Welcker, "Meetings with Joyce," trans. Wolfgang Dill, in *Portraits of the Artist in Exile,* ed. Willard Potts (Seattle: University of Washington Press, 1979), 264-65.

2. Nino Frank, "The Shadow That Had Lost Its Man," trans. Jane Carson, in Potts, 89.

3. Letter to Ruth Bauerle from Albert Hubbell, 10 March 1990.

4. Cheryl Herr, *Joyce's Anatomy of Culture* (Urbana: University of Illinois Press, 1986), 2.

5. In neither city was Joyce's life "settled" in any conventional sense, as the list of his addresses in either Dublin or Paris bears witness. But an internationalized Paris formed his mature years as Dublin formed his youth.

6. For a map illustrating how Howth resembles the United States in its geographical outline, see Louis Mink, *A "Finnegans Wake" Gazetteer* (Bloomington: Indiana University Press, 1978), facing p. 346.

7. Fritz Senn, "A Throatful of Allusions," *Joycenotes* 1:1. "White Wings" was first written by a Joseph Gulick in 1882, the year of Joyce's birth. Gulick sold rights to Banks Winter, who tried unsuccessfully to market the song with a new tune and new words. It became a hit in 1884. Sigmund Spaeth, *A History of Popular Music in America* (New York: Random House, 1948), 229; David Ewen, *All the Years of American Popular Music* (Englewood Cliffs, N.J.: Prentice-Hall, 1977), 102.

8. The difficulty of knowing when Joyce intends a musical allusion has been discussed elsewhere (Ruth Bauerle, *The James Joyce Songbook* [New York: Garland, 1982, 1984], xx-xxii; see also discussions of allusion above in Introduction and Timothy Martin's essay). To the difficulties there listed may be added the inability of generations of scholars to agree on all suggested allusions.

9. To these will be added more than two thousand newly identified references in the forthcoming volume *Opera Allusions in "Finnegans Wake,"* by Matthew J. C. Hodgart and Ruth Bauerle.

10. Zack Bowen, *Musical Allusions in the Works of James Joyce, Early Poetry through "Ulysses"* (Albany: State University of New York Press, 1974), index listing of song titles.

11. This number includes the operatic material listed in Hodgart and Bauerle, *Opera Allusions in "Finnegans Wake."*

12. American musician Otto Luening, for instance, remembers Joyce as always fond of music that had a good melodic line for singing. Timothy Martin and Ruth Bauerle, "A Voice from the Prompt Box: Otto Luening Remembers James Joyce in Zurich," *Journal of Modern Literature* 17 (Summer 1990): 35–48.

13. Spaeth, *A History of Popular Music,* 278-79.

14. Adaline Glasheen identifies the Dreiser name at *FW* 55.23 in the term "rundreisers," though that is also from the German *Rundreise,* or "tour" (*Third Census of "Finnegans Wake,"* [Berkeley: University of California Press, 1977]), 78.

15. For a survey of the content and attitudes in these songs, see William H. A. Williams, "From Lost Land to Emerald Isle: Ireland and the Irish in American Sheet Music, 1800-1920," *Éire-Ireland* 26:1: 19-45.

16. Carole Brown [Knuth], "Will the Real Signor Foli Please Stand up and Sing 'Mother Machree'?" (*A Wake Newslitter* n.s. 27 [Dec. 1980]: 99-100). Carole Brown [Knuth] and Leo Knuth, *The Tenor and the Vehicle: A Study of the*

John McCormack/James Joyce Connection (Colchester, Essex: A Wake Newslitter Press, 1982. *A Wake Newslitter* Monograph no. 5). Knuth and Knuth, "More Wakean Memories of McCormack: A Centenary Tribute" (*A Wake Newslitter Occasional Paper No. 4,* September 1984).

17. Sigmund Spaeth, *Read 'Em and Weep: The Songs You Forgot to Remember* (Garden City, N.Y.: Doubleday, Page and Co., 1927, [© 1926]). Spaeth apparently took the subtitle, which has the kind of paradox with which Joyce filled *Finnegans Wake,* from the last line of Irving Berlin's "Remember." Joyce's copy of Spaeth's volume has survived in the Special Collections of the Stanford University Library. See Thomas J. Kenney, "James Joyce's System of Marginal Markings in the Books of His Personal Library," *Journal of Modern Literature* 6 (April 1977): 264-76.

18. Danis Rose, ed., *James Joyce's The Index Manuscript FINNEGANS WAKE Holograph Workbook VI.B.46* (Colchester, Essex: *A Wake Newslitter,* 1978), 235-46; hereafter referred to as the *Index Manuscript.* The few errors in Rose's transcription of Joyce's difficult handwriting affect the count in only one instance.

19. Although Rose transcribes the word "O'Reilly" (Buffalo Notebook VI.B.46, p. 111 top), he does not treat it as part of the *Read 'Em and Weep* entries, passing instead from the notebook's page 110 to page 112. Yet the notation by Joyce probably refers to "Are You the O'Reilly?" given in Spaeth, 184, and alluded to by Joyce at *FW* 93.30 and 578.10-11.

20. Songs in *Read 'Em and Weep* that appear in *FW:* * preceding the title indicates Danis Rose identified the note in *Finnegans Wake;* # indicates an English song; +, an Irish song.

Abdul Abulbul Amir
*Adams and Liberty
*Adams and Clay
After the Ball
*Animal Fair
Are You the O'Reilly?
The Band Played On
*Call Me Pet Names
*Camptown Races
Captain Kidd
Casey Jones
The Cat Came Back
#Champagne Charlie
*Come Home, Father
Cubanola Glide
Down Went McGinty
The Eastern Train
#Elsie from Chelsea
The Erie Canal

The Fatal Wedding
*Frankie and Johnnie
*Free America
The Free-Lunch Cadets
The Girl I Left behind Me
*The Gipsy's Warning
Hamlet, Prince of Denmark
Has Anybody Here Seen Kelly? (American version)
The Hat Me Father Wore
Her Golden Hair Was Hanging down Her Back
Hot Time in the Old Town Tonight
In the Baggage Coach Ahead
Just Break the News to Mother
Kafoozalem
Lardy Dah
*Lincoln and Liberty
*Listen to the Mocking Bird

*Little Brown Jug
*The Lone Fish Ball
Major Gilfeather
*#The Man on the Flying Trapeze
#The Man That Broke the Bank at Monte
   Carlo
*A Married Woman's Lament
*Menagerie
*The Mermaid
*The Mill-Boy of the Slashes
Mona ("You Shall Be Free")
*The Monkey Married the Baboon's Sister
*My Last Cigar
The New Bully
*#Not for Joe
Oh, Didn't He Ramble?
*Oh, Fred, Tell Them to Stop
*Old Hal o' the West
* + Old Rosin the Beau
Only a 'ittle Dirly Dirl
*Over There (Pratie Song)
P. T. Barnum's Show
Paddy Duffy's Cart
The Picture That is Turned toward the
   Wall

*Polly-Wolly-Doodle
Sam Hall
Shoo, Fly, Don't Bother Me
*The Son of a Gambolier
*The Song of All Songs
*The Sorrow of Marriage
The Straight-out Democrat
Tammany
Ta-ra-ra-boom-der-e
*There is a Tavern in the Town
*To Anacreon in Heaven (melody for Star-
   Spangled Banner)
Two Little Girls in Blue
*#Vilikins and His Dinah
Waste Not, Want Not
*Water Boy
*We Never Speak as We Pass By
Where Did You Get That Hat?
The Widow Nolan's Goat
*#Wife, Children, and Friends
Willie, the Weeper
With All Her Faults I Love Her Still
*Woodman, Spare That Tree
*Yankee Doodle
*Zip Coon

Titles used by Joyce, for which *Read 'Em and Weep* prints no words or music:

Beth-Gelert
*#Come Back to Erin
*Marching through Georgia
My Little Chimpanzee
*On the Raging Canal

*On the Other Side of Jordan
Over There (Cohan)
Under the Yum-Yum Tree
*Turkey in the Straw

21. Seven of the Spaeth songs Joyce used are English, not American; finding them in Spaeth, however, Joyce may have considered them American.

22. Philippe Soupault, "James Joyce," trans. Carleton W. Carroll, in Potts, 117.

23. Louis Gillet, "Farewell to Joyce" and "The Living Joyce," trans. George Markow-Totevy, in Potts, 194.

24. A. Walton Litz, "'Ithaca'" in *James Joyce's "Ulysses"* (Berkeley: University of California Press, 1974), 387.

25. Stuart Gilbert, "Paris Diary," *Joyce Studies Annual* 1990, 17.

26. James Joyce, *Index Manuscript*, 235-51.

27. Gilbert, "Diary," 17.

28. Jacques Mercanton, "The Hours of James Joyce," trans. Lloyd C. Parks, in Potts, 234.

29. Anthony Burgess repeatedly makes a similar point in his memoir *You've Had Your Time* (New York: Grove Weidman, 1991), as he protests that readers and scholars pass over musical elements in studying the texts of Joyce, Shakespeare, and Burgess himself.

30. The resentment that lyricists may feel about this situation is exemplified in the remark attributed to Mrs. Oscar Hammerstein II, that it was her husband who wrote "Old Man River." All Jerome Kern contributed, she claimed, was "Tum tum tumtum, ta tum tum tumtum."

31. Mercanton, 213, 234.

32. Bauerle, *James Joyce Songbook*, 423-25, 592-94.

33. Mabel Worthington points to a similar blending of the American "John Brown's Body" with the Irish "Shan Van Vocht." Mabel Worthington, "American Folk Songs in Joyce's *Finnegans Wake*," *American Literature* 28 (May 1956): 197-210, at p. 204.

34. Joyce being Joyce and the *Wake* the *Wake,* he often does two or three of these things simultaneously.

35. Worthington, "American Folk Songs," 197-210. For a detailed analysis of Worthington's article, see "Laughing Words" section.

36. Because *girl* derives, according to Webster's, from the Middle English *gurle* or *girle,* meaning a young person of either sex, the language seems to have accomplished the sex change already for this word.

37. On Joyce's knowledge of John Scotus Erigena (ca. 800-ca. 877) see Alessandro Francini Bruni, "Joyce Stripped Naked in the Piazza," trans. Lido Botti, in Potts, 37.

38. Mercanton, 221, 237.

39. Otto Jespersen, *Growth and Structure of the English Language* (New York: Doubleday Anchor Books, 1955, reprint of 9th Macmillan edition of 1938), ii, iv. It is a Joycean coincidence that Danish pronunciation of the scholar's name makes him, like Molly Bloom, a "yes-person."

40. Jespersen, 177 (paragraph 173).

41. If Joyce is following Jespersen here, he is not being slavish. For where Jespersen was commenting on a shift in the final consonant of the word, Joyce frequently changes the initial consonant.

42. Spaeth, *Read 'Em and Weep* (88-90) spells the title "Gambolier," and acknowledges its Irish origin. Joyce at *FW* 317.14-15 spells it "gombolier." Matthew J. C. Hodgart and Mabel Worthington, *Song in the Works of James Joyce* (New York: Columbia University Press for Temple University Publications, 1959) followed Joyce.

43. "I'm a rambling wreck from Georgia Tech and a Hell of an engineer. A helluva helluva helluva helluva helluvan engineer." On "wandering" see also

Martin's essay in this volume, on Wotan, and the listings for Wotan in Hodgart and Bauerle, *Opera Allusions in "Finnegans Wake."*

44. Spaeth's chorus repeats two lines. The version I have known for half a century varies the repetition as "Ho ho ho, me and you, Little brown jug I love you too."

45. In addition to the American "On the Raging Canal" and "The Other Side of Jordan," Foster also names in this tour de force several English songs used by Joyce in *Finnegans Wake*. The song, whose lyric consists entirely of titles of other popular songs, is a kind of antecedent of *Finnegans Wake*, which might be conceived as a song made up of thousands of other songs.

46. Mercanton, 237.

47. For a list see Worthington, "American Folk Songs," 198, citing Padraic Colum.

48. Hodgart and Worthington, *Song in the Works of James Joyce*, 155.

49. Worthington, "American Folk Songs," 197-210. In this pioneering article, Worthington discusses eight songs in detail: "Home, Sweet Home"; "Woodman, Spare That Tree"; "Yankee Doodle"; "Mademoiselle from Armentières"; "Tramp, Tramp, Tramp"; "One More Drink for the Four of Us"; "John Brown's Body"; and "Old Man River." For the rest of her forty-nine songs, Worthington lists as "folk" such genuine folk melodies as "Frankie and Johnny"; popular nineteenth-century ballads (John Howard Payne's "Home, Sweet Home," Stephen Foster's "Old Folks at Home," or Charles K. Harris's "After the Ball"); spirituals ("Certainly, Lord" and "Swing Low, Sweet Chariot"); and minstrel songs ("Won't You Come Home, Bill Bailey?"). She also counted songs that, though extremely popular in America, were not American ("Abdul the Bulbul Amir" by Percy French; "The Man on the Flying Trapeze" by Leybourne and Lee; or "Mademoiselle from Armentières" by the Canadian Gitz-Rice). A portion of her commentary was included in the essay "Songs in *Finnegans Wake*" in Hodgart and Worthington, *Song in the Works of James Joyce*, 24-58.

50. It is nevertheless true that the *Index Manuscript* entries transcribed by Rose are almost completely in order as the songs occur in Spaeth's *Read 'Em and Weep*, suggesting that Joyce was selecting them because they were American, rather than for any thematic reasons. The additional Spaeth songs identified here but not listed in Joyce's *Index Manuscript* are drawn from throughout Spaeth.

51. Spaeth, *Read 'Em and Weep* (42) urges that "Old Rosin the Beau" was Scots in origin. Yet it lent its melody to at least four nineteenth-century American political songs, and is still sung, as Irish, by the Clancy Brothers. This is also the air for the Irish song, "Men of the West."

52. Worthington, "American Folk Songs," 202.

53. *Encyclopaedia Britannica*, s.v. "Cromwell," dates the fall of Oxford to

the rebel troops as 24 June 1646, without stating whether Cromwell led the rebels into the city.

54. Spaeth, *Read 'Em and Weep*, 55-56. Lyricist Frances Sargent Locke Osgood (1811-50) was a well-known American popular poet of the nineteenth century, and a close friend of Edgar Allan Poe. Her poem was set to music by Charles H. Jarvis (1837-95), a pianist and teacher active in Philadelphia music circles, who left his considerable music library to the Drexel Institute. Osgood and Jarvis are listed in the *DAB*.

55. Joyce, *Index Manuscript* VI.B.46, 110; reproduced in *James Joyce Archive* 40:206. Danis Rose, in editing the *Index Manuscript*, transcribes this line as "W.I.M 2 M I W 3" (237) and passes it over without comment, both because this transcription is not translatable, and because Joyce did not cross it out as incorporated in the *Wake* manuscript.

56. From "Way down upon the Swanee River":

> All up and down the whole creation
> Sadly I roam,
> Still longing for the old plantation
> And for the old folks at home.

and from "My Old Kentucky Home":

> The corn top's ripe and the meadow's in the bloom,
> While the birds make music all the day. . . .
>
> CHORUS:
> We will sing one song for the old Kentucky home
> For the old Kentucky home far away.

57. "*Black Birds* May Be Hit of Summer Season in Paris," Paris *Tribune*, 10 June 1929, rpt. *The Left Bank Revisited: Selections from the Paris "Tribune," 1917-1934*, ed. Hugh Ford (University Park: Pennsylvania State University Press, 1972), 236-37. See also Janet Flanner, *Paris Was Yesterday* (New York: Viking, 1972), 156 on Marian Anderson; Martin Duberman, *Paul Robeson* (New York: Knopf, 1988), 109, on Alberta Hunter and Roland Hayes at Robeson's recital. See also n. 60 below. Armstrong was in Paris in 1932 and 1933-34, and Ellington during Armstrong's second visit. On Taylor Gordon and Rosamund Johnson, brother of James Weldon Johnson and composer of "O, Didn't He Ramble" (*FW* 355.18, 506.13-14) and "My Little Chimpanzee" (*FW* 590.11), see Samuel Putnam, *Paris Was Our Mistress* (New York: Viking Press, 1947), 49.

58. B. J. Kospoth, "Paul Colin's 'Black Tumult,'" Paris *Tribune*, 20 January 1929; rpt. Ford, 201. Under review was Paul Colin, *Le Tumulte Noir* (Paris: Editions Succès, 1929).

59. As this volume was going to press, Vincent Deane's transcription of

Joyce's notes on Marc Connelly's play *The Green Pastures* arrived on my desk. This raises the number of identifiable sources to four. Vincent Deane, *"The Green Pastures" A "Finnegans Wake" Circular* 4 (Spring 1989), 56-60.

60. Duberman, 92. Richard McDougall, ed. and trans., *The Very Rich Hours of Adrienne Monnier* (New York: Charles Scribner's Sons, 1976), 56. Paul Shinkman in the Paris *Tribune,* 13 November 1925; rpt. Ford, 103.

61. Robeson did the inaugural concert of a year's tour of Europe at Salle Gaveau, 29 October 1927. Mrs. Robeson had also written Gertrude Stein in advance. Others attending were Caterina Jarboro, Johnny Hudgins, Mrs. Cole Porter, Ludwig Lewisohn, Naomia Bercovici, Michael Strange, Sylvia Beach, Baroness Erlanger, and Georges Auric. Duberman, 109.

62. Moorland-Spingarn Research Center, Howard University, Washington, D.C., and the Paul Robeson Archive at the Akademie der Künste, [East] Berlin, kindly provided me copies of this program. My thanks are due Joellen ElBashir, senior manuscript librarian at Howard University, and Christine Naumann, scientific assistant at the Akademie der Künste for their help. Although Lawrence Brown is listed on the program as a "tenor," Martin Duberman says in *Paul Robeson* that Brown was the piano accompanist.

63. Other music Robeson performed that evening [with dialect spelling as given on the program] included the spirituals "Wade in De Water," "On Ma Journey," "Ezekiel Saw De Wheel," "By and By," "Deep River," "I Know De Lord's Laid His Hands On Me," "Every Time I Feel De Spirit," "Nobody Knows De Trouble I've Seen," and "Joshua Fit De Battle of Jericho." The folksongs Joyce heard, without including them in *FW,* were "Sometimes I Feel Like a Motherless Child" and "Little David."

64. I am grateful to my friend Hugh Staples for pointing out this allusion. Joe Hill was a labor organizer executed in 1915 for murder. Fellow unionists insisted he was framed. "Joe Hill," (lyrics by Alfred Hayes, music by Earl Robinson) was copyrighted by two different owners in 1938: MCA Music and Bob Miller, Inc. Nevertheless, the lyrics' statement, "But Joe, you're ten years dead," suggests the song was written about 1925. Settings of the song may be found in Wanda W. Whitman's *Songs That Changed the World* (New York: Crown, 1969), 75; and Margaret Bradford Boni's *Fireside Book of Folksongs* (New York: Simon and Schuster, 1947), 50-51. Paul Robeson recorded it.

65. Flanner, 156.

66. Mercanton, 242.

67. James Weldon Johnson, *The Book of American Negro Spirituals* (New York: Viking, 1925) and *The Second Book of Negro Spirituals* (New York: Viking, 1926), republished as a single volume, *The Books of American Negro Spirituals* (New York: Viking, 1951). Musical arrangements in these volumes are by Johnson's brother, J. Rosamund Johnson, and Lawrence Brown. Both Rosa-

mund Johnson and Brown performed in Paris in the 1920s, the latter as Robeson's accompanist at the Salle Gaveau recital of 1927. Each arrangement in these volumes has its own dedication, and these, as a group, constitute a mini-history of 1920s culture, including Roland Hayes, Paul Robeson, W. E B. Du Bois, Walter and Gladys White, Ruth Hale and Heywood Broun, Marian Anderson, Walter Damrosch, John McCormack, Henry Krehbiel, Carl Van Vechten, Rebecca West, Otto H. Kahn, Eslanda Robeson, George Gershwin, Will C. Handy, Franklin P. Adams, the memory of Bob Cole, Alain Locke, Witter Bynner, Countee Cullen, H. L. Mencken, David Belasco, the Alfred Knopfs, Irita Van Doren, and Mr. and Mrs. Eugene Goosens. Goosens set several of Joyce's poems to music.

68. Johnson, 1:47. The movement was aided by the Fisk University collections of the songs, and the concerts by the Fisk Jubilee Singers in both the United States and Europe. H. E. Krehbiel, music critic for the *New York Tribune,* collected data for years and published *Afro-American Folksongs* in 1914, according to Johnson, 1.47-48. Johnson goes on to describe the spirituals as having a "vogue" in the mid-twenties.

69. Johnson, 1.29, 47. See also Ulrich Schneider's comments on the popularity of black American music, above.

70. An early version of the material in this section was presented at the 1983 Joyce conference in Provincetown, Mass.

71. Letter to Ruth Bauerle from Albert Hubbell, 10 March 1990.

72. Mary and Padraic Colum, *Our Friend James Joyce* (Garden City, N.Y.: Doubleday, 1958), 184.

73. Frank, 93-94.

74. Albert McCarthy, *The Dance Band Era* (London: November Books, Ltd., 1971; rpt. Radnor, Pa.: Chilton Book Company, 1982), 132.

75. McCarthy, 132.

76. McCarthy, 132; *Grove's Dictionary of Jazz,* s.v. "Hawkins."

77. McCarthy, 120, lower photo.

78. *James Joyce Archive,* vols. 44, 49, 50.

79. Frank, 98.

80. Soupault, 113.

81. Ellmann (*JJ2*) mentions in passing, for instance, Joyce's presence at the following restaurants and cafes: Gypsy Bar (515); Brasserie Lutétia (516); Café d'Harcourt; Ferrari's (524); Café Weber (525); Hôtel Léopold at Les Vaux-de-Cernay (615); Imperial Hotel, Torquay (616), and the Alhambra Music Hall, London (518).

82. Albert Hubbell, letter to Ruth Bauerle, 10 March 1990. At the time he was seeing Lucia, Hubbell recalls, the Joyces lived in the Square Robiac. Ellmann places the family there from 1 June 1925 to 10 April 1931 (*Letters 2,*

lx). Armstrong did not perform in Europe until 1932, so the couple's enjoyment of "Satchmo" must have been from records, movies, shortwave radio, or European players imitating the style.

83. Worthington, "American Folk Songs," 198.

84. Sylvia Beach, *Shakespeare and Company* (New York: Harvest-Harcourt Brace, 1956, 1959), 125-26.

85. Charles Schwartz, *Gershwin: His Life and Music* (Indianapolis: Bobbs-Merrill, 1973), 158.

86. Beach, 125-26.

87. Unsigned note, the Paris *Tribune,* 3 April 1928; rpt. Ford, 224-25.

88. Schwartz, 155.

89. Frank, 74-75.

90. Schwartz, 155, 157-58. See also George Wickes, *Americans in Paris* (New York: Doubleday for Paris Review Editions, 1969), chapter 5, "Virgil Thomson and Other Musical Saints," 193-233.

91. David Ewen, *American Popular Songs* (New York: Random House, 1966), 246. Alec Wilder, *American Popular Song: The Great Innovators, 1900-1950* (New York: Oxford University Press, 1972), 129-30.

92. Bruce Cook, *Listen to the Blues* (New York: Scribner's, 1973), 147-48.

93. Irving Schwerké, "Paris Audience Thrilled by Antics of Paul Whiteman's Jazz Orchestra," Paris *Tribune,* 2 July 1926; rpt. Ford, 221.

94. Cook, 148-49.

95. George Seldes in the Paris *Tribune,* 15 March 1921; rpt. Ford, 228-29.

96. Eugene Jolas, "Stravinsky Predicts Musical Future for America; Jazz Thrilled Him," Paris *Tribune,* 21 March 1925; and "Influence of Jazz in American Music Greatly Over-rated, Says Koussevitsky," Paris *Tribune,* 31 May 1925; rpt. Ford, 213-14, 217.

97. Mercanton, 227.

98. Robert McAlmon and Kay Boyle, *Being Geniuses Together,* rev. and enlarged ed. (Garden City, N.Y.: Doubleday, 1968), 30-31.

99. McAlmon and Boyle, 56.

100. Ibid., 40-41.

101. Joyce spelled the name "Nanette"; the song's title is "Nannette." Though at odds with his many additions of double letters to other words in *FW,* the change allows a simultaneous allusion to Nanetta in Verdi's opera *Falstaff.*

102. On the *Wake's* tea theme, see, for instance, Clive Hart, *Structure and Motif in "Finnegans Wake"* (London: Faber and Faber, 1962), 194-97, 200, 206-7; William York Tindall, *A Reader's Guide to "Finnegans Wake,"* (New York: Farrar Straus Giroux, 1969), 103, 156; and Frances Bolderoff, *Reading "Finnegans Wake"* (Woodward, Pa.: Classic Nonfiction Library, 1959), 182 ff.

It might be noted, too, that "tea" is an anagram of Greek "eta" or "H," and therefore is one of H. C. Earwicker's initials.

103. Mercanton, 213.

104. Ibid., 206-7, 225-26. I can find no American song of this title, though it may be a European ballad. Possibly Mercanton misremembered the title of the Gershwins' 1937 song, "Nice Work If You Can Get It."

105. Joyce quoted by Mercanton in Potts, 226-27.

Appendix 1

Songs, Chiefly American, from Sigmund Spaeth's *Read 'Em and Weep* in *Finnegans Wake*

Key:

page/line no. in *FW,* text from *FW;* song title (W: lyricist; M: composer, date)

/ indicates end of line in *FW*

// indicates end of page in *FW*

Finnegans Wake, Book I.1:

007.34, bom, tarabom, tarabom; Ta-Ra-Ra Boom-der-é (W&M: Henry J. Sayers, 1891)

009.17, Drink a sip, drankasup; Little Brown Jug (W&M: Joseph Eastburn Winner, 1869)

009.28, .33, .35, This is jinnies rinning away . . . the jinnies they left behind them . . . the rinnaway jinnies; The Girl I Left behind Me (W&M: trad., 1758)

012.13, beardsboosoloom; Kafoozalem (W: S. Oxon; M: Frederick Blume, arranger [and composer?], 1866)

015.14–15, pollyfool / fiansees; Polly Wolly Doodle (W&M: anon., 1883)

019.28–29, sons of the sod, sons, littlesons, yea and lealittle- / sons; Free America (W: Joseph Warren; M: tune of British Grenadiers, ca. 1775)

024.12–14, Have / you whines for my wedding, did you bring bride and bedding, / will you whoop for my deading is a? Wake; The Fatal Wedding (W: W. H. Windom; M: Gussie L. Davis, 1893)

029.4–5, showm!), the height of Brew- / ster's chimpney and as broad below as Phineas Barnum; P. T. Barnum's Show (W&M: anon., 1870s)

Finnegans Wake, Book I.2:

033.27–28, Hay, hay, hay! Hoq, hoq, hoq! / Faun and Flora on the lea love that little old joq; Little Brown Jug (W&M: Joseph Eastburn Winner, 1869)

033.30, .32–33, .36, 034.1–3, vicefreegal . . . beard / on prophet . . . stambuling // . . . Dumbaling . . . tarrk . . . Abdul- / lah Gamellaxarksky; Abdul Abulbul Amir (W&M: Percy French, 1877, based on a traditional English song from the Crimean War)

040.11–13, when lavinias had her mens / lease to sea in a psumpship doodly show whereat he was looking / for fight niggers with whilde roarses; Polly Wolly Doodle (verse 3; W&M: anon., 1883)

042.20, Spare, woodmann, spare; Woodman, Spare That Tree (W: George Pope Morris; M: Henry Russell, 1837)

043.35, decentsoort hat; The Hat Me Father Wore (W: Ferguson; M: Daniel McCarthy, 1876)

043.35, decentsoort hat; Where Did You Get That Hat? (W&M: Joseph J. Sullivan, 1888)

Finnegans Wake, Book I.3:

061.6–11, her vowelthreaded syllabelles: Have you evew thought, wepow- / tew, that sheew gweatness was his twadgedy? Nevewtheless ac- / cowding to my considewed attitudes fow this act he should pay / the full penalty, pending puwsuance, as pew Subsec. 32, section / 11 of the C.L.A. act 1885, anything in this act to the contwawy / notwithstanding; Only a 'ittle Dirly Dirl (W&M: Addison Fletcher Andrews, 1878)

061.25, Puellywally; Polly Wolly Doodle (W&M: anon., 1883)

069.18, .34, 070.33, cadet . . . free . . . lunch- / eonette; The Free Lunch Cadets (W&M: John Philip Sousa, 1877)

071.25, *O'Reilly's Delights to Kiss the Man / behind the Borrel;* The Man That Broke the Bank at Monte Carlo (W&M: Fred Gilbert, 1892)

071.32, *Flunkey Beadle Vamps the Tune Letting on He's / Loney;* Yankee Doodle (W: Oxonian Cavaliers; M: nursery rhyme, 1646)

072.2, Twitchbratschballs; The Lone Fish Ball (W&M: anon., 1855. It appears in C. Wistar Stevens, *College Song Book* [Boston: Russell & Tolman, 1860] as a Harvard song.)

073.8, like Potts Fracture did with Keddle Flatnose; The Mermaid (W&M: folk, ca. 1868)

Finnegans Wake, Book I.4:

077.16, wouldmanspare; Woodman, Spare That Tree (W: George Pope Morris; M: Henry Russell, 1837)

079.33–34, as her weaker had / turned him to the wall; Picture That Is Turned towards the Wall (W&M: Charles Graham, 1891)

085.1–2, and all his crewsers stock locked in the / burral of the seas; Down Went McGinty (W&M: Joseph Flynn, 1889)

090.24, Like the crack that bruck the bank in Multifarnham; The Man That Broke the Bank at Monte Carlo (W&M: Fred Gilbert, 1892)

093.30, I am the Sullivan; Are You the O'Reilly? (W&M: Pat Rooney, 1883)

102.24, For her holden heirheaps hanging down her back; Her Golden Hair Was Hanging down Her Back (W: Monroe H. Rosenfeld; M: Felix McGlennon, 1894)

103.9–10, we / have hanged our hearts in her trees; There is a Tavern in the Town (W&M: William H. Hills, 1883)

Finnegans Wake, Book I.5:

104.7, *Here's to the Relicts of All Decencies;* The Hat Me Father Wore (W: Ferguson; M: Daniel McCarthy, 1876)

104.7, *Here's to the Relicts of All Decencies;* Where Did You Get That Hat? (W&M: Joseph J. Sullivan, 1888)

104.10–11, *Ik / dik dopedope et tu mihimihi;* Little Brown Jug (W&M: Joseph Eastburn Winner, 1869)

104.23–24, *Where Portentos they'd Grow Gonder how / I'd Wish I Woose a Geese;* Over There (W&M: folk, 1844)

104.24, *Gettle Nettie, Thrust him not;* The Gipsy's Warning (W&M: Henry A. Coard)

105.1, *Myrtles of Venice Played to Bloccus's Line;* To Anacreon in Heaven (W: Anacreontic Society of London; M: John Stafford Smith, 1771)

105.1–2, *To Plenge Me High / He Waives Chiltern on Friends;* Wife, Children, and Friends (W: William Robert Spencer, 1770–1834; M: Humors of the Glen air, 1856)

106.17, *Welikin's Douchka Marianne;* Villikins [or Villikens, or Vilikins] and his Dinah (W: John Parry; M: folk, 1800s)

Finnegans Wake, Book I.6:

133.27–28, emirate . . . babu; Abdul Abulbul Amir (W&M: Percy French, 1877, based on a traditional English song from the Crimean War)

135.12–13, while he has trinity left / behind him like Bowlbeggar Bill; The Girl I Left behind Me (W&M: trad., 1758)

135.22–23, O sorrow / the . . . Mairie; The Sorrow of Marriage (W&M: folk, 1850 or earlier)

135.24–26, who / repulsed from his burst the bombolts of Ostenton and falchioned / each flash downsaduck in the deep; Adams and Liberty (W: Robert Treat Paine, Jr.; M: John Stafford Smith, 1796)

153.6–7, *My, my, my! Me and me! Little down dream / don't I love thee;* Little Brown Jug (W&M: Joseph Eastburn Winner, 1869)

158.23–24, *O! O! O! Par la / pluie;* Little Brown Jug (W&M: Joseph Eastburn Winner, 1869)

159.17–18, *Why, why, why! Weh, O weh! / I'se so silly to be flowing but I no canna stay;* Little Brown Jug (W&M: Joseph Eastburn Winner, 1869)

160.28, Mr Wist is thereover beyeind the wantnot; Waste Not, Want Not (You Never Miss the Water till the Well Runs Dry) (W&M: Rollin Howard, 1874)

Finnegans Wake, Book I.7:

170.3, not for a dinar! not for jo; Not for Joe [or Not for Joseph] (W&M: Arthur Lloyd, 1860s)

173.21–22, and one moment tarabooming great / blunderguns; Ta-Ra-Ra Boom-der-é (W&M: Henry J. Sayers, 1891)

176.14, *Zip Cooney Candy;* Zip Coon (W&M: folk, 1834; Irish melody: The Old Rose Tree)

176.15–17, Turkey in the Straw . . . Pat Farrel; Turkey in the Straw (W: Bob Farrell and George Washington Dixon; M: Irish melody: The Old Rose Tree, 1834 as Zip Coon)

177.2–3, tarned long and then a nation / louder; Yankee Doodle (W: Oxonian Cavaliers; M: nursery rhyme, 1646)

177.21, this hambone dogpoet pseudoed himself; Mona (You Shall Be Free) (W&M: anon., nineteenth century)

177.21–22, this hambone dogpoet pseudoed himself under / the hangname he gave himself of Bethgelert; Beth-Gelert, the Good Greyhound (W&M: William Robert Spencer, ca. 1800)

179.18, from pulling himself on his most flavoured canal the huge chest- / house of his elders; Erie Canal (W&M: folk, after 1825, when the Canal opened)

184.25, the legs he left behind with Litty fun Letty fan Leven; The Girl I Left behind Me (W&M: trad., 1758)

185.8, Sam Hill; Sam Hall (Sammy Hall, Samuel Hall) (W&M: folk)

191.12–13, I pose you know why possum hides is / cause he haint the nogumtreeumption; Zip Coon (W&M: folk, 1834; Irish melody: The Old Rose Tree)

Finnegans Wake, Book I.8:

206.36, jellybelly; Polly Wolly Doodle (W&M: anon., 1883)

209.13, or efter the ball; After the Ball (W&M: Charles K. Harris, 1892)

209.31, pollynooties; Polly Wolly Doodle (W&M: anon., 1883)

Finnegans Wake, Book II.1:

228.29–30, He would, with the greatest of ease . . . by dear home; The Daring Young Man on the Flying Trapeze (W: Alfred Lee or George Leybourne; M: Alfred Lee, 1868)

228.30, by dear home trashold on the raging canal; Erie Canal (W&M: folk, after 1825, when the canal opened)

238.30, on the raging canal; On the Raging Canal (W&M: anon., 1863 or earlier)

228.30–31, on the raging canal, / for othersites of Jorden; The Song of All Songs (W&M: Stephen C. Foster, 1863)

238.31, for othersites of Jorden; On the Other Side of Jordan (W&M: anon., 1863 or earlier)

228.31, heave a hevy, waterboy; Water Boy (W&M: folk, 1800s)

228.36, 229.13, .25, Free leaves for eribadies! . . . Luncher out . . . free; The Free Lunch Cadets (W&M: John Philip Sousa, 1877; in conjunction with two Spaeth songs, Son of a Gombolier at 229.14 and The New Bully at 229.15)

229.14, A Wondering Wreck; Son of a Gambolier (W&M: anon., 1800s)

229.15, .23, Bullyfamous . . . meataxe; The New Bully (W: Charles E. Trevathan; M: old Negro melody, says Spaeth, 1896; in conjunction with two other Spaeth songs on same page: Son of a Gambolier and The Free Lunch Cadets)

231.15, dense floppens mugurdy; Down Went McGinty (W&M: Joseph Flynn, 1889)

231.29, An oldsteinsong; Stein Song (W: W. Lincoln Colcord; M: M. E. A. Fenstad, 1901, arr. A. W. Sprague 1910; identified here in conjunction with Spaeth's word "Ratskellers," also included in the Joycean variant "Ratskillers" at 231.33 and "readyos" [radios, where Rudy Vallee used The Stein Song as his theme] at 231.34)

231.31, hopjoimt; Frankie and Johnnie (W&M: folk, 1870–75)

231.32, ladle broom jig; Little Brown Jug (W&M: Joseph Eastburn Winner, 1869)

231.32, locofoco; Old Hal O' the West (W: anon.; M: air of Old Rosin the Beau, ca. 1844)

231.32–33, when a redhot / turnspite he; The Mermaid (W&M: folk, ca. 1868)

231.33, Under the reign of old Roastin the Bowl; Old Rosin the Beau (W&M: folk, ca. 1830)

231.34, Why was that man for he's doin her wrong; Frankie and Johnnie (W&M: folk, 1870–75)

231.34–232.1, Lookery / looks, how he's knots in his entrails! Mookery mooks, it's a / grippe of his gripes. Seekeryseeks, why his biting he's head off? // Cokerycokes, it's his spurt of coal; Casey Jones (W: T. Lawrence Seibert; M: Eddie Newton, 1909)

232.2–3, For the mauwe that blinks you blank is / mostly Carbo; The Man That Broke the Bank at Monte Carlo (W&M: Fred Gilbert, 1892)

232.10–13, When (pip!) a message / interfering intermitting interskips from them (pet!) on herzian / waves, (call her venicey names! call her a stell!) a butterfly from / her zipclasped handbag, a wounded dove astarted from, escaping / out her forecotes. Isle wail for yews, O doherlynt! The poetesser; Call Me Pet Names (W: Charles N. Jarvis; M: Mrs. Frances Sargent Locke Osgood, ca. 1860)

233.1–3, if he hadn't got it toothick he'd a telltale tall of his pitcher / on a wall with his photure in the papers for cutting moutonlegs / and capers; Picture That Is Turned towards the Wall (W&M: Charles Graham, 1891)

234.7–8, the kerl he left / behind him; The Girl I Left behind Me (W&M: trad., 1758)

240.9, .12, 241.5, No more singing all the dags . . . dooly . . . pollygameous; Polly Wolly Doodle (W&M: anon., 1883)

244.33, cockeedoodle; Yankee Doodle (W: Oxonian Cavaliers; M: nursery rhyme, 1646)

246.7–9, With / lightning bug aflash from afinger. My souls and by jings, should / he work his jaw to give down the banks and hark from the tomb; Adams and Liberty (W: Robert Treat Paine, Jr.; M: John Stafford Smith, 1796; allusion to final stanza: "[War's] bolts could n'er rend Freedom's temple asunder; For unmoved at its portals would Washington stand, And repulse with his breast the assaults of the thunder; Of its scabbard would leap, His sword from the sleep, And conduct, with its point, every flash to the deep!")

247.28, Tarara boom decay; Ta-Ra-Ra Boom-der-é (W&M: Henry J. Sayers, 1891)

249.19, The boy which she now adores. She dores; O! Fred, Tell Them to Stop (W&M: George Meen, 1860s?)

250.12–13, For / you've jollywelly dawdled all the day; Polly Wolly Doodle (W&M: anon., 1883)

250.30–31, And what do you think / that pride was drest in; The Monkey Married the Baboon's Sister (W&M: anon., 1800s)

250.30–31, And what do you think / that pride was drest in! Voolykins' diamondinah's vestin; Villikins [or Villikens, or Vilikins] and his Dinah (W: John Parry; M: folk, 1800s)

250.36–251.1, We haul minymony on that piebold nig. Will any dubble dabble // on the bay; Camptown Races (W&M: Stephen C. Foster, 1850)

251.1, Nor far jocubus? Nic for jay; Not for Joe [or Not for Joseph] (W&M: Arthur Lloyd, 1860s)

251.35, But listen to the mocking birde to micking barde making bared; Listen to the Mocking-Bird (W&M: Septimus Winner, 1854)

258.5, buncskleydoodle; Yankee Doodle (W: Oxonian Cavaliers; M: nursery rhyme, 1646)

258.8, To Mezou- / zalem with the Dephilim; Kafoozalem (W: S. Oxon; M: Frederick Blume, arranger [and composer?], 1866)

Finnegans Wake, Book II.2:

260.n.1, blue / canaries; My Last Cigar (W&M: anon., 1830s. It appears in C. Wistar Stevens, *College Song Book* [Boston: Russell & Tolman, 1860] identified as a Harvard song.)

262.13, When shoo, his flutterby; Shoo, Fly, Don't Bother Me! (W: Billy Reeves; M: Frank Campbell, 1869)

267.n.5, but I thinks more of my pottles and ketts; The Mermaid (W&M: folk, ca. 1868)

274.1–2, For the man that / broke the ranks on Monte Sinjon; The Man That Broke the Bank at Monte Carlo (W&M: Fred Gilbert, 1892)

274.32–275.1, a broken breached meataerial // from Bryan Awlining; The Man That Broke the Bank at Monte Carlo (W&M: Fred Gilbert, 1892)

278.n.7, Strutting as proud as a great turquin weggin that cuckhold on his Eddems / and Clay's hat; Adams and Liberty (W: Robert Treat Paine, Jr.; M: John Stafford Smith, 1796)

279.n.1.11, Your are me severe; A Married Woman's Lament (W&M: folk, 1850 or earlier)

279.n.1.11, Then rue; The Sorrow of Marriage (W&M: folk, 1850 or earlier)

279.n.1.11, jr; American usage of Sr./Jr. to designate father and son of same name. Note that a song from Spaeth, by composer Robert Treat Paine, Jr., appears at 278.n.7.

279.n.1.28–29, slapping my straights till the sloping ruins, postillion, postallion, a / swinge; Yankee Doodle (W: Oxonian Cavaliers; M: nursery rhyme, 1646)

279.n.1.32, like anegreon in heaven; To Anacreon in Heaven (W: Anacreontic Society of London; M: John Stafford Smith, 1771)

288.17, P. T. Publikums; P. T. Barnum's Show (W&M: anon., 1870s)

294.17–19, like your Bigdud . . . turvku; Abdul Abulbul Amir (W&M: Percy French, 1877, based on a traditional English song from the Crimean War)

299.n.4, Hoodle doodle, fam.; Yankee Doodle (W: Oxonian Cavaliers; M: nursery rhyme, 1646)

301.n.5, Very glad you are going to Penmark; Hamlet, Prince of Denmark (W&M: anon., before 1868). H. R. Waite in *Carmina Collegensia* (Boston: Oliver Ditson, 1868) identifies this as popular at Hamilton College; so Joyce might have heard it from Ezra Pound. It was also known in Dublin in Joyce's childhood, for Watters and Murtagh (*Infinite Va-*

riety: Dan Lowrey's Music Hall 1879–97 [Dublin: Gill and Macmillan, 1975], 50) quote the first stanza of this as having been a feature of Tom Maglagan's performance at the Star of Erin in 1882. Maglagan, in turn, had borrowed it from a Sam Cowell.

Finnegans Wake, Book II.3:

311.6, lives thor a toyler in the tawn; There is a Tavern in the Town (W&M: William H. Hills, 1883)

316.18, down to the button of his seat; Down Went McGinty (W&M: Joseph Flynn, 1889)

317.13–14, One fish- / ball with fixings; The Lone Fish Ball (W&M: anon., 1855. It appears in C. Wistar Stevens, *College Song Book* [Boston: Russell & Tolman, 1860] as a Harvard song.)

317.14–15, For a dan of a ven of a fin of a son of a gun of a gombolier; Son of a Gambolier (W&M: anon., 1800s)

323.6–7, voyag- / ing after maidens, belly jonah hunting the polly joans; Polly Wolly Doodle (W&M: anon., 1883)

323.23, and that hell of a hull of a hill of a camelump bakk; Son of a Gambolier (W&M: anon., 1800s)

328.3, be me fairy fay; Polly Wolly Doodle (W&M: anon., 1883)

328.5, wiry eyes and winky hair; Polly Wolly Doodle (W&M: anon., 1883)

328.10, roundsabouts; O! Fred, Tell Them to Stop (W&M: George Meen, 1860s?)

328.10, .12, donochs . . . and were he laid out on that counter there; Old Rosin the Beau (W&M: folk, ca. 1830)

328.11, the volumed smoke; My Last Cigar (W&M: anon., 1830s. It appears in C. Wistar Stevens, *College Song Book* [Boston: Russell & Tolman, 1860] identified as a Harvard song.)

328.11, the clonk in his stumble strikes warn; Come Home, Father (W&M: Henry Clay Work, 1864)

328.12, a Slavocrates; Lincoln and Liberty (W: anon.; M: air of Old Rosin the Beau, 1860)

329.1, Yinko Jinko Randy; Yankee Doodle (W: Oxonian Cavaliers; M: nursery rhyme, 1646)

340.15, *to the relix of old decency;* The Hat Me Father Wore (W: Ferguson; M: Daniel McCarthy, 1876)

340.15, *to the relix of old decency;* Where Did You Get That Hat? (W&M: Joseph J. Sullivan, 1888)

340.31, Hyededye, kittyls, and howdeddoh, pan; Willie the Weeper (W& M: folk, ca. 1885)

340.31, Hyededye, kittyls, and howdeddoh, pan; The Mermaid (W&M: folk, ca. 1868)

341.4, *the little brown jog;* Little Brown Jug (W&M: Joseph Eastburn Winner, 1869)

341.7, Why the gigls he lubbed beeyed him; The Girl I Left behind Me (W&M: trad., 1758)

346.18, *pollyvoulley foncey;* Polly Wolly Doodle (W&M: anon., 1883)

349.35–350.1, *hereis cant came back saying he codant steal no lunger, yessis, // catz come buck beques he caudant stail awake;* Casey Jones (W: T. Lawrence Seibert; M: Eddie Newton, 1909)

349.35–350.1, *hereis cant came back saying he codant steal no lunger, yessis, // catz come buck beques he caudant stail awake;* The Cat Came Back (W&M: Henry S. "Harry" Miller, 1893)

351.19–20, buckoo / bonzer, beleeme; Abdul Abulbul Amir (W&M: Percy French, 1877, based on a traditional English song from the Crimean War)

355.10–11, Abdul Abulbul / Amir or Ivan Slavansky Slavar. In alldconfusalem; Kafoozalem (W: S. Oxon; M: Frederick Blume, arranger [and composer?], 1866)

355.10–11, Abdul Abulbul / Amir or Ivan Slavansky Slavar. In alldconfusalem; Abdul Abulbul Amir (W&M: Percy French, 1877, based on a traditional English song from the Crimean War)

355.12, major guiltfeather; Major Gilfeather (W: Ned "Pete" Harrigan; M: David Braham, 1881)

355.16–18, rollicking rogues / from, rule those rackateer romps from, rein their rockery rides / from. Rambling; O Didn't He Ramble (W: Bob Cole; M: J. Rosamond Johnson, 1902)

355.25–27, sats and suns, / the sat of all the suns . . . sats of his sun; Son of a Gambolier (W&M: anon., 1800s)

360.23,—Bulbul, bulbulone; Abdul Abulbul Amir (W&M: Percy French, 1877, based on a traditional English song from the Crimean War)

365.16, Amir; Abdul Abulbul Amir (W&M: Percy French, 1877, based on a traditional English song from the Crimean War)

366.32–33, And dong wonged Magongty till the bombtomb of the warr, / thrusshed in his whole soort of cloose; Down Went McGinty (W&M: Joseph Flynn, 1889)

368.10–14, okey boney . . . porker but, porkodirto . . . rolies out of the Monabella . . . cullebuone . . . arraky bone; Mona [You Shall Be Free] (W&M: anon., nineteenth century)

368.27–30, K.C. jowls, they're sodden in the secret. K.C. jowls, they sure / are wise. K.C. jowls, the justicestjobbers, for they'll find another / faller if their ruse won't rise; Casey Jones (W: T. Lawrence Seibert; M: Eddie Newton, 1909)

368.29, Whooley the Whooper; Willie the Weeper (W&M: folk, ca. 1885)

368.31–32, Peaky booky nose over a / lousiany shirt; Polly Wolly Doodle (W&M: anon., 1883)

376.24, Scaldhead pursue! Before you bunkledoodle / down; Yankee Doodle (W: Oxonian Cavaliers; M: nursery rhyme, 1646)

377.25, to brake the news to morhor; Break the News to Mother (W&M: Charles K. Harris, 1897)

379.12, volleyholleydoodlem; Polly Wolly Doodle (W&M: anon., 1883)

379.19, ho, ho, ho, ah, he, he; Little Brown Jug (W&M: Joseph Eastburn Winner, 1869)

379.34, Timmotty Hall; Tammany (W: Vincent P. Bryan; M: Gus Edwards, 1905)

380.31–32, witht the widow Nolan's / goats; The Widow Nolan's Goat (W: Ned "Pete" Harrigan; M: David Braham, 1882)

Finnegans Wake, Book II.4:

397.17–18, their bowl of brown shackle and milky and boterham clots, a potion a peace, a piece aportion; Yankee Doodle (W: Oxonian Cavaliers; M: nursery rhyme, 1646)

397.24, the phlegmish hoopicough; Polly Wolly Doodle (W&M: anon., 1883)

Finnegans Wake, Book III.1:

404.27–28, a starspangled zephyr / with a decidedly surpliced crinklydoodle front; Yankee Doodle (W: Oxonian Cavaliers; M: nursery rhyme, 1646)

418.2–3, Flunkey Footle / furloughed foul, writing off his phoney; Yankee Doodle (W: Oxonian Cavaliers; M: nursery rhyme, 1646)

418.30, *We are Wastenot with Want;* Waste Not, Want Not (You Never Miss the Water till the Well Runs Dry) (W&M: Rollin Howard, 1874)

420.10–11, Bauv Betty Famm and Pig / Pig Pike; Sweet Betsy from Pike (W: folk ballad; M: tune of Villikens and His Dinah, 1853, possibly 1840)

421.18, penmarks; Hamlet, Prince of Denmark (W&M: anon., before 1868. H. R. Waite in *Carmina Collegensia* [Boston: Oliver Ditson, 1868] identifies this as popular at Hamilton College; so Joyce might have heard it from Ezra Pound. See also note for *FW* 301.n.5)

427.15–16, And the lamp went out as it couldn't glow on burning, yep the / lmp wnt out for it couldn't stay alight; Casey Jones (W: T. Lawrence Seibert; M: Eddie Newton, 1909)

427.15–16, And the lamp went out as it couldn't glow on burning, yep the / lmp wnt out for it couldn't stay alight; The Cat Came Back (W&M: Henry S. "Harry" Miller, 1893)

Finnegans Wake, Book III.2:

431.17, tarnelly; Yankee Doodle (W: Oxonian Cavaliers; M: nursery rhyme, 1646)

431.35, erigenal house; Erie Canal (W&M: folk, after 1825, when the canal opened)

435.3–5, and asking with whispered offers in a very low bearded / voice, with a nice little tiny manner and in a very nice little tony / way; The Eastern Train (Riding down from Bangor) (W&M: Louis Shreve Osborne?, 1871, *The Harvard Advocate*)

442.2–3, and I don't / care a tongser's tammany hang who the mucky is; Tammany (W: Vincent P. Bryan; M: Gus Edwards, 1905)

443.14, federal in my cup; Yankee Doodle (W: Oxonian Cavaliers; M: nursery rhyme, 1646)

452.13, th'other over th'ether; Over There (The Pratie Song) (W&M: folk, 1844)

454.27–28, Fare thee / well, fairy well; Polly Wolly Doodle (W&M: anon., 1883)

464.21–22, and yunker / doodler wanked to wall awriting off his phoney; Yankee Doodle (W: Oxonian Cavaliers; M: nursery rhyme, 1646)

469.1–2, And whinn muinnuit flittsbit twinn her ttittshe cries / tallmidy; The Girl I Left behind Me (W&M: trad., 1758; McHugh identifies these lines as a parody of "Girl I Left behind Me," "But when moonlight flits between her tits, Jesus Christ, Almighty!")

469.10–11, I'll travel / the void world over; Old Roisin the Beau (W&M: folk, ca. 1830)

Finnegans Wake, Book III.3:

476.2, the bulbul; Abdul Abulbul Amir (W&M: Percy French, 1877, based on a traditional English song from the Crimean War)

476.27, the ass that lurked behind him; The Girl I Left behind Me (W&M: trad., 1758)

479.1, overthere; Over There (The Pratie Song) (W&M: folk, 1844)

479.6, Polldoody; Polly Wolly Doodle (W&M: anon., 1883)

486.30–31, I ahear of a hopper behidin the door slappin his feet in a / pool of bran; Polly Wolly Doodle (W&M: anon., 1883)

496.2, Lordy Daw and Lady Don; Lardy Dah (W&M: anon., 1870s)

497.16–17, afeerd he was a gunner but afaird to stay away; The Cat Came Back (W&M: Henry S. "Harry" Miller, 1893)

506.13–14, Psalmtimes it grauws on me to ramble, / ramble, ramble; O Didn't He Ramble (W: Bob Cole; M: J. Rosamond Johnson, 1902)

508.19, pollywollies; Polly Wolly Doodle (W&M: anon., 1883)

509.1, Where do you get that wash; Where Did You Get That Hat? (W&M: Joseph J. Sullivan, 1888)

509.7, About his shapeless hat; Where Did You Get That Hat? (W&M: Joseph J. Sullivan, 1888)

509.22, his haliodraping het; Where Did You Get That Hat? (W&M: Joseph J. Sullivan, 1888)

510.35, bride eleft; The Girl I Left behind Me (W&M: trad., 1758)

513.12, Taranta boontoday; Ta-Ra-Ra Boom-der-é (W&M: Henry J. Sayers, 1891)

513.13, .23–24, .35, polcat . . . Noeh / Bonum's shin do . . . elephants; P. T. Barnum's Show (W&M: anon., 1870s)

514.5–6,—All our stakes they were astumbling round the ranky roars / assumbling when Big Arthur flugged the field at Annie's courting; The Man That Broke the Bank at Monte Carlo (W&M: Fred Gilbert, 1892). Also, of course, the Irish song "Enniscorthy."

515.28, that bamboozelem mincethrill voice of yours; Kafoozalem (W: S. Oxon; M: Frederick Blume, arranger [and composer?], 1866)

526.20–21, Woman / will water the wild world over. And the maid of the folley will go; Old Rosin the Beau (W&M: folk, ca. 1830)

538.28–29, The man what shocked his shanks at contey / Carlow's; The Man That Broke the Bank at Monte Carlo (W&M: Fred Gilbert, 1892)

539.32, Champaign Chollyman; Champagne Charlie (W: George Leybourne; M: Alfred Lee, 1868)

542.4, hurusalaming; Kafoozalem (W: S. Oxon; M: Frederick Blume, arranger [and composer?], 1866)

551.14, .29, .31, to rodies . . . sophister agen sorefister . . . gregos and democriticos; The Straight-out Democrat (W: anon.; M: air of Old Rosin the Beau, 1872)

557.10, fisstball; The Lone Fish Ball (W&M: anon., 1855. It appears in C. Wistar Stevens, *College Song Book* [Boston: Russell & Tolman, 1860] as a Harvard song.)

561.36, petnames; Call Me Pet Names (W: Charles N. Jarvis; M: Mrs. Frances Sargent Locke Osgood, ca. 1860)

Finnegans Wake, Book III.4:

570.7–8, Some wholetime in / hot town tonight; Hot Time in the Old Town Tonight (W: Joe Hayden; M: Theodore Metz, 1896)

578.10–11, Can thus be Misthra / Norkmann that keeps our hotel; Are You the O'Reilly? (W&M: Pat Rooney, 1883)

579.7, .21, free . . . lunch; The Free Lunch Cadets (W&M: John Philip Sousa, 1877)

584.34, O I you O you me; Little Brown Jug (W&M: Joseph Eastburn Winner, 1869)

587.5, No kidd, captn; Captain Kidd (W&M: anon., Spaeth terms "very old." Alan Lomax, *Folk Songs of North America* [Garden City, N.Y.:

Doubleday, 1960], 7–8, 15–16, dates this version of "Captain Kidd" from at least 1872 with a melody possibly as early as the sixteenth century, and words possibly from the time of Kidd's execution in 1701; he also prints a hymn version from 1825.)

587.14–15, the pitchur that he's turned to / weld the wall; Picture That Is Turned towards the Wall (W&M: Charles Graham, 1891)

587.26, Elsies from Chelsies; Elsie from Chelsea (W&M: Harry Dacre [Decker], 1896)

587.26–27, the two leggle- / gels in blooms; Two Little Girls in Blue (W&M: Charles Graham, 1893)

588.13, Jimmy, my old brown freer; Paddy Duffy's Cart (W: Ned "Pete" Harrigan; M: David Braham, 1881)

589.14–15, with the boguey which he snatched in the / baggage coach ahead; In the Baggage Coach Ahead (W&M: Gussie L. Davis, 1896)

589.18, Duffy's; Paddy Duffy's Cart (W: Ned "Pete" Harrigan; M: David Braham, 1881)

589.19, the band played on; The Band Played On (W: John E. Palmer; M: Charles B. Ward, 1895)

589.20, Ofter the fall; After the Ball (W&M: Charles K. Harris, 1892)

590.11, Mista Chimepiece? You got nice yum plemyums; My Little Chimpanzee [In Zanzibar] (W: Bob Cole; M: J. Rosamond Johnson, 1904)

590.11, You got nice yum plemyums; Under the Yumyum Tree (W: Andrew B. Sterling; M: Harry von Tilzer, 1910)

Finnegans Wake, Book IV:

597.13–19, Moskiosk Djinpalast . . . bazaar, allahallahallah . . . alcovan . . . Shavarsanjivana; Abdul Abulbul Amir (W&M: Percy French, 1877, based on a traditional English song from the Crimean War. This instance refers to Abdul's opponent, the Muscovite Ivan Skavinsky Skavar)

598.21–22, the pitcher go to aftoms on the wall; Picture That Is Turned towards the Wall (W&M: Charles Graham, 1891)

599.21–22, There's / a tavarn in the tarn; There Is a Tavern in the Town (W&M: William H. Hills, 1883)

601.6, under wasseres of Erie; Erie Canal (W&M: folk, after 1825, when the canal opened)

601.17–18, A dweam of dose innocent dirly / dirls; Only a 'ittle Dirly Dirl (W&M: Addison Fletcher Andrews, 1878)

604.25, the onebut thousand insels; "the Thousand Islands": phrase used in Spaeth's description of first hearing "The Eastern Train." Identification furnished by Vincent Deane.

606.26, inked with penmark; Hamlet, Prince of Denmark (W&M: anon., before 1868. H. R. Waite in *Carmina Collegensia* [Boston: Oliver Ditson, 1868] identifies this as popular at Hamilton College; so Joyce might have heard it from Ezra Pound. See also note for *FW* 301.n.5.)

607.19, Mees is thees knees. Thi is Mi; Little Brown Jug (W&M: Joseph Eastburn Winner, 1869)

618.22, my cubarola glide; The Cubanola Glide (W: Vincent P. Bryan; M: Harry von Tilzer, 1909)

622.5, sookadoodling; Yankee Doodle (W: Oxonian Cavaliers; M: nursery rhyme, 1646)

624.35, Howsomendeavour, you done me fine; Frankie and Johnnie (W&M: folk, 1870–75)

627.34, For all their faults. I am passing out; With All Her Faults I Love Her Still (W&M: Monroe H. Rosenfeld, 1888)

Appendix 2

Spirituals in *Finnegans Wake*

Following are the songs listed in Hodgart and Worthington's *Song in the Works of James Joyce* as spirituals, with a few additional citations. Some, as noted below, are minstrel songs rather than spirituals; several are not spirituals in the sense of folk songs, but melodies composed by or associated with African-Americans in the American theater.

Key:
Page/line in *FW,* text from *FW;* title alluded to (W: lyricist, if any; M: composer, if any)
/ indicates end of line in *Finnegans Wake*
// indicates end of page in *Finnegans Wake*

055.5, deeds bounds going arise again; These Bones Gwine to Rise Again
074.5, roll, orland, roll; Roll Jordan, Roll
100.21, swinglowswaying; Swing Low, Sweet Chariot
185.8, Sam Hill; Joe Hill (W: Alfred Hayes; M: Earl Robinson, 1925? Wanda Whitman [*Songs That Changed the World,* 75] calls this "the 'spiritual' of the union movement.")
228.31, for othersites of Jorden; Jordan Am a Hard Road to Trabbel (W&M: Dan Emmett or T. F. Briggs, 1853; minstrel song, not spiritual)
228.31, heave a hevy, waterboy; Water Boy (Paul Robeson's Salle Gaveau program included this as a folk song; but Sigmund Spaeth in *A History of Popular Music in America* [New York: Random House, 1948], 534, lists it as by Avery Robinson.)
232.21–23, Is you / zealous of mes, brother? . . . Satanly, lade; Certainly, Lord!
233.7, he maun't know ledgings here; Ain't No Hiding Place Down There

243.24−25, massa / dinars; Massa Dear

243.26, glory cloack; Glory Road (W: Clement Wood; M: Jacques Wolfe, 1928)

245.12, Junoh and the whalk; Jonah and the Whale

264.23, By this riverside; Down by the Riverside

279.n.1.32, sing loud, sweet cheeriot; Swing Low, Sweet Chariot

312.12, dinned he raign; O, Didn't it Rain! (W&M: Eddie Leonard, 1923; American popular song)

313.5−6, Godeown moseys and skeep thy beeble / bee; Go Down, Moses

320.30−31, didn't he / drain; O, Didn't It Rain! (Eddie Leonard, 1923; American popular song)

323.7, belly jonah hunting the polly joans; Jonah and the Whale

330.28−29, He goat a berth. And she cot a manege. And wohl's gorse / mundom ganna wedst; All God's Chillun Got Wings

333.30, hush lillabilla lullaby; My Curly-Headed Baby (W&M: George H. Clutsam, 1926)

334.22−24, He / banged the scoop and she bagged the sugar while the whole / pub's pobbel done a stare; All God's Chillun Got Wings

339.4−5, He gatovit and me gotafit and Oalgoak's Cheloven gut / a fudden; All God's Chillun Got Wings

359.19, singaloo sweecheeriode; Swing Low, Sweet Chariot

363.12−13, You known that tom? . . . Soothinly low; Certainly, Lord!

372.18, rainydraining; O, Didn't It Rain (Eddie Leonard, 1923; American popular song)

434.27, Jonas in the Dolphin's Barncar; Jonah and the Whale

442.24, bringthee balm of Gaylad; Balm of Gilead (W&M: H. T. Bryant; minstrel, 1861; this is not the hymn, "There Is a Balm in Gilead")

458.5, forty ways in forty nights; O, Didn't It Rain (Eddie Leonard, 1923; American popular song)

463.31−32, Jonas wrocked in / the belly of the whaves; Jonah and the Whale

467.22, down on the river airy; Ain't Gwine Study War No More (Down by the Riverside)

506.11−14, Were you there . . . ramble; Were You There When They Crucified My Lord?

536.32−33, Jonah Whalley; Jonah and the Whale

588.19, 588.33, were you there . . . they trembold, humbild; Were You There When They Crucified My Lord?

601.18−19, Keavn! Keavn! And they all setton voicies about singsing / music was Keavn; All God's Children Got Wings

Appendix 3

American Popular Songs, 1913–38, in *Finnegans Wake*

These allusions have been checked against Joyce's drafts, typescripts, and corrected proofs for *Finnegans Wake* in the volumes of the *James Joyce Archive* (New York: Garland, 1978 and after); each appears in Joyce's text after the song's publication date. Most have not previously been listed as musical allusions in the *Wake*.

Key: page/line no. in *FW*, text from *FW;* song title (W: lyricist; M: composer, date of publication)
/ indicates end of line in *FW*
// indicates end of page in *FW*

Finnegans Wake, Book I.1:
005.23, bedoueen the jebel and the jpysian sea; Between the Devil and the Deep Blue Sea (W: Ted Koehler; M: Harold Arlen, 1931)
007.3, O carina! O carina; O Katharina (W: L. Wolfe Gilbert; M: Richard Fall, 1924)
007.36, when the clouds roll by, jamey; Missouri Waltz (W: J. R. Shannon [pseud for W. James Royce]; M: Frederick Knight Logan, 1914)
007.36, Hence when the clouds roll by, jamey, a proudseye view; Till the Clouds Roll By (W: P. G. Wodehouse, Jerome Kern, and Guy Bolton; M: Jerome Kern, 1917)
012.6–7, And we all like a marriedann because she is mer- / cenary; Mercenary Mary (W&M: Con Conrad, 1925)
020.3, his cousin charmian; Charmaine (W: Lew Pollack; M: Erno Rapee, United States 1926, Europe 1914)
026.14, And that's ashore as you were born; You're in Kentucky, [Sure as You're Born] (W&M: George A. Little, Larry Shay, and Haven Gillespie, 1923)

Finnegans Wake, Book I.2:

037.17–18, between / Druidia and the Deepsleep Sea; Between the Devil and the Deep Blue Sea (W: Ted Koehler; M: Harold Arlen, 1931)

038.30, the writress of Havvah-ban-Annah; Yes, We Have No Bananas (W: Frank Silver; M: Irving Cohn, 1923)

Finnegans Wake, Book I.3:

064.25, puddywhackback to Pamintul; Mademoiselle from Armentières (W&M: Lt. Gitz Rice, 1917?)

064.35–36, There are 29 sweet reasons / why blossomtime's the best; *Blossom Time* (W: Dorothy Donnelly; M: Sigmund Romberg, 1921)

065.8, share good times way down west in a / guaranteed happy lovenest; Let the Rest of the World Go By (W: J. Keirn Brennan; M: Ernest R. Ball, 1919)

065.28–32, with their cherrybum / chappy (for he is simply shamming dippy) if they all were afloat / in a dreamlifeboat . . . / in his tippy, upindown dippy, tiptoptippy canoodle; Ciribiribin (W: Rudolf Thaler, 1909, 1934; M: A. Pestalozza, 1909, 1934)

065.30–32, hugging two by two in his zoo-doo-you-doo, / a tofftoff for thee, missymissy for me and howcameyou-e'enso for / Farber; Tea for Two (W: Irving Caesar; M: Vincent Youmans, 1924)

065.32, in his tippy, upindown dippy, tiptoptippy canoodle; My Little Canoe (W: Otto Harbach; M: Louis H. Hirsch, 1921)

071.11–12, *Yass We've Had His / Badannas;* Yes, We Have No Bananas (W: Frank Silver; M: Irving Cohn, 1923)

Finnegans Wake, Book I.4:

075.3, Marmarazalles from Marmeniere; Mademoiselle from Armentières (W&M: Lt. Gitz Rice, 1917?)

078.31–32, Bellona's Black / Bottom; Black Bottom (W: Bud G. DeSylva and Lew Brown; M: Ray Henderson, 1926)

092.20, dindy dandy sugar de candy; Fine and Dandy (W: Paul [Warburg] Jones; M: Swift, Kay, 1930)

092.25, all all alonely; All Alone (W&M: Irving Berlin, 1924)

092.30, shey'll tell memmas when she gays whom; Go Home and Tell Your Mother (W: Dorothy Fields; M: Jimmy McHugh, 1930)

094.14–16, "Ena milo melo- / mon, frai is frau and swee is too, swee is two when swoo is free, ana mala woe is we; Tea for Two (W: Irving Caesar; M: Vincent Youmans, 1924)

096.10–11, in Milton's Park under lovely Father Whisperer / and making her love; Whispering (W: Malvin Schonberger; M: John Schonberger, 1920; recorded by Whiteman)

098.13, bumbashaws; Becky, Do the Bombashay (W&M: anon., 1910; Jewish song, says Mark Sullivan in *Our Times*, 3:403)

Finnegans Wake, Book I.5:

106.2–3, *He's Hue to Me Cry, I'm the Stitch / in his Baskside You'd be Nought Without Mom;* You're the Cream in My Coffee (W: Bud G. DeSylva and Lew Brown; M: Ray Henderson, 1928)

117.16, Since nozzy Nanette tripped palmyways; No No, Nannette (W: Irving Caesar; M: Vincent Youmans, 1924)

117.17–19, there's a spurtfire turf a'kind o'kindling when oft as the / souff-souff blows her peaties up and a claypot wet for thee, my / Sitys, and talkatalka tell Tibbs has eve; Tea for Two (W: Irving Caesar; M: Vincent Youmans, 1924)

119.30–31, a tea anyway for a tryst / someday; Tea for Two (W: Irving Caesar; M: Vincent Youmans, 1924)

121.12–14, *ingperwhis through the hole of his hat,* indicating that the / words which follow may be taken in any order desired, hole of / Aran man the hat through the whispering his ho; Whispering (W: Malvin Schonberger; M: John Schonberger, 1920; recorded by Whiteman)

123.2, why, O why, O why; Why Did I Kiss That Girl? (W: Lew Brown; M: Robert A. King [born Keiser] and Ray Henderson, 1924)

123.4, when all is zed and done; Margie (W: Benny Davis; M: Con Conrad and J. Russel Robinson, 1920)

Finnegans Wake, Book I.6:

131.14–16, married / with cakes and repunked with pleasure; till he was buried how- / happy was he; When We Are Married (W: Zelda Sears; M: Vincent Youmans, 1924)

133.7, Roseoogreedy (mite's); The Daughter of Rosie O'Grady (W: Walter Brice or Gus Kahn; M: Walter Donaldson, 1918)

139.15, Does your mutter know your mike; Cecelia (W: Herman Ruby; M: Dave Dreyer, 1925)

143.1–2, Sweet / Peck-at-my-Heart; Peg o' My Heart (W: Alfred Bryan; M: Fred Fisher, 1913)

145.5, Tay for thee; Tea for Two (W: Irving Caesar; M: Vincent Youmans, 1924)

145.34, I'll beat any sonnamonk to love; Sheik of Araby (W: Harry B. Smith and Francis Wheeler; M: Ted Snyder, 1921)

145.35–36, halve a ban- / nan in two; Yes, We Have No Bananas (W: Frank Silver; M: Irving Cohn, 1923)

146.5–6, I'm only any / girl, you lovely fellow of my dreams; Girl of My Dreams (W&M: Sunny Clapp, 1927)

146.21–22, when you / are married to reading and writing; When We Are Married (W: Zelda Sears; M: Vincent Youmans, 1924)

147.31–34, with the / proof of love . . . when you learned / me the linguo to melt; Sheik of Araby (W: Harry B. Smith and Francis Wheeler; M: Ted Snyder, 1921)

147.36–148.1, Why do you like my // whisping; Whispering (W: Malvin Schonberger; M: John Schonberger, 1920; recorded by Whiteman)

159.12–13, her muddied name was Missis- / liffi; Mississippi Mud (W&M: Harry Barris, 1927)

164.14, .18–20, Margareen . . . I / cream for thee, Sweet Margareen. . . . O Mar- / gareena! O Margareena; Margie (W: Benny Davis; M: Con Conrad and J. Russel Robinson, 1920)

164.14, .18–20, Margareen . . . I / cream for thee, Sweet Margareen. . . . O Mar- / gareena! O Margareena; O Katharina (W: L. Wolfe Gilbert; M: Richard Fall, 1924)

Finnegans Wake, Book I.7:

170.3, not for a dinar! not for jo; Dinah (W: Sam Lewis and Joe Young; M: Harry Akst, 1925)

170.20, yea, he hath no mananas; Yes, We Have No Bananas (W: Frank Silver; M: Irving Cohn, 1923)

175.35, with Dina and old Joe kicking her behind; Dinah (W: Sam Lewis and Joe Young; M: Harry Akst, 1925)

176.12, *Ducking Mammy;* My Mammy (W: Sam Lewis and Joe Young; M: Walter Donaldson, 1918)

Finnegans Wake, Book I.8:

197.21, Sabrine asthore; Eileen Alannah Asthore (W: Henry Blossom; M: Victor Herbert, 1917)

199.14, Dubber Dan; Dapper Dan, the Sheik of Alabam' (W: Lew Brown; M: Albert von Tilzer, 1921)

203.29, Why a why; Why Did I Kiss That Girl? (W: Lew Brown; M: Robert A. King [born Keiser] and Ray Henderson, 1924)

208.30–31, Missus, be good and don't / fol in the say; Lady, Be Good (W: Ira Gershwin; M: George Gershwin, 1924)

209.16, And I don't mean maybe; Yes Sir, That's My Baby (W: Gus Kahn; M: Walter Donaldson, 1925)

209.22, making chattahoochee; Making Whoopee (W: Gus Kahn; M: Walter Donaldson, 1928)

212.16, a moonflower; Moonlight & Roses (W&M: Edwin H. Lemare, Ben Black, and Neil Moret [pseud of Chas. N. Daniels], 1925)

Finnegans Wake, Book II.1:

223.17, in Glenasmole of Smiling Thrushes Patch Whyte; Smilin' Through (W&M: Arthur Penn, 1915)

224.35, that thong off his art; Song o' My Heart (W: Joseph McCarthy; M: James Hanley, 1930)

226.2–3, For always down in Carolinas lovely Dinahs vaunt their / view;
Dinah (W: Sam Lewis and Joe Young; M: Harry Akst, 1925)

226.2–3, For always down in Carolinas lovely Dinahs vaunt their / view;
Carolina in the Morning (W: Gus Kahn; M: Walter Donaldson, 1922)

226.14–15, Mammy / was, Mimmy is; My Mammy (W: Joe Young and Sam
Lewis; M: Walter Donaldson, 1918)

228.12, Byebye, Brassolis; Bye, Bye, Blackbird (W: Mort Dixon; M: Ray
Henderson, 1925)

229.11, To Wildrose LaGilligan; Wild Rose (W: Clifford Grey; M: Jerome
Kern, 1920)

230.15, Mademoisselle from Armentières; Mademoiselle from Armentières
(W&M: Lt. Gitz Rice, 1917?)

232.13, Isle wail for yews; I Cried for You (W: Arthur Freed; M: Gus Arn-
heim and Abe Lyman, 1923)

232.19, I have soreunder from to him now, dear- / mate ashore; I Surrender,
Dear (W: Gordon Clifford; M: Harry Barris, 1931)

232.35–36, elazilee him / on her knee; Tea for Two (W: Irving Caesar; M:
Vincent Youmans, 1924)

233.3, and his tail cooked up; Horsey Keep Your Tail Up (W&M: Walter
Hirsch and Bert Kaplan, 1923)

234.7, with eyes white open; With My Eyes Wide Open (W&M: Mack Gordon and Harry Revel, 1934)

236.1, Charmeuses chloes; Chloe (W: Gus Kahn; M: Neil Moret [pseud of
Charles N. Daniels], 1927)

236.1, Charmeuses chloes; Charmaine (W: Lew Pollack; M: Erno Rapee,
United States 1926, Europe 1914)

246.1, who over comes ever for Whoopee Weeks; Making Whoopee (W: Gus
Kahn; M: Walter Donaldson, 1928)

246.34–35, Teaseforhim. Toesforhim. / Tossforhim. Two; Tea for Two (W:
Irving Caesar; M: Vincent Youmans, 1924)

247.15, Teapotty. Teapotty; Tea for Two (W: Irving Caesar; M: Vincent Youmans, 1924)

249.27, nobody loves me but you; Nobody But You (W: Arthur Jackson and
Bud G. DeSylva; M: George Gershwin, 1919)

249.27, nobody loves me but you; Nobody Wants Me (W: Philip Charig; M:
Irving Caesar, 1929)

249.27, nobody loves me but you; Nobody Wants Me (W: Morrie Ryskind;
M: Henry Souvaine, 1926)

249.27, nobody loves me but you; Somebody Loves Me (W: Ballard Mac-
Donald and Bud G. DeSylva; M: George Gershwin, 1924)

257.2, laughs her stella's visperine; Whispering (W: Malvin Schonberger; M:
John Schonberger, 1920; recorded by Whiteman)

258.9–10, Yip! Yup! Yar-/rah; *Yip, Yip, Yaphank* (W&M: Irving Berlin, 1918)

Finnegans Wake, Book II.2:

260.1–3, As we there are where are we are we there / from tomtittot to teetootomtotalitarian. Tea / tea too oo; Tea for Two (W: Irving Caesar; M: Vincent Youmans, 1924)

264.n.3, Porphyrious Olbion, redcoatliar, we were always wholly rose marines on our side every time; Rose Marie (W: Otto Harbach and Oscar Hammerstein, II; M: Rudolph Friml, 1924)

267.10, briefest glimpse from gladrags, pretty / Proserpronette; Glad-Rag Doll (W: Dan Daugherty; M: Jack Yellen and Milton Ager, 1929)

267.15–16, with the blewy blow and / a windigo; Mood Indigo (W&M: Duke Ellington, 1930)

270.n.2, Lang Wang Wurm; Wang, Wang Blues (W: Leo Wood; M: Gus Mueller, "Buster" Johnson, and Henry Busse, 1921)

271.n.5, that slippering snake charmeuse; Charmaine (W: Lew Pollack; M: Erno Rapee, United States 1926, Europe 1914)

273.7–11, So / wrap up your worries in your woe (wumpum- / tum!) and shake down the shuffle for the / throw. For there's one mere ope for down- / fall ned; Bye, Bye, Blackbird (W: Mort Dixon; M: Ray Henderson, 1925)

276.n.4, Parley vows the Askinwhose; Mademoiselle from Armentières (W&M: Lt. Gitz Rice, 1917?)

277.7, the mountain mourning his duggedy dew; Dig-adig-a-do (W: Dorothy Fields; M: Jimmy McHugh, 1928)

277.n.4, McEndicoth as one of the "lays of ancient homes" = "indigo" as "lay" or song; Mood Indigo (W&M: Duke Ellington, 1930)

282.n.4, That's his whisper waltz I like from Pigott's with that Lancydancy step; Whispering (W: Malvin Schonberger; M: John Schonberger, 1920; recorded by Whiteman)

285.n.6, Indiana Blues; Blues (W: various lyricists; M: various composers)

288.5–6, to don't say / nothing; Old Man River (W: Oscar Hammerstein, II; M: Jerome Kern, 1927)

288.10, the charmhim girlalove; Charmaine (W: Lew Pollack; M: Erno Rapee, United States 1926, Europe 1914)

290.3, peg-of-my-heart; Peg o' My Heart (W: Alfred Bryan; M: Fred Fisher, 1913)

291.5–6, .10, a lonely peggy, . . . thirt sweet of her face! . . . O'Kneels; Peggy O'Neil (W&M: Harry Pease, Ed G. Nelson, and Gilbert Dodge, 1921)

291.20, for merry a valsehood whisprit he to manny a / lilying earling; Whispering (W: Malvin Schonberger; M: John Schonberger, 1920; recorded by Whiteman)

295.5–6, purr lil mur- / rerof myhind; Little Mother of Mine (W: Walter Brown; M: H. T. Burleigh, 1917)

304.9, seeing rayingbogeys rings round me; There's a Rainbow Round My Shoulder (W: Al Jolson and Billy Rose; M: Dave Dreyer, 1928)

Finnegans Wake, Book II.3:

309.22, bawling the whowle hamshack; Ballin' the Jack (W: Jim Burris; M: Chris Smith, 1913)

312.12, dinned he raign; Oh! Didn't It Rain! (W&M: Eddie Leonard, 1923)

312.24, had he hows would he keep her as niece as a fiddle; Fit as a Fiddle and Ready for Love (W: Arthur Freed and Al Hoffman; M: Al Goodheart, 1932)

315.26, wagger with its tag tucked. Up; Horsey Keep Your Tail Up (W&M: Walter Hirsch and Bert Kaplan, 1923)

320.30–31, didn't he / drain; Oh! Didn't It Rain! (W&M: Eddie Leonard, 1923)

332.1, Snip, snap, snoody. Noo err historyend goody; Goody Goody (W: Johnny Mercer; M: Matt Malneck, 1936)

332.2–3, for he put off the ketyl and they / made three (for fie!); Tea for Two (W: Irving Caesar; M: Vincent Youmans, 1924)

333.30, hush lillabilla lullaby; Ma Curly-Headed Baby (W&M: George H. Clutsam, 1926)

337.10, A truce to lovecalls; Indian Love Call (W: Otto Harbach and Oscar Hammerstein, II; M: Rudolph Friml, 1924)

337.13–14, written in smoke and blurred by mist and signed of / solitude; In My Solitude (W&M: Duke Ellington, 1933)

340.31, Hyededye, kittyls, and howdeddoh, pan; Minnie the Moocher (W&M: Cab Calloway and Irving Mills, 1931)

344.12, *bleyes bcome broon;* Brown Eyes, Why Are You Blue? (W: Alfred Bryan; M: George W. Meyer, 1925)

352.3, the same old domstoole story; The Same Old Story (W: Bud G. DeSylva; M: George Gershwin, 1924)

361.15–16, Call Kitty / Kelly! Kissykitty Killykelly; Pretty Kitty Kelly (W: Harry Pease; M: Ed Nelson, 1920)

363.10, Heat wives rasing. They jest keeps rosing; Heat Wave (W&M: Irving Berlin, 1933)

363.10–11, They jest keeps rosing. He jumps leaps rizing. / Howlong; Old Man River (W: Oscar Hammerstein, II; M: Jerome Kern, 1927)

364.9–10, his shool comes merg- / ing along; Old Man River (W: Oscar Hammerstein, II; M: Jerome Kern, 1927)

367.28–30, lighning leaps from the numbulous . . . see what follows; Look for the Silver Lining (W: Bud G. DeSylva; M: Jerome Kern, 1920, but written earlier)

367.34, vode's dodos; Vo-de-do-de-o Blues (W: Jack Yellen; M: Milton Ager, 1920s?)

372.18, rainydraining; Oh! Didn't It Rain! (W&M: Eddie Leonard, 1923)

377.19–20, the brideen Alan- / nah; Eileen Alannah Asthore (W: Henry Blossom; M: Victor Herbert, 1917)

377.27, Shonny Bhoy; Sonny Boy (W: Bud G. DeSylva and Lew Brown; M: Ray Henderson, 1928)

379.13, Boohoohoo it oose; Boo-Hoo! (W: Edward Heyman; M: Carmen Lombardo and John Jacob Loeb, 1937)

379.34, Tem for Tam at Timmotty Hall; Tea for Two (W: Irving Caesar; M: Vincent Youmans, 1924)

380.35, all alone by himself in his grand old handwedown pile; All by Myself (W&M: Irving Berlin, 1921)

Finnegans Wake, Book II.4:

384.30, kissing her, tootyfay charmaunt; Charmaine (W: Lew Pollack; M: Erno Rapee, United States 1926, Europe 1914)

384.31–32, Isolamisola, / and whisping and lisping her about Trisolanisans; Whispering (W: Malvin Schonberger; M: John Schonberger, 1920; recorded by Whiteman)

384.32–33, how one was / whips for one was two and two was lips for one was three; Tea for Two (W: Irving Caesar; M: Vincent Youmans, 1924)

387.19–20, Lally / in the rain; Lilacs in the Rain (W: Mitchell Parish; M: Peter DeRose, ca. 1934, ca. 1939)

388.4, Mild aunt Liza is as loose as her neese; Liza (W: Ira Gershwin and Gus Kahn; M: George Gershwin, 1929)

393.24, they used to be getting up from under; Get Out and Get Under (W: Grant Clarke and Edgar Leslie; M: Abrahams, Maurice, 1913)

398.21–22, thoh the dayses / gone still they loves young dreams; When Day Is Done (W: Bud G. DeSylva; M: Robert Katscher, 1926)

Finnegans Wake, Book III.1:

404.3, I was jogging along in a dream; Drifting Along with the Tide (W: Arthur Jackson; M: George Gershwin, 1921)

405.19–20, fourale to the / lees of Traroe. Those jehovial oyeglances! The heart of the rool; When You Look into the Heart of a Rose (W: Marian Gillespie; M: Florence Methven, 1918)

418.31, *Bruneyes come blue;* Brown Eyes, Why Are You Blue? (W: Alfred Bryan; M: George W. Meyer, 1925)

421.35, She, the mammy far; My Mammy (W: Joe Young and Sam Lewis; M: Walter Donaldson, 1918)

426.4, moother of mine; That Old Irish Mother of Mine (W: William Jerome; M: Harry von Tilzer, 1920)

427.14, It was sharming! But sharmeng; Charmaine (W: Lew Pollack; M: Erno Rapee, United States 1926, Europe 1914)

427.21, undfamiliar faces; Old Familiar Faces (W: Rose; M: Edwards, 1920s? A Hodgart and Worthington listing on which I have been unable to find more information.)

427.28, tootoo too; Toot, Toot, Tootsie (W: Gus Kahn and Ernie Erdman; M: Dan Russo, 1922)

Finnegans Wake, Book III.2:

434.5, Give back those stolen kisses; Stolen Kisses (W: Francis Wheeler; M: Ted Snyder, 1921)

436.33–34, Lay your lilylike long his shoulder but buck / back if he buts bolder; Sweetie Pie (W&M: John Jacob Loeb, 1934)

439.29–30, No cheeka- / cheek with chipperchapper; Cheek to Cheek (W&M: Irving Berlin, 1935)

441.16–17, the wish is on her rose marine and the lunchlight in her / eye; Rose Marie (W: Otto Harbach and Oscar Hammerstein, II; M: Rudolph Friml, 1924)

444.29, Up Rosemiry Lean; Rose Marie (W: Otto Harbach and Oscar Hammerstein, II; M: Rudolph Friml, 1924)

446.25, suirland and noreland; Your Land and My Land (W: Dorothy Donnelly; M: Sigmund Romberg, 1927)

452.13, th'other over th'ether; Over There (W&M: George M. Cohan, 1917)

453.13, bluemoondag; Blue Monday Blues (W: Bud G. DeSylva; M: George Gershwin, 1922)

453.15, Ole Clo goes through the wood with Shep; Chloe (W: Gus Kahn; M: Neil Moret [pseud of Charles N. Daniels], 1927)

454.16–18, Thou pure! / Our virgin! Thou holy! Our health! Thou strong! Our victory! / O salutary; Thou Swell (W: Lorenz Hart; M: Richard Rodgers, 1927)

455.14, one finel howdiedow; Minnie the Moocher (W&M: Cab Calloway and Irving Mills, 1931)

457.19–20, Someday duly, oneday truly, twosday newly, / till whensday; The Man I Love (W: Ira Gershwin; M: George Gershwin, 1924)

457.21, A tear or two in time is all there's toot; Tea for Two (W: Irving Caesar; M: Vincent Youmans, 1924)

457.28–30, as she tactilifully grapbed her male corrispondee to flusther / sweet nunsongs in his quickturned ear, I know, benjamin brother, / but listen, I want, girls palmassing, to whisper my whish; Whispering (W: Malvin Schonberger; M: John Schonberger, 1920; recorded by Whiteman)

458.5, forty ways in forty nights; Oh! Didn't It Rain! (W&M: Eddie Leonard, 1923)

459.11, she says sossy while I say sassy; Let's Call the Whole Thing Off (W: Ira Gershwin; M: George Gershwin, 1937)

462.18, a dear old man pal of mine too; Dear Old Pal of Mine (W: Robe; M: Lt. Gitz Rice, 1918) There was also a music hall song titled "Dear Old Pals."

464.24, dapper dandy; Dapper Dan, the Sheik of Alabam' (W: Lew Brown; M: Albert von Tilzer, 1921)

466.1–2, Yipyip! To pan! To / pan! To tinpinnypan. All folly me yap to Curlew; Yip, Yip, Yaphank (W&M: Irving Berlin, 1918)

466.20, Dauber Dan; Dapper Dan, the Sheik of Alabam' (W: Lew Brown; M: Albert von Tilzer, 1921)

469.21, Solo, solone, solong; So Long! Ooo Long! (W: Bert Kalmar; M: Harry Ruby, 1920)

Finnegans Wake, Book III.3:

490.26, Toot! Detter for you, Mr Nobru. Toot toot; Toot, Toot, Tootsie (W: Gus Kahn and Ernie Erdman; M: Dan Russo, 1922)

490.31–32, What though it be for the sow of his heart? If even she / were a good pool Pegeen; Song o' My Heart (W: Joseph McCarthy; M: James Hanley, 1930)

490.31–32, What though it be for the sow of his heart? If even she / were a good pool Pegeen; Peg o' My Heart (W: Alfred Bryan; M: Fred Fisher, 1913)

498.6, *Horsibus, keep your tailyup;* Horsey Keep Your Tail Up (W&M: Walter Hirsch and Bert Kaplan, 1923)

514.22–23, at A Little Bit of / Heaven Howth; A Little Bit of Heaven (W: J. Keirn Brennan; M: Ernest R. Ball, 1914)

527.8, He's gone on his bombashaw; Becky, Do the Bombashay (W&M: anon., 1910; Jewish song, says Mark Sullivan in *Our Times* 3:403)

527.18, nue charmeen cuffs; Charmaine (W: Lew Pollack; M: Erno Rapee, United States 1926, Europe 1914)

531.7, do dodo doughdy dough; Do, Do, Do (W: Ira Gershwin; M: George Gershwin, 1926)

531.22, Shusies-with-her-Soles-Up; Horsey Keep Your Tail Up (W&M: Walter Hirsch and Bert Kaplan, 1923)

533.23–24, ye litel chuch rond / ye coner; Little Church around the Corner (W: Bud G. DeSylva; M: Jerome Kern, 1920)

533.23–24, ye litel chuch rond / ye coner; Little Church around the Corner (W: Alexander Gerber; M: Sigmund Romberg, 1919)

Finnegans Wake, Book III.4:

556.11–12, for she was the only girl they / loved; If You Were the Only Girl
in the World (W: Clifford Grey; M: Nat D. Ayer, 1925)

556.11–12, for she was the only girl they / loved; If You Were the Only Girl
(W: Lew Brown; M: George W. Meyer, 1916)

556.31, wan fine night and the next fine night and last find night; Keep Your
Head Down, Fritzi Boy (W&M: Lt. Gitz Rice, 1918)

562.16, crazedledaze; Pal of My Cradle Days (W: Marshall Montgomery; M:
Al Piantadosi, 1925)

567.15, Nan Nan Nanetta; No No, Nannette (W: Irving Caesar; M: Vincent
Youmans, 1924)

577.16, peg of his claim and pride of her heart; Peg o' My Heart (W: Alfred
Bryan; M: Fred Fisher, 1913)

581.6, the swanee her ainsell; Swanee (W: Irving Caesar; M: George Gershwin, 1919)

584.10–11, Three for two will do for me and he / for thee and she for you;
Tea for Two (W: Irving Caesar; M: Vincent Youmans, 1924)

Finnegans Wake, Book IV:

599.34–35, that the old man of / the sea and the old woman in the sky if
they don't say nothings; Old Man River (W: Oscar Hammerstein, II;
M: Jerome Kern, 1927)

601.11–12, From thee to thee, thoo art it thoo, that / thouest there. The like
the near, the liker nearer; Tea for Two (W: Irving Caesar; M: Vincent
Youmans, 1924)

603.4, and as fat as a fuddle; Fit as a Fiddle and Ready for Love (W: Arthur
Freed and Al Hoffman; M: Al Goodheart, 1932)

603.12–13, shay for shee and / sloo for slee; Tea for Two (W: Irving Caesar;
M: Vincent Youmans, 1924)

603.16, Heard you the crime, senny boy; Sonny Boy (W: Bud G. DeSylva
and Lew Brown; M: Ray Henderson, 1928)

603.34, Tyro a tora; Tea for Two (W: Irving Caesar; M: Vincent Youmans,
1924)

607.19, Mees is thees knees, Thi is Mi; Tea for Two (W: Irving Caesar; M:
Vincent Youmans, 1924)

615.8–9, Cockalooralooraloo- / menos; Toora Loora Loora (W&M: J. R.
Shannon [pseud for W. James Royce], 1914)

617.15–16, Music, me / ouldstrow, please; Music, Maestro, Please (W: Herb
Magidson; M: Allie Wrubel, 1938)

618.6–7, Just a prinche for to- / night; Just for Tonight (W: Clifford Grey;
M: Maury Rubens, 1926)

618.18, when love walks in; Love Walked In (W: Ira Gershwin; M: George
Gershwin, 1937)

620.33, He's for thee what she's for me; Tea for Two (W: Irving Caesar; M: Vincent Youmans, 1924)

622.17, You remember; Remember (W&M: Irving Berlin, 1925)

625.28–29, If I lose my breath for a minute or two don't / speak, remember; Remember (W&M: Irving Berlin, 1925)

626.8, The day. Remember; Remember (W&M: Irving Berlin, 1925)

626.19–20, There'll be others but non / so for me; But Not for Me (W: Ira Gershwin; M: George Gershwin, 1930)

627.34, For all their faults; It Had to Be You (W: Isham Jones; M: Gus Kahn, 1924)

Appendix 4

It Ain't Necessarily So:
Musical Delusions in *Finnegans Wake*

Some phrases in *Finnegans Wake* seem to wave flags and toot horns to call attention to their allusive nature, even though Joyce inserted them in his manuscripts before the song to which they "allude" was published or, indeed, even written. To save time for other students of Joyce, a group of these musical delusions is listed here. Each of these "allusive" passages can be found in the drafts or revisions of *Finnegans Wake* prior to the existence of the song that seems to be alluded to.

Key:
page/line no. in *FW*, text from *FW*; song title (W: lyricist; M: composer, date)
/ indicates end of line in *FW*

010.32–34, a runalittle, doalittle, preealittle, pouralittle, / wipealittle, kicksalittle, severalittle, eatalittle, whinealittle, kenalittle, / helfalittle, pelfalittle gnarlybird; The Glory of Love (W&M: Billy Hill, 1936)
065.31, missymissy for me; Goody Goody (W: Matt Malneck; M: Johnny Mercer, 1936)
071.12, *Funnyface*; Funny Face (W: Ira Gershwin; M: George Gershwin, 1927)
096.14–15, meeting waters most improper (peepette!) ballround the garden, / trickle trickle trickle triss, please, miman, may I go flirting; Yes, My Darling Daughter (W&M: Jack Lawrence, 1940; the late Victory Pomeranz said this song was based on a Yiddish song, "Go Way Back in the Water," to which Joyce may have alluded here.)

143.25–26, blue out of the ind of / it; Mood Indigo (W&M: Duke Ellington, 1931)

146.7, my trysting of the tulipies; Tiptoe through the Tulips (W: Al Dubin; M: Joseph A. Burke, 1929)

148.1, divinely deluscious; It's De-Lovely (W&M: Cole Porter, 1936; Alan Cohn identified this anachronism.)

184.23, and stardust; Star Dust (W: Mitchell Parrish; M: Hoagy Carmichael, 1929; Alan Cohn identified this anachronism.)

209.22, chattahoochee; Chattanooga Choo Choo (W: Mack Gordon; M: Harry Warren, 1941; Alan Cohn identified this anachronism.)

240.5, But low, boys low, he rises; What Shall We Do with a Drunken Sailor? (W&M: sea chanty, arranged David W. Guion, 1933)

246.35, Else there is danger of. Solitude; In My Solitude (W&M: Duke Ellington, December 1933)

247.12–13, Boo, you're through! / Hoo, I'm true; Boo-Hoo! (W: Edward Heyman; M: Carmen Lombardo and John Jacob Loeb, 1937)

253.4–5, slove look at / me now; Look at Me Now (W: John DeVries; M: Joe Bushkin, 1941)

264.11, Between a stare and a sough; Between a Kiss and a Sigh (W: Burke; M: Johnston, 5 December 1938. Alan Cohn identified the anachronism.)

330.30–32, Knock knock. War's where! Which war? The Twwinns. / Knock knock. Woos without! Without what? An apple. Knock / knock; Knock, Knock (W: Jimmy Tyson, Bill Davies, Johnny Morris; M: Vincent Lopez, 1936; before the song appeared, however, there was a nationwide craze for "knock-knock" jokes in the United States, and Joyce may have been alluding to these. *FW* phrase inserted in 1935 typescript.)

380.32–36, wait till I tell you, / what did he do, poor old Roderick O'Conor Rex, the aus- / picious waterproof monarch of all Ireland, when he found him- / self all alone by himself in his grand old handwedown pile after / all of them had all gone off with themselves to their castles; All Alone (W&M: Irving Berlin, 1924)

380.33, what did he do; What'll I do? (W&M: Irving Berlin, 1924)

393.24, they used to be getting up from under; Get Out and Get Under [the Moon] (W: W. C. Tobias and William Jerome; M: Larry Shay, 1928)

404.3, I was jogging along in a dream; Breezing Along with a Breeze (W: Haven Gillespie; M: Seymour Simone and Richard Whiting, 1926)

453.13, bluemoondag; Once in a Blue Moon (W: Anne Caldwell; M: Jerome Kern, 1933; Joyce used this phrasing in *transition 13* 1928. The Knuths say John McCormack recorded the song in 1932, but *Variety Musical*

Cavalcade dates the song 1933. It is possible that McCormack was invited to record the song prior to its publication, to help its sales.)

457.5–6, leave you biddies till / my stave is a bar; Beat Me Daddy, Eight to the Bar (W&M: Don Raye, Hugh Prince, and Eleanor Sheehy, 1940; Alan Cohn identified the anachronism.)

457.18–19, And you'll miss me more as the narrowing / weeks wing by; Autumn Leaves (W: Johnny Mercer and Jacques Prevert; M: Joseph Kosma, 1947 in United States; orig. French)

461.29, we are doing to thay one little player; Say a Little Prayer for Me (W: Joseph George Gilbert; M: Horatio Nicholls, 1930)

495.4, a deepsea dibbler; Between the Devil and the Deep Blue Sea (W: Ted Koehler; M: Harold Arlen, 1931)

495.4, like a deepsea dibbler; The Dipsy Doodle (W&M: Larry Clinton, 1937)

522.27–28, But this is no / laughing matter; This Is No Laughing Matter (W&M: Buddy Kaye and Al Frisch, 1941)

531.26–29, Fuddling fun for Fullacan's sake! . . . fiddling with / his faddles; Fiddle Faddle (W: no lyrics; M: Leroy Anderson, 1948)

540.21–22: Redu Negru may be black in tawn but under them lintels / are staying my horneymen meet each his mansiemagd; Lulu's Back in Town (W: Al Dubin; M: Harry Warren, 1935)

561.3, .6, for little Porter babes . . . this is the other one nighadays; Night and Day (W&M: Cole Porter, 1932)

571.12, O ma ma; Oh, Ma-ma! (The Butcher Boy) (W: Lew Brown; M: Rudy Vallee, 1938)

581.35–36, so early in the / morning; What Shall We Do with a Drunken Sailor? (W&M: sea chanty, arranged David W. Guion, 1933; allusion appeared as "so realy [*sic*] in the morning" in the *transition* proofs of 1929.)

582.6–7, between the devil's punchbowl and the deep / angleseaboard; Between the Devil and the Deep Blue Sea (W: Ted Koehler; M: Harold Arlen, 1931)

586.7, Omama; Oh, Ma-ma! (The Butcher Boy) (W: Lew Brown; M: Rudy Vallee, 1938; phrasing in 1929 *transition* proofs. Song was based on a popular Italian song, *Luna merro mare* with music by Paolo Citorello, according to *American Popular Song*. Joyce may have alluded to the Italian song.)

586.13, din a ding or do; Dig-adig-a-do (W: Dorothy Fields; M: Jimmy McHugh, 1928)

587.4, me and my auxy (in section dealing with shadows and darkness); Me and My Shadow (W&M: Billy Rose, Al Jolson, and Dave Dreyer, 1927)

588.25, Listen, misled peerless, please; Music, Maestro, Please (W: Herb Magidson; M: Allie Wrubel, 1938)

620.15, So oft. Sim. Time after time; Time after Time (W: Sammy Cahn; M: Jule Styne, 1947)

Contributors

RUTH BAUERLE (Ohio Wesleyan University) has previously published *A Word List to Joyce's "Exiles"* and *The James Joyce Songbook*. She organized the first panel on women in Joyce's work at the 1973 Symposium.

ZACK BOWEN (University of Miami) is the author of *Musical Allusions in the Works of James Joyce: Early Poetry through "Ulysses"* and *"Ulysses" as a Comic Novel*, and producer-director of five recordings of episodes from Joyce's *Ulysses* in dramatic form with background music.

TIMOTHY MARTIN (Rutgers University) wrote *Joyce and Wagner: A Study of Influence*, and co-edited *Joyce in Context*. He directed 1989's "Joyce in Philadelphia" conference. For sixteen years he has also sung professionally in Philadelphia.

HENRIETTE LAZARIDIS POWER (Harvard University) was a contributor to *Coping with Joyce: Essays from the Copenhagen Symposium* and has published other articles on Joyce and on Mary Shelley. She is working on a social history of the British pantomime in the nineteenth century.

ULRICH SCHNEIDER (University of Erlangen/Nuremberg), who has published widely on Joyce, is author of *Die Londoner Music Hall und ihre Songs* and co-author of *British Music Hall, 1840–1923: A Bibliography and Guide to Sources*.

General Index

Index of Citations of Joyce's Works